Complete Elementary
Physical Education Guide

ROSALIE BRYANT
ELOISE McLEAN OLIVER

PARKER PUBLISHING COMPANY, INC. / WEST NYACK, NEW YORK

Library of Congress Cataloging in Publication Data

Bryant, Rosalie.
    Complete elementary physical education guide.

    1. Physical education for children. I. Oliver,
Eloise McLean, joint author. II. Title.
GV443.B76   613.7'042   74-5188
ISBN 0-13-159939-9

Printed in the United States of America

We dedicate this book to that special kind of teacher—the one who loves children, who values the relationship that exists between mind and body, who sees the whole child, who plans so that each child finds both success and challenge, and who provides an environment that always reflects the human element and is filled with an atmosphere of trust.

Rosalie Bryant and Eloise Oliver have done it again. They have given the classroom teacher yet another complete book on teaching physical education. It is more than a what-to-do book. It is full of how-to-do-it and why.

Yes, it is, in part, a book for the classroom teacher. But it is also a philosophy of physical education jampacked with all the practical day-to-day advice that a busy generalist classroom teacher needs. Though it is of most obvious help to the teacher who has not had an in-depth background in physical education, it is also a time-saver even for the teacher with physical education training. Here, in a ready-made document, is that "lesson plan" all wrapped up in a pink ribbon; yet for the ingenious, innovative teacher, every activity is flexible and adaptable, lending itself to more creative approaches.

This is a humanistic book, aimed at strengthening the student's self-image, his mind-body relationships, assessment of himself, and individual and group sportmanship through activities that provide for both success and challenge. The pièce-de-résistance, however, is that special touch of advice to teachers and students, and the remarkable quotes that make this book one you'll want to keep on your shelves forever.

If you believe in the philosophy of a sound mind in a healthy body, if you believe in developing interests and skills for worthy use of leisure time, if you believe in the value of lead-up skills for a later athletic life, if you believe in the value of perceptual, visual, auditory, motor coordination, then you are in for a very special treat.

Rosalie and Eloise give you more than an academic exercise. These lessons were tested in the field. Physical education is one of the programs that distinguishes the Charlotte-Mecklenburg School System. Now you will find the reason why our teachers are so enthusiastic about physical education.

Because I believe so strongly that the development of a positive self-concept is the most important single ingredient necessary for good education, I'm especially grateful for this book, which does that job so well.

Dr. Rolland W. Jones
Superintendent, Charlotte-Mecklenburg
   Schools
Charlotte, North Carolina

This book gives the teacher new and meaningful ideas in physical education that are practical to use in everyday situations. It blends traditional ideas with the more current trends in an effort to preserve the very best that both philosophies offer. The resulting program recognizes the value in guided discovery and problem-solving styles of teaching, which allow each child to succeed at his own pace. It also places value in there being times when children conform to predetermined sets of rules and standards that are designed for the good of the group.

If your classroom reflects the belief that children learn by doing and that learning can be fun, you will find new and exciting ideas throughout the book. If your teaching includes the use of learning centers, you will be particularly interested in those suggested for the open classroom. These stations or centers not only add more meaning to other curriculum areas, such as mathematics, social studies, and language arts, but also free you to provide the individual help that might not otherwise be possible. And, perhaps most importantly, the child becomes more involved in the learning process and progresses according to his ability.

You will find that the organization of the book will be most helpful. The material is arranged into months of the school year so that there is sequential development in an easy-to-use form. Each activity is preceded by a quick review of its highlights, the equipment needed, suitable area for play, and the number of suggested players. Within each month there are several suggestions for appropriate holiday themes that will be fun for your students as well as yourself. Included also are games designed especially for the classroom. These are invaluable to have at your finger tips as relief from physical inactivity. In addition, there are lesson plans for each month; these may be followed or used as examples of the types of activities that may be combined within a regular thirty-minute period. Your plans should be according to the needs and interests of your particular class.

If you like definite ideas, yet desire flexibility in adjusting the

ideas to your individual personality and situation, you will be pleased with the "Points to Ponder" section following each activity. It includes several hints in the areas of planning, organizing, and correlating with other subjects. In addition, directions are given for improvising most of the materials needed for each of the activities so that you may have a quality program regardless of budgetary conditions.

As a teacher, you know that children enjoy repetition. Therefore, many activities that are introduced at the beginning of the year may well be enjoyed with improved skills throughout the year. Often, children will think of ways to change a particular activity and should be encouraged to do so if it produces desirable results.

Perhaps the most opportune time to really see how a child feels about himself and others is when he is engaged in play. Play is second nature to most children; in fact, it is their "business in life." With your guidance, this "business" could pay dividends that extend far beyond the activity room or playground.

Rosalie Bryant
Eloise McLean Oliver

ACKNOWLEDGMENTS

To the many teachers and children who contributed ideas used in our book, we extend our heartfelt thanks.

We are especially grateful and wish to express our appreciation to Dr. Rolland W. Jones, Superintendent of the Charlotte-Mecklenburg Schools for reviewing the book, writing the foreword, and encouraging us in our endeavors.

We are particularly indebted to our friend Emily Campbell and extend a special thanks to her for typing the manuscript, illustrating the book, and sharing her knowledge with us.

Contents

June *(cont.)*

P rovide a variety of activities.

H elp each child develop a positive self-image.

Y our attitude is contagious.

S tudents appreciate a teacher who can admit, "I don't know. Let's find out."

I magination and ingenuity can solve many equipment and space problems.

C reative activities should be included throughout the year.

A ll children need daily vigorous activity organized for maximum participation.

L ook for ways to involve the handicapped child.

E xcluding a child for punishment should be avoided unless other efforts fail.

D evelop good safety habits and attitudes.

U se children's ideas in planning and implementing their activities.

C reate an atmosphere that is conducive to fun and relaxation.

A dapt activities to individual situations and needs.

T he child is the one who is being taught—activities are only the tools.

I t is not whether you win or lose, but how you play the game.

O pportunities to develop leadership abilities should be given to each child.

N othing improves a program more than periodic evaluations.

If you should tell me once, and for some reason
I do not understand you, tell me that I did not listen—
and I'll doubt that you can reach me.

If you should tell me once, and for some reason
I do not understand you, tell me that perhaps you did not
explain it well—and I'll know that you can teach me.

—Rosalie Bryant

Suggestions

ORGANIZATION

Recognizing the role that organization plays in helping to reach desired objectives, teachers are searching for better ways to insure involvement for each child in all areas of learning. Lack of involvement has sometimes occurred during physical education activities because we often get so engrossed in teaching a game that we fail to see each child. Therefore, too many children may spend far more time awaiting a "turn" during the physical education class than they do in participation. This usually results from an honest effort to teach a particular activity, or from thinking that there is not enough equipment available to organize into more than one or two groups.

The purpose of the following types of organizational patterns is to help you provide maximum participation for the children according to specific objectives. The descriptive name given to each type is purely for clarification in this book.

(1) *Individually*. If the primary objective is for each child to become more physically skilled and to succeed according to his individual ability, the organization needs to be such that each child is working independently, but in relation to others in the area, to boundaries, and to objects. In this type of arrangement, you would structure the lesson so that sometimes children could explore different ways to solve a particular problem, and other times they would be asked to do specific things. Examples are: (a) "See how many different ways you can control the ball and carry it with you as you travel without touching anyone." (b) "Using only your feet to control the ball, carry it with you as you travel without touching anyone."

These are only two examples of the literally hundreds of opportunities for children to work independently on the same problem and to succeed according to each child's ability.

Note: Inexpensive ways to provide each child with the necessary equipment are given throughout the book.

(2) *With a Partner*. If the primary objective is for each child to become more physically skilled in situations that depend upon the

movements of another person, then organize so that two children work together. They should sometimes be asked to work in opposition and sometimes in supportive roles. Examples are: (a) "Take turns trying to keep your partner from being able to tag you—remember, we're working on dodging, not turning and running away from your partner." (b) "You and your partner are to continuously move in and out of the spaces you occupy as you pass the ball back and forth. Work on moving in different directions—sometimes close together, sometimes farther apart. Remember, you're working on throwing the ball so that your partner can catch it, but you both must keep moving."

Again, these are only two examples of partner-type activities.

(3) *Small Groups.* If the primary purpose is for each child to learn to use his skills in situations depending upon the movements of a few other people, or simply to learn or play a game, organizing into small groups offers tremendous possibilities. Children should be given opportunities to create their own small-group activities as well as to learn traditional ones with specific rules to follow. Small-group play, therefore, refers to organizing a class so that each small group is engaged in the *same* activity. In certain games, two small groups may join to make a team. The number of children on a team should be the minimum number necessary to accomplish the objective, otherwise too many children are left anxiously waiting to join the action.

(4) *Stations.* Station play refers to organizing so that children are in small groups, but each group is engaged in a *different* activity. The majority of the activities should be those that the children have learned previously as a whole class and played in small groups so that there will not be too many new things to learn at one time. Stations not only provide a variety of activities within a class period, but also offer solutions to limited equipment and supplies. If only a few individual ropes are available, for instance, they could be used as a station activity. The same would be true for balls, hoops, beanbags, and small or large apparatus. Stations also provide you with the opportunity to introduce a new activity, and the time to help each group as it rotates to the new station. Depending upon the type of activity and your personal preference, the new activity may be introduced to the entire class before organizing into stations or to each group as it arrives at the station.

If there are four or five stations, each group rotates to the next station after a few minutes. The number of stations and length of

time at each depends upon the activities as well as the number of children in the class.

(5) *Large Groups.* There are few activities that provide maximum participation regardless of the number of participants. These include some of the chasing-tagging games that involve every child all or almost all of the time. There are still others that depend on a large number of participants for success. Included in this category are those using the parachute, and some of the more complicated dodging games.

(6) *Interest Centers.* With this type of organization, children are given opportunities to explore and pursue their interests. Equally important, you have a chance to learn a little more about a particular child, join a group, observe interests of the class, or help on a one-to-one basis. The only difference between interest centers and stations is that with interest centers each child is free to choose and to move to another center when he is ready, rather than rotating with a group as in stations. This type of freedom demands responsibility for oneself and respect for the rights of others, otherwise chaos could result. In establishing an atmosphere conducive to learning, children will need much on-going guidance. They should be involved in making specific rules regarding such things as how many may be at a particular center at the same time, what to do if too many choose the same one, when they may choose a different center, and so on.

The number of centers will depend on the types of experiences planned, the available space, and the amount of equipment needed. If the centers are geared to individual or partner play, the number of centers and the amount of equipment at each should be enough to accommodate the group, and still allow choices. If, however, the centers are geared to small-group play, the number of centers and the amount of equipment needed would, in most cases, be less. Centers may also be mixed—some designed for small-group play and others for individual or partner play.

With interest centers, the equipment and space are provided, children are free to explore or to pursue their interests, and your role is to give any necessary help.

(7) *Learning Centers.* The organization for learning centers is basically the same as for stations or interest centers. However, learning centers are structured more toward the individual's learning specific concepts and skills. They are also designed so that, in most cases, each child works independently and progresses according to his

ability. The directions for each station or center may be given verbally, written on cards, illustrated through drawings, or combinations of these, depending on the group as well as the tasks.

Examples of learning centers for upper grades may include: (1) throwing at a target from various distances and recording the number of hits out of five tries, (2) dribbling (with hands or feet) a ball to a designated point and back, and recording the score in seconds, (3) running the bases and recording, in seconds, the time taken to touch every base, (4) attempting the standing broad jump and recording the best of three tries, (5) hitting a ball repeatedly against the wall with a paddle, and recording the best score (timed or consecutive hits), and (6) jumping rope and recording the number of different ways a child successfully jumps. There should be enough equipment at each center to allow each child to work on his own. Some children will complete their tasks sooner than others, and may move to another center of their choice.

Examples of centers for primary grades may be: (1) running the bases touching each in order, (2) dribbling a ball (with hands or feet) to a designated place and back without losing control of the ball, (3) jumping a rope five times without missing, (4) trying to keep a ball from bouncing more than once after each hit with a paddle, (5) tossing the ball into a circle (box, trash can, etc.) from a specified distance—with no limit to the number of tries, and (6) skipping to the tree, going around it twice, and galloping back. Again, the equipment should be adequate so that no child is waiting in line. As each finishes his task to his satisfaction, he moves to another center.

Specific ideas for learning centers in the open classroom are given in another section. Although they are geared toward quietness and small spaces, many of them may be used as centers in a regular physical education class. Children need experiences in a variety of skills and in a variety of learning situations. There is no one best way to teach all children because of the simple truth that no two people are alike. Therefore, there is no one best way to organize all activities. The purpose and the readiness of the group should be the determining factors in deciding the organizational pattern to follow for specific activities.

STUDENT LEADERS

The practice of involving children in leadership responsibilities is not new. It has been the secret of much of the success that many dedicated teachers have enjoyed through the centuries. Children

learn well from each other and, in many instances, much more readily than from an adult. Children should be given many opportunities to help and be helped by each other in literally every phase of school life. Not only is the practice educationally sound, but it also changes many of your time-consuming tasks into meaningful learning experiences for children.

Two responsible positions suggested for students in the area of physical education are *Squad Leaders* and *Equipment Managers.*

(1) *Squad Leaders.* These are boys and girls who are given the responsibility of helping to plan and provide leadership during physical education. Usually, one leader for every five to eight students is feasible. The duration of service will depend on the ages of the students as well as what works best in a particular class. However, the time should be long enough for a good experience in leadership. Between four and six weeks is usually adequate in the upper grades and a shorter period of time in the primary grades.

The position should be regarded as one of importance, with the class not only electing its leaders, but also establishing some rules or guidelines to be observed. The students will probably arrive at most of the points needed for discussion. The following are given as suggestions to offer only if necessary.

—*Qualities of a good leader:* Leading without "bossing"; being fair; helping courteously; setting a good example; being a good sport; including everyone in the activity; recognizing and overcoming obstacles; solving arguments; planning a variety of activities; being prepared; keeping the activity going; being responsible for the group; being patient; respecting abilities, rights, and feelings of others; accepting criticism . . . add others.

—*Qualities of a good follower:* Accepting criticism; being a good sport; offering suggestions without demanding; remembering directions; asking questions only when necessary; helping others; sharing turns willingly; accepting the leader's decisions and instructions . . . add others.

—*Election of squad leaders:* Nominations from the class; names submitted from former leaders; those who feel "ready" volunteering; . . . add others.

—*Selection of squad members:* Both boys and girls; boys and girls on separate squads; each leader choosing his own members; each leader choosing members for a squad and then "drawing" for the one he will lead. (Whatever method of selection is used, take care to do it in privacy so as not to expose any unpopular children to the recurring embarrassment of being chosen last.)

—*What to do about irresponsible leadership:* Class discussion; private session with the teacher; number of chances given to improve; replacements during office held; . . . add others.

(2) *Equipment Managers.* These are students who have the

responsibility for the equipment used in physical education. Usually two students per class are sufficient to do the job. Their duration of service need not coincide with that of squad leaders; it may need to be for a longer period of time. This, too, should be regarded as a position of importance with all students involved in the election and establishment of guidelines and rules to be followed. Use suggestions made by the class, adding those that follow only if necessary.

—*Qualities of a good manager:* Knowing where the equipment is located; securing it in advance; setting it up for play; accounting for it at the end of the period; returning it to its proper place; keeping it clean, repaired, inflated, etc. . . . add others.

—*Responsibilities of classmates:* Letting the equipment managers do their jobs; feeling responsible for equipment during play; reporting any lost or found items; . . . add others.

—*Election of equipment managers:* This may be the same procedure as that used with squad leaders.

—*What to do about irresponsible management:* This may also be the same procedure as that used with squad leaders.

Periodic meetings for brief sessions with the squad leaders and equipment managers will be necessary for their planning and communication and will add prestige to their positions. More time will be needed for the squad leaders to plan together and to decide when you or they may introduce new activities.

A good leadership program can be one of the highlights of an elementary school. There is no richer soil in which to plant the seeds necessary to grow responsible citizens.

EVERYDAY HINTS

—If necessary, hand signals are preferred over a whistle for getting children's attention. Teach them to recognize that two hands raised means *gather informally in front of the teacher so that all can see and hear.* One hand means *stop the activity and listen for further instructions.* A whistle may be needed for immediate response in only those few games involving much action, large distances, or a great deal of noise.

—To avoid a delay caused in certain games by a child's not choosing someone quickly, by a player's running too far away from the group, by a few monopolizing the game instead of including others—or wherever it is applicable— teach students to count slowly, "1-2-3." On the count of 3, the necessary changes must have begun or the leader or teacher will make the desired changes. Children enjoy this self-discipline and the responsibility of keeping the game "alive." They seem to sense when it is time to count.

—In chasing games, help children assume the responsibility for choosing replacements when they become too tired to be "it."

—In certain types of games requiring an official, discuss the need to respect

the official's decision, whether favorable or unfavorable. If each child is allowed to have many chances to *call* a game, he will learn how it feels to quickly "call it as he sees it." Respect for and acceptance of decisions usually becomes much more pronounced than before.

—When games requiring speed involve two people meeting each other, teach them to keep to the right, just as cars are driven on the right side of the road. When there are several players running in the same direction, discuss staying in lanes as cars do on roads that have several lanes for cars traveling in the same direction.

—Spend some time working on movements that involve responses to: *right, left, up, down, around, over, under, in, out,* etc. *Parallel, perpendicular, opposite, vertical, horizontal, diagonal,* and so on may be added according to grade or ability.

—When giving directions to a group outdoors on a sunny day, face the sun so that the children's backs are to it. This eliminates their squinting in order to see you. If you are wearing sunglasses, remove them; children listen better when they can see your eyes.

—If hand-squeezing, pinching, and arm-pulling become apparent when the children form circles, eliminate the joining of hands. Have them form a circle without touching, or perhaps by touching only finger tips.

—If it is necessary for students to form lines, help them realize that being first in line does not necessarily mean being first to do whatever is planned. In the upper grades, you may find that the competition to be *last* in line is equally great. In order to eliminate this needless jockeying for position, make it a regular policy to reverse the line so that the back end goes first, to divide it in the middle and re-form it, to have every other one step out and go to the end (or front) of the line, and so forth.

—Make a special effort to organize so that every child is as active as possible. Often, the reason for rushing to be first or for being dishonest about sharing "turns" is due to the organization of the activity. If organization is poor, the child may find that the only sure way to be recognized or have a turn is either to be first or not to tell the truth about already having had a turn (see *ORGANIZATION*).

—For efficiency in certain activities, teach children to count off by 2's, 3's, 4's, and so on. However, opportunities should also be given for children to assume the responsibility to arrange themselves quickly in groups of a given number.

—Don't try to give directions when the group is talking. Trying to talk over them only causes frustration for you and the children.

—Make directions easy on yourself and the children. *Effective:* "When I say, 'Go!' I'd like you to run as fast as you can to the tree and back. When you return, get a rope and find a space on the paved area." *Ineffective:* "Run as fast as you can to the tree and . . ." (They'll be off and running before you get the chance to finish your instructions.)

—Children need opportunities to explore and respond creatively and individually. Some suggestions for these types of responses are found throughout

the book. Intersperse them with group play, and review them often to work toward self-improvement throughout the year.

—Be aware of the shy or timid child, and try to find a way to involve him without embarrassment. Threat or force never solves the real problem.

—Unless all other efforts fail, a child should not be eliminated from physical education as a means of punishment. The temptation to use or threaten to use this punishment usually results from disciplinary problems that arise in the classroom. To eliminate a child from physical education is the same as denying that it is a part of the curriculum, and setting it apart as a reward for good behavior. However, a child should not be allowed to be disruptive and create a difficult situation for others during physical education. A temporary and on-the-spot solution is to have him walk back and forth within your view between two designated objects. He should understand that he may return to the activity when he feels that he can participate constructively.

—Children should not be expected to sit still for long periods of time. Letting them have a few minutes of vigorous physical activity periodically during the day pays big dividends.

—Every child is gifted in some way. Try to help children realize this by commenting not only on the more physically coordinated child, but also on other often unnoticed abilities—leadership, preparation of equipment, sportsmanship, organization, or officiating.

—Plan times when children have free play. This may be built into the period as a station to which they rotate from other activities, or it may be the last few minutes of the period.

—Let the children help accumulate materials and equipment to keep on hand for convenience and for saving time. Examples: (1) plastic detergent, bleach, and milk bottles to make bowling pins, markers, boundaries, and scoops; (2) carpet samples or squares cut from discarded rugs to make bases, markers, boundaries, and hopscotch patterns; (3) plow line, cotton cord, and plastic clothesline to jump rope, make boundaries, or obstacles to go over, around, in, out, etc.; (4) corrugated cardboard to cut into squares, stack, and secure with tape or cord to make boxes to jump off, over, onto, etc.; (5) paper balls to use for nearly every activity requiring a ball that does not have to bounce. Paper balls may be made any size. Open a double page of newspaper, start at one corner, and roll it into a round shape. Enlarge the ball by adding pages—one at a time—until the desired size is reached. Work it into a round shape after each sheet is added. Secure it with masking tape or a nylon stocking. (Push the ball into the toe of the stocking, stretch the stocking, twist it several times, and push the ball back through. Repeat this process as many times as possible and secure with masking tape or thread.)

—Praise is probably the most powerful motivator there is—everyone likes and needs it. Compliment your class and each child individually as often as possible, but be sincere because no one, not even a child, appreciates false praise.

—Remember that the same skill that may be easy for one child may require

a tremendous amount of effort for another child. This refers to skills requiring physical coordination and to those involving social, emotional, and intellectual stages of development.

—Children grow and learn best in an atmosphere filled with love, acceptance, and trust.

—Life has been referred to as a series of "games." Help each child learn to perform well in all roles—as the star, the teammate, the winner, the loser, the offensive, the defensive—but most of all, to perform in a manner of which he can be proud.

—Some of the wisest people known include a time every day to be quiet and still, and think happy thoughts. The period of time may be brief, but the results are long-lasting. Try to help children establish this habit by frequently providing such a period. Many fears and pressures have been overcome by simply lying on the grass, putting thoughts into proper perspective, and concentrating on those things for which to be thankful.

—Add others.

September

TO THE TEACHER—On Moving to Learn

You have only to watch a baby exploring his body and his world to see "moving to learn" in constant action. We accept his curiosity and perpetual motion as necessary in his development. Then, all too often, when he enters school, the close relationship that exists between mind and body is overlooked. Because the thinking process is so deeply involved with motor activity, and because they have such a pronounced effect on each other, we cannot afford to ignore either of them. Language has much more meaning to a child when he can relate the words to movement that he understands—over, under, around, in, out, beside, greater than, less than, in front of, and behind.

Research indicates that, in most cases, children with a higher degree of motor development are more receptive to learning and tend to excel in their academic efforts. Studies also support the fact that more than three-fourths of a child's basic motor movements are acquired during the first twelve years of his life.

BALL-HANDLING SKILLS (K-6)

At first glance the activities in this section may not attract your attention as quickly as a game with a "catchy" name. However, as you read the material and visualize it, you will immediately see the value of providing these experiences for children. Although more balls than usual are required, you will find inexpensive solutions in the section, Points to Ponder. If there is still a doubt, only one serious attempt is all that is usually required before both you and the children are completely sold on the value of these activities. You will see individual learning taking place, each child experiencing success according to his individual ability, many solutions to a given problem being discovered, and complete involvement of all students occurring.

Because of the depth of understanding and the quality of movements that are possible, the experiences suggested are *much more than games* and should never be considered finished. Instead, they should be provided continuously throughout the year.

The more experiences children have in handling a ball, the more likely they will be successful in games in which ball handling is a part. Although any of several methods may be used to promote understanding of the body movements necessary to best receive or pass a ball, the following suggestions are given to serve as a starting point. Although certain grade levels are suggested, these would vary according to the degree to which an idea is explored and the abilities of the children.

(1) *Toss and catch at different levels. (K-6).*   Give each child a beanbag or a small paper ball (as described in Points to Ponder) and ask him to toss the ball so that he can catch it *within reaching distance*—without moving out of the space around him. The class should be kept within a limited area for easy communication. Ask them to space themselves as well as possible to avoid interfering with each other. Keep working on the idea of *controlling* the ball. Offer individual help where needed, but rather than telling him to "do it this way," make every effort to guide each child toward *his* solutions: "Why do you think the beanbag or ball is going too far in front of [or behind] you? . . . Where are your hands when they release the ball? . . . Where would they have to release a ball in order for it to go overhead? . . . to one side?" Try to get the child to respond through action (tossing the ball) rather than just a verbal response.

After the group has some understanding of what *control* means, work on tossing the ball so that it goes to a different height or level each time it is tossed. At all times, the key word is *control!* Keep working on this until it is apparent that they understand not only the level that is barely above the floor and the one that is as high as each can toss with control, but also the many levels in between. In order to get the idea of "giving with the ball" (absorbing the force with the hands), ask them to catch the ball or beanbag as softly or quietly as possible. Good results are almost instant!

Once levels of tossing an object are understood, add the task of *receiving* it at different levels: "Toss the ball and catch it so that your hands are at a different level each time it is caught." This idea is a little more difficult to grasp. Demonstrate the very highest level they can reach (by jumping) to the lowest level their hands can be above the floor. Some of them will probably catch the ball at the same level each time, and then move their hands to a different level after the ball is caught. Watch for this, and emphasize that the *first* contact the hands make with the ball should be at different levels.

As tossing and receiving at different levels are understood, ask them to combine the two—toss to a different level each time *and* catch at a different level each time. Work toward tossing the ball from the level at which it was caught.

Note: You may need to discuss the term "reaching distance" so that children know that they may jump, stretch, step, slide, etc. in order to catch the ball.

(2) *Catch ball using all of personal space (1-6).* In tossing and catching at different levels, most children have explored or used the space above them and immediately in front of them. The objective now becomes to toss and catch the ball using *all* of the space around them within their reach (front, back, sides, high, low). "Toss the ball so that you have to reach or stretch as far as possible to catch it." Let them keep working on the idea for a short period of time as you give individual help where needed: "You have the idea . . . now can you toss it a little farther away so that you really have to stretch to catch it?" or, "That's it; now can you toss it to another space (side, behind, etc.) so that you have to *reach* way back (out) to catch it?" or (for those who are not stretching or extending fully), "Toss it far enough away from you that it is *just outside* your reach when you try to catch it."

(3) *Pass and receive ball using all of personal space (4-6).* With two children per ball, ask them to toss it to each other so that each has to receive it at a different level or height each time. Watch for those who toss the ball so that it makes an arc but falls in their partner's hands at the same level each time. Help them understand that their partner's hands should be at a different level when they first contact (catch) the ball: "How must you toss the ball so that your partner catches it as high as he can reach [jump]? . . . as close to the floor [ground] as he can? . . . think of all the levels in between." Give individual help and encouragement as needed to get the idea across. When feasible, add the task of passing the ball so that each partner not only receives it at different levels, but also in different spaces around him (high, low, right side, left side). Emphasize making each partner stretch to reach the ball. At first it is difficult to pass and receive a ball while concentrating on levels. Some may need to take turns, letting one partner concentrate on passing the ball as the other works on receiving it. Give them time to practice so that eventually they can do it together. Work toward their being able to pass the ball from the same level at which they received it.

(4) *Pass and receive ball in constantly changing situations*

(4-6). Have one ball for every pair of students: "While both of you move constantly, pass the ball back and forth to each other. Sometimes you will be very close together—try not to get more than approximately 10 feet apart, but keep moving constantly. You may not be very accurate at first, but keep working on it—don't worry if you miss." When they are ready, progress to: "I'd like for you to *think* about what I'm going to ask you to do next. You and your partner are to join another pair of players. Keep one of the two balls and put the other one away. When you are still, I'll know you're ready. Any questions? . . . Off you go!" When they are in groups of four, ask them to do the same thing they were doing in pairs—to constantly move as they pass the ball to each other. Encourage them to keep changing directions (so that they are not just going around in a circle). Emphasize anticipating directions and making an honest effort to pass the ball so that it can be caught.

(5) *Pass and receive ball in competition (4-6).* As players become more skilled in handling a ball in constantly changing situations as explained in (4) above, occasionally give them experiences with a competitive element added: "In your groups of four, take turns letting one person try to deflect or intercept the ball as the other three pass it among themselves. Remember, the three passing the ball must keep moving as before." The moment competition is added (a person trying to intercept the ball), there is usually a noticeable lapse in skillful ball handling as well as a tendency to stop moving. This is a normal reaction. Be aware of it and give help as needed; with experience, these skills will gradually improve. Once the players become more skillful, challenge them to make five passes before changing the person attempting to intercept the ball.

Points to Ponder

If there is a choice between small paper balls and beanbags for (1) and (2), beanbags are preferable. However, if paper balls are used, they may be easily made by loosely rolling only one double sheet of newspaper into the shape of a ball and securing it with masking tape or cellophane tape. For (3), (4), and (5), the balls should be approximately 8" in diameter. Balls made of paper actually work as well, if not better, than other kinds. If others are available and desired, the lighter weight volleyball, playground ball, or plastic ball are preferred.

If there is an odd number of children, use a group of three or five players, as the case may be.

Keep the objective in mind—If the children are working on receiving the ball as far away from them as possible, keep aiming toward that goal. Be patient and always offer words of encouragement for improvement.

Remember that these experiences are geared toward a much wider range of understanding of movement than is usually emphasized in any one game. Therefore, they should be viewed differently. They should be considered the necessary foundation for improving skills in many game situations requiring the use of a ball.

ROPE JUMPING (K-6)

Highlights—hand-eye-foot coordination, jumping lightly with a lift, landing softly; *Equipment*—short ropes, approximately 8' long—1 per child or enough for one group of 6-8 children; long ropes, approximately 16' long—1 per group of 4-6 children; *Area*—activity room, playground, paved area, or classroom.

Rope jumping is one of the most valuable exercises. It involves skills that are simple enough for a four- or five-year-old to master, as well as skills that are complex enough to challenge a champion athlete. It is relatively inexpensive, is suitable for both boys and girls, and requires little space. It may be enjoyed individually or in small groups, with or without music.

For Beginners

Without a rope, begin with all children in front of you. Clap your hands in a steady and rhythmical 4/4 time. Continue this until all can clap rhythmically together. Then let some clap while others jump lightly in place to the same rhythm. As progress is made, encourage a slightly higher jump on *every other* jump to get a smooth jump-bounce-jump-bounce rhythm (you may prefer to say high-low-high-low). The bounce is the intervening movement of the body after each jump over the rope to maintain the rhythm. Encourage light and easy jumps that lift the body. Encourage landing on the balls of the feet and "giving" with knees and ankles to make the landing soft. This need not be described, because usually the response is perfect when you ask something like, "Can you jump so softly to the rhythm that I can't hear a sound? What did you have to do to make your landings so quiet?"

Long Ropes

Once the jump without the rope is mastered, the long rope may be added using many different methods that will vary with individual

children. One method is to have the jumper stand at the center of the rope and begin his rhythmical jump (jump-bounce-jump-bounce) while you and one child turn the rope to the rhythm set by the jumper: "Bill, do you think you could continue jumping while Jane and I try to turn the rope so that it goes under your feet? . . . If you land on the rope or it hits your legs, it will be our fault. You just keep on jumping until we get it right, understand? Go!" You and your helper should be able to turn to his rhythm after only a few misses, if any. Since some children lose the rhythm once they see the rope being turned, many have found it helpful to close their eyes and jump until they have successfully jumped the rope several times. As soon as they open their eyes, these children will often miss at first.

At a later time, after they gain confidence in jumping, let them progress to running in, jumping, and running out as the rope is being turned: "Watch the rope as it turns toward you [turn the rope as you talk]. If you were going to run in and jump while it is turning, where would the rope be when you go in? Right, on the other side. Where on the other side should it be to give you the most time to get in and be ready to jump? That's right, at the *bottom* of the other side."

Let one at a time try to run in and jump. It may be helpful to say that as soon as the rope hits the *third* time, they must run in and jump. Let those who are successful try jumping a designated number of times and running out the other side (back door).

Short Ropes

After children understand the rhythmical jumping and can jump a long rope, they usually progress rather easily to an individual rope. If there is difficulty, it is usually in coordinating the movements of hands and feet. Without a rope, let them practice what the hands must do to make the rope go smoothly ('round and 'round or over and over) without stopping. This takes time and practice. Some children get the "feel" of the turn better if they turn it backward. This prevents their slamming it down on the ground as they turn. They often learn faster by observing and helping each other.

Additional Skills

Perhaps the most meaningful skills are those that originate with your students. Give them a few minutes to experiment with another way to use their feet as they jump the rope. When they have worked this out, let them show it to the class to see if others can do it. Another time, the children might experiment with other ways they

can turn the rope and jump it. Many of the skills may be done with long ropes or individual ropes. When the students are ready, let some or all of them work with partners or in small groups to create different skills and routines that could be done with or without music.

Some skills that children have created are as follows:

Jump-Bounce: Both feet—With feet together, jump with an intervening bounce. One foot—Lift one foot and jump-bounce on the other.

Rock: Place one foot in front of the other. Clear the rope with the front foot, then the back foot—the weight shifts forward and back, producing a rocking motion.

Skip: Skip as the rope turns.

Run*: Run as the rope turns. (Clear the rope with every other step, or turn the rope quickly and clear it with each step.)

Cross Feet: Jump and land with feet crossed on every other jump.

Slip*: Swing the rope vertically beside the body (right or left side). Hands are kept close together to keep the rope closed.

Fast Jump: Jump rope without an intervening bounce. Turn rope quickly (Hot Potato).

Cross Hands*: Cross arms about chest high on every other jump. Arms will be uncrossing every other jump, thus forming a figure eight with each hand. This may be done while turning the rope forward or backward.

Alternate: Jump on one foot and swing the other leg forward on the bounce. Repeat, alternating feet.

Travel*: Do any skill while moving forward, backward, diagonally, or sideways.

There are many other skills and activities that your class and you will discover as you explore rope jumping.

Points to Ponder

Plow line (3/8") is relatively inexpensive and makes good jump ropes. To keep it from unravelling, wrap a few inches with masking or plastic tape at the desired length and cut in the center of the tape, thus securing two ends at a time when making many jump ropes.

Usually, many students in every class already know the basic skills of jumping rope. They could be discovering new ways to jump while you work with the beginners. Rope jumping could also be one of several stations of activities through which all groups rotate. At this station, you could work with the beginners in the group, and have individual ropes for the others.

---

*Try only with individual ropes.

With good organization, it is possible to teach rope jumping even if you have only one long rope and a few individual ropes. However, there is much more that could be done creatively as a class if there could be several long ropes, and enough individual ropes for each child to have one.

Jumping rope is vigorous activity. Organize and plan so that less strenuous activities are interspersed during a class period. This may be done by using rope jumping as one of the stations through which all groups rotate, by letting small groups work out skills or routines together (which automatically provides physically inactive periods) or by beginning or ending less vigorous activities with rope jumping as a physical workout.

I SEE (K-2)

Highlights—listening and responding to a verbal signal, creative interpretations; *Equipment*—none; *Area*—playground, activity room, paved area, or classroom; *Number of players*—unlimited.

"We are going to play a game today called *I See*. There are only three rules to the game: listening at a certain time, stopping at a certain time, and not touching anyone. Do you think you could do those three things? . . . Good, I think you can, too. The game begins when I say, 'I see!' All together, you will shout to me, 'What do you see?' Whatever I tell you that I see, you will pretend to be or do. Suppose I said, 'I see boys and girls jumping high in the air and not making any noise'—could you do that? Remember, every time you hear me shout, 'I see,' you must stop and yell, 'What do you see?' I will then tell you what else I see. Any questions? . . . Here we go . . . 'I see!' [Children respond, 'What do you see?'] 'Fairies running quietly all around.' "

This action continues until the teacher says, "I see." at which time the children stop and respond, "What do you see?"—and the game continues.

Points to Ponder

If playing on a large playground, it may be wise to limit the area so as to stay within hearing distance.

Be sensitive to the involvement of the children, and always stop the activity while the interest level is high. This is a favorite game to repeat if it is played only a brief period at a time.

Encourage children to think of things they would like the class

to do, and give volunteers an opportunity to be leaders. Some favorites enjoyed by many classes are: "Indians dancing all around," "old, old men and women," "all the teachers in the school," "a strong man cutting down a tree," "a baseball player sliding into home," "boys and girls on vacation."

The game may be used as a brief warm-up activity, making the phrases more and more active with the last one being: "boys and girls sitting quietly in front of me" (or whatever arrangement is best suited to lead into the next activity). It may also be used effectively at the end of the class period with the last phrase being: "boys and girls walking quietly back to the room," or "boys and girls getting ready for lunch" (or whatever is planned next).

V-R-R-ROOM (K-2)

Highlights—running safely in a large group, chasing/tagging, chanting with a group; *Equipment*—none; *Area*—playground or activity room; *Number of players*—unlimited.

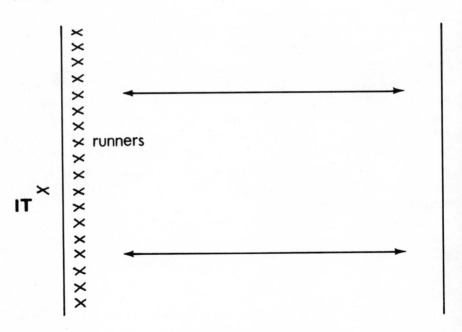

Figure 1 V-R-R-ROOM

Before playing the game, let children have as many experiences as possible in moving (walking, running) within a given area without

touching anyone. Discuss staying within boundary lines and not getting into a space where someone else is or is going. Discuss ways to avoid collisions.

With children standing or sitting informally, teach them the chant "Spaceships headed for the moon!...3...2...1...V-r-r-room!" Explain that they will all be standing side by side on a line and facing IT, as shown in Figure 1. On the word, "V-r-r-room," they will turn around and run to the other line while IT chases them, trying to tag as many as possible. From those *not* tagged, IT will choose someone to replace him before they finish slowly counting "1-2-3." The game will continue from this line back to the original line. Make sure that everyone understands where the two lines are, choose an IT to begin the game, and play for a brief period of time.

Points to Ponder

Make sure that everyone understands that a tap is all that is necessary in tagging. There is no need to hold onto the person or his clothes.

Common faults include arguing whether or not a person was tagged, and stopping *on* the "finish" line instead of running past it to leave space for others. Discuss these points and try to keep them from occurring.

Plastic bottles set in the four corners, ropes laid on the ground, or drawn lines may be used to indicate boundaries. Whatever is used, make sure that the children understand where the boundaries are and why they must run beyond them during the game (for safety).

SPUD (3-6)

Highlights—wise judgment, accuracy in hitting a stationary target, quick response to signals, leisure-time activity; *Equipment*—one ball—6"-10" in diameter, and one base per game; *Area*—playground; *Number of players*—suited best for 8-10 per game.

Grades 3-4

While the others watch, use one group for demonstration purposes. The game begins with one person holding the ball and standing on the base as the others stand around informally. He calls the name of the player to be IT and tosses the ball straight overhead. All players scatter except IT, who retrieves the ball and yells, "Spud!"—the signal for other players to freeze. IT calls the name of a

player he thinks he can hit and throws the ball in an attempt to hit that person. If successful, all return to the base, and IT tosses the ball overhead, calling the name of the next IT who will continue the game. If he is *not* successful, all return to the base, and the player who was thrown at and missed tosses the ball and calls the name of a new IT. When everyone understands, play the game in groups, or use it as a station to which groups rotate during the period.

Note: When IT yells, "Spud!" each player must come to a dead stop and may not move in an attempt to dodge a ball thrown at him except to protect his face should a ball be thrown too high.

Points to Ponder

Encourage players to be daring by staying just close enough to IT to be thrown at and far enough away to be a challenge. Some players will seek attention by trying to be closest to IT. However, this situation has a way of solving itself, because IT will usually seek out a greater challenge. IT should throw the ball hard enough to hit his target, but not hard enough to hurt.

To lessen the impact of the ball, use one made of paper, or one that is punctured or has been slightly deflated.

The suggested base (plastic bottle, marker, etc.) is necessary only as a means of keeping the game in a given area.

Opportunities for each child to experience success in tossing the ball overhead should be given prior to playing *Spud.* This may easily be done in earlier sessions. Give each child a ball made of paper and let him explore, with guidance, the many directions the ball will go, depending on where his hands are at the point of release. In *Spud,* a common error is throwing the ball to the person who is to be IT, rather than throwing it straight overhead.

Grades 5-6

With a few modifications, *Spud* can be an entirely different game, offering challenge to older boys and girls as well as adults. The main difference is that once the game begins, it is fast and continuous for a given time limit—no one returns to the base to call another name. In a nutshell, the directions are:

—One person tosses the ball and names an IT.

—IT retrieves the ball and calls, "Spud!"—freezing all players.

—IT names the player he wishes to hit, and throws the ball in an attempt to do so.

—If he is successful, IT retrieves the ball immediately, and the others scatter until IT calls, "Spud!"

—If he is unsuccessful, IT becomes a regular player and the one at whom he threw becomes IT, retrieving the ball, and the game continues.

Note: To maintain a high interest level, restrict play to a given area and to approximately five minutes' time.

SOCK IT TO ME (K-6)

Highlights—alertness and quick response, continuously throwing balls; *Equipment*—one paper ball per child, a volleyball net (or long rope or string), and a whistle, drum or loud voice; *Area*—activity room, playground, paved area, or classroom; *Number of players*—unlimited.

Very few directions are necessary for *Sock It to Me*. Make sure that each player has a ball; then divide the group into two even teams. Place one team on each side of the net (rope or string) bisecting the area. Explain that when the starting signal is given, everyone will throw his ball over the net and throw back any that come from the other team as fast as he can. This will continue until the whistle (drum beat or "Stop!") is heard. No balls may be thrown after this time. Each team will gather the balls on its side and count them aloud. The team with the fewest balls on its side wins. If there are no questions, assign one player to give the starting signal by saying, "Sock it to me! Sock it to me!"

Points to Ponder

If there is an uneven number, use the extra player to give the signals for starting and stopping. The signal to stop should be loud and clear.

If balls are being deliberately thrown after the signal to stop is given, let the class decide the penalty.

This game is *very* active and is a good way to end the class period. Playing it no more than one or two minutes at the most will insure its being one of the favorites for frequent play throughout the year.

DEFROST (3-6)

Highlights—quick starts, stops, and changes of direction, chasing/tagging in a large group; *Equipment*—none; *Area*—playground or activity room; *Number of players*—unlimited.

The game of *Defrost* is played quite successfully by third graders as well as sixth graders. The physical skills involved are running, tagging, and dodging, but the differences in the older students' game are mostly in strategy and tactics.

Choose five students to be taggers and two to be defrosters. Explain that the five taggers will start the game by getting in a huddle and counting aloud to five as all other players scatter. On the count of five, the taggers try to tag as many players as possible. Any player tagged must freeze and remain frozen until one of the two defrosters touches him and shouts, "Defrost!" To add more spice to the game, the defrosters must be careful not to be tagged because they, too, may be frozen. The object of the game is to see how many players are frozen at the end of a given period of time.

Points to Ponder

The playing area should be well defined—for an average-sized class, an area approximately 60' x 60' works well. Any players running out of bounds should be considered tagged; otherwise, those being chased would have an unfair advantage, and the game would probably lose the dodging element entirely, becoming one of only chasing and running.

The game is made much more effective by selecting five taggers who have something easily identifiable to others: plaid shirts, green jeans, and so forth. The same could be done with the defrosters. Of course, any distinguishing feature is feasible—colored armbands, for example.

Since *Defrost* is an extremely active game, it should not be continued for long periods of time. Play it before or after a less active game, or for a few minutes at the end of a class period.

Players who stand still but have not been tagged will confuse the taggers and defrosters. If this becomes a problem, ask all untagged players to keep moving even when they are not being chased.

CAPTURE THE FLAG (4-6)

Highlights—independent thinking and self-responsibility, decision-making, team strategy; *Equipment*—two flags (markers or handkerchiefs); *Area*—playground; *Number of players*—suited best for 10-40 players.

Divide the class into two teams, and start each in its own half of the field as shown in Figure 2. The object of the game is to capture

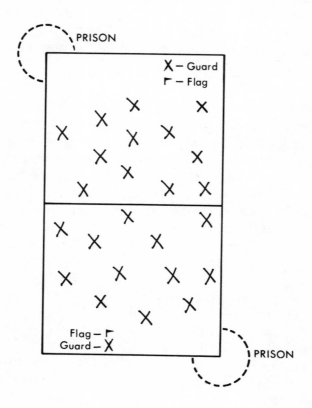

Figure 2 CAPTURE THE FLAG

the opponents' flag and bring it "home" (to one's own half of the field) without being tagged by an opponent. Students can make individual attempts to capture the flag, or they can work together to accomplish this. Play must remain within the boundaries. Any time a player is in the opponents' territory, he can be tagged by them and put in their prison where he must stay until he is tagged by one of his teammates. Any number of players may be confined in a prison, but each one must be tagged to be freed. One player may release any number of prisoners as long as he himself remains untagged. When a player is freed from prison, he *walks* home outside the playing area and begins aggressive play only *after* he has first returned to his half of the field. The player who releases the prisoners may not have a

free walk home because he is subject to being tagged himself. Freed prisoners may not be tagged as they walk home.

One player from each team guards the flag. Others may chase those threatening the flag, but only the guard stays by or close to the flag. He may not hold or touch the flag while guarding it.

The game starts on a given signal and is over when one team succeeds in capturing the opponents' flag.

Points to Ponder

Fourth graders will play a teasing kind of game; half of the fun for them is sticking a foot over the center line to see if they can get it back before being tagged. Fifth graders concentrate more on the objective at hand, getting the flag, but have not as yet learned to use much caution or teamwork. A sixth-grade game can be a work of art, because sixth graders usually discover that strategy pays, that working together is the only way to win, and that an individual sacrifice can win the game for the team. Guide students in discovering these keys to success. Remind them that protecting their own flag is as important as capturing their opponents' flag.

Let students modify any rule to suit the situation or add any they feel are needed (such as no guard for the prison). The rules of the game are not as important as a successful game. It should be fair. It should be safe. It should be fun.

The playing field need not be marked off as such. Placing plastic bottles or markers to indicate the four corners, to designate the center line, and to define the area of the prisons is usually quite satisfactory.

TRUE OR FALSE (3-6)

Highlights—correlation with other subject areas, independent thinking, alertness, and quick reaction; *Equipment*—For classroom—none, For playground or activity room—4 long ropes or 4 lines or 8 markers; *Area*—playground, activity room, or classroom; *Number of players*—suited best for 10-35 players.

For Classroom

Divide the class to form two teams. Add interest by having each team choose an appropriate name. A leader stands in front of the class and makes a statement. If the statement is true, players *stand*; if it is false, they shout, "false!" The leader decides which team is first to respond correctly and awards that team one point.

For Playground or Activity Room

Two equal teams of players stand behind two parallel lines placed 6'-8' apart. Players are side by side, facing the opposing team. One team is the *true* team; the other is the *false* team. Approximately 30' behind each team is another line. A leader stands at one end of the two lines of players and makes a statement (Examples: "Today is Monday." Mr. Ledford is our principal." "Agnew is the Vice President of the United States." "5 x 3 = 20." "There are 50 states in the Union.") If the statement is true, the true team turns and runs to the line behind it, pursued by the false team, which tries to tag as many true members as possible; if false, the false team runs back to its own line, pursued by the true team. Each time the game is played, tagged players join the opposing team, and all players return to the starting lines. The winning team is the one with the greater number of players at the end of a given period of time.

Points to Ponder

Before playing the game suggested for playground or activity room, students should know how to tag (tap) and how to run in a group. Discuss with them what they should do if two players disagree on whether or not one tagged the other.

When in the classroom, scorekeeping at the chalkboard can be a visual stimulation. Try keeping score by 4's and 5's instead of single points as a good exercise in arithmetic.

The leader of the game need not be the teacher. Part of the fun is in making the statements and judging the winner. Let students take turns doing this, choosing replacements after each point is scored.

Try restricting statements to a specific area, such as math, language arts, social studies, or health. After a session in a given area, spend the last part of the period playing *True or False* as a fun way to review.

TOUCHÉ TURTLE (K-2)

Highlights—falling safely, running in a large group, chasing/tagging; *Equipment*—none; *Area*—playground or activity room; *Number of players*—unlimited.

"Have you ever seen a turtle turned over on his back? . . . Could you show me with your bodies what he looks like? All of you don't have to be just alike, but your feet and arms (representing four legs) must be up during part of the game we're going to learn today. Sometimes you won't have much time to get in that position because

you will be running or dodging. Let's all sit down for a minute, because I want you to think with me.

"The game we're going to play is called *Touché Turtle*. Touché has a friend who is a dog, and his name is Dum Dum. In the game, Touché and Dum Dum will try to tag as many of you as possible. You must stay within this area [designate an area] and dodge them, if possible. When you cannot keep from being tagged by dodging, there is a way for you to be 'safe'—guess what you could do so that Touché and/or Dum Dum cannot tag you? . . . Good, lie flat on your back and raise all fours. And we're going to add *one* more thing—you must say, "Dead turtle!" When Touché and Dum Dum go away to chase others, you may get up and join the game. Now, we have one problem to solve—you may be running or moving quickly, and won't have time to stop before you lie down. How could you get down? . . . Yes, and that's where more fun comes in—you actually get to fall down in this game. Stay seated now, but *think* how you could fall without hurting yourself or anyone else. Do you think you know? Who could show all of us? [Let one volunteer show as others watch.] Why do you think he fell so smoothly? . . . That's right, he made his body *soft* and didn't fall flat on his back. When I say 'Go,' I want all of you to stand up and run around the [designated] area doing two things: one is to be sure you don't run into anyone or anything; the other is to fall, lift all fours, and say, 'Dead turtle!' You will continue this over and over until you see my arms raised. Then come back and sit down. Any questions? . . . Ready? . . . Go!"

When all have done this a couple of minutes, raise both arms. After the children are seated, discuss whatever seems necessary: "That was great! I saw no accidents [or, I saw only one (two) accidents]. What *must* you do to avoid bumping into others? . . . hurting yourself when you fall?" Practice again, *if necessary*.

"Mary, you be Touché Turtle and Jimmy will be your friend, Dum Dum. Remember, everyone must stay within the area. When Touché or Dum Dum has tagged you, keep one hand raised while you're *walking* over to stand by me so that we will know you're out of the game. After eight of you are tagged, Touché and Dum Dum will choose replacements from those *not* tagged before we slowly count 1-2-3. All tagged players will re-enter the game, and we start again. Any questions? . . . While I'm counting to 3, everyone will scatter except Touché and Dum Dum; when I finish counting, they're free to chase you. Ready? . . . 1—2—3!"

Points to Ponder

Consider the available surface for play. A dry, grassy area, a gymnasium, multipurpose room, or activity room are suitable. Clay, cement, asphalt, or dirty surfaces are obviously unsatisfactory.

Consider the weather; there is vigorous movement involved in the game, which makes it an excellent outdoor game when the temperature is appropriate.

Some inexpensive way to distinguish Touché and Dum Dum would be helpful. One suggestion is to tie a brightly colored strip of cloth or crepe paper around their necks, upper arms, or waists. You and your class could think of others.

The number of players tagged before the game starts over should vary according to the number playing the game, the size of the area, and the skills of the children. Adjust this as necessary to maintain interest, challenge, and still allow no one to remain out of the game very long after being tagged.

If the girls are not dressed appropriately to "raise all fours," let all children raise only their arms and say, "Dead turtle!"

Generally, children love to fall down; it is simply part of their nature. This is one of the few games of which falling is a part; therefore, it is usually a real favorite.

The game need not be played until every child has a chance to be Touché or Dum Dum because it provides vigorous activity for all. It may be played in small groups or as a whole class. Once the children know the game, it is a good one to use as a quick workout at the beginning or end of a class period.

STRIDE BALL (K-6)

Highlights—alertness in response to a moving object, leisure-time activity; *Equipment*—one ball—6"-10" in diameter—for each group of 5-8 players; *Area*—playground, activity room, paved area, or classroom; *Number of players*—suited best for 5-8 players per game.

The game of *Stride Ball* is very exciting to young children, and, with a few modifications, becomes quite challenging to older boys and girls. The basic game is one in which a small number of players stands in circle formation with feet spread a little more than shoulder-width apart, touching the feet of the players on either side. The ball is in the center.

The object of the game is to push (roll) the ball so that it passes

through the legs (goal) of another player. Players may use both hands to defend their goals. On signal, any of the players may push the ball to start the game. Each time a player allows the ball to pass through his goal, a point is scored against him. The player with lowest score at the end of a given time wins.

Note: A player may not lower his body to the ground or floor to defend his goal.

Points to Ponder

Since the ball does not need to bounce, it may be one with a puncture or may be made of paper.

This is one of the few games in which the winner is the one with the lowest score. If golf is well known in your area, the comparison of scoring may help in understanding.

If the students are highly skilled and more challenge is needed, make modifications in the game. One that many older students like is that only one hand may be used to defend the goal or to play the ball. Another is that their hands must remain on their knees at all times except when they are defending their goals or pushing the ball.

MOON MAN (K-2)

Highlights—dramatization of a current interest, running in a large group, chanting with a group, chasing/tagging; *Equipment*—none; *Area*—playground; *Number of players*—unlimited.

"One day a group of boys and girls were playing outside when suddenly one of them said, 'Oh, look!' and pointed toward something. Then another saw it and pointed, too. And guess what; there *was* something! It was an awfully strange looking creature—everybody just stood still and looked at him. 'Could he be from outer space? Could he be from the moon?' Zoom, all of the children ran right up behind the funny little creature. They were glad to see him; but as they got closer, he ran away. The children chanted, 'Space Man, Space Man, glad you've come! Space Man, Space Man, where're you from?' The creature turned around and made funny faces at the children and said, 'I'm from Mars.' [or anywhere in space] and ran away again. The children followed and chanted again. This time the Space Man turned around and made funny faces and said, 'I'm from the moon!' and chased all the children home, catching as many as he could.

"We can make a game out of the story if you'd like. Johnny, would you be our Moon Man? You can be from anywhere at all, but

when you say you're 'from the moon,' catch as many of us as you can before we get back home. You will choose a new Moon Man from those *not* tagged before we count 1-2-3. Those tagged will re-enter the game and play again."

Points to Ponder

Let the children practice running to and from a designated place. Discuss safe ways to run, tag, and so forth.

The line for "home" should be wide enough so that players do not have to bunch together to be safe, and it should be far enough from a wall or fence to allow for running past it, rather than stopping on it. An imaginary line between two plastic bottles, markers, or bases set approximately 40' apart makes a good "home."

Discuss other names from outer space that the Space Man could give. He may say, "I'm from the Moon!" any time he wishes—it does not have to be the second answer.

BACK AWAY (K-6)

Highlights—hand-eye coordination, cooperation between two people, throwing and catching a ball, judgment of distance; *Equipment*—one ball for every two players; *Area*—playground; *Number of players*—two per game.

Back Away offers a dual kind of challenge to the individual. In order to advance in the game, he must not only be concerned with his skill in catching a ball, but also with his skill in throwing the ball so that his partner can catch it.

Each pair of partners starts facing each other with only a couple of feet separating them. They toss the ball back and forth one time. If neither of them misses, one partner takes a big step backward (back away), and the tossing and catching is repeated. This continues—gradually throwing the ball farther distances—until one of them misses. They may have three tries at any distance. When unsuccessful (three tries), the procedure is reversed. That is, after each successful throw and catch, partners move closer together until they are tossing and catching as in the beginning. The game may be repeated as often as desired.

Points to Ponder

Because of the small number of players per ball, *Back Away*

would probably be most practical when used as a station to which groups rotate during the physical education period.

Any type of ball may be used. However, in the lower grades, balls should be 6"-10" in diameter—volleyballs, playground balls, vinyl balls, or balls made of paper. In the upper grades, other types may be added for variety—softballs, basketballs, footballs.

EXPLOSION (K-6)

Highlights—vigorous activity, stopping, starting, and changing directions quickly, moving in a large group without touching anyone; *Equipment*—none; *Area*—playground or activity room; *Number of players*—unlimited.

The game begins with all children spaced so that they are not crowded. The leader calls a way to move (walk, run, skip, hop, slide, crawl, gallop, march, tiptoe, etc.), and points in any direction. The children use the type of movement called, and move in the given direction until the leader calls, "Change!" and points in a different direction. Each time the leader calls and indicates a change in direction, the children respond accordingly. When the leader calls: "Explosion!" each child uses his body to interpret the word "explosion," and *runs* anywhere within the area until the leader raises two hands. This is the signal to stop and listen. At this time the leader may ask them to interpret a word such as *sink, collapse, melt, freeze,* and so forth. However, he may call a different way to move and repeat the game.

Points to Ponder

Before playing the game, spend parts of several class periods working on being able to move slowly within an area without touching anyone. Gradually *increase* the speed of movement and *decrease* the size of the area.

Each time the game is repeated, call a different way to move throughout the game until "Explosion!" is called—at this time they run.

If there is a child who is unable to participate, he could be the leader.

This is a favorite game and a good one to end or begin the class period.

JUMPING BROOKS (K-6)

Highlights—running, jumping, and landing safely, leisure-time activity; *Equipment*—two short ropes per 4 players (See Points to Ponder for substitutes for ropes); *Area*—playground; *Number of players*—unlimited.

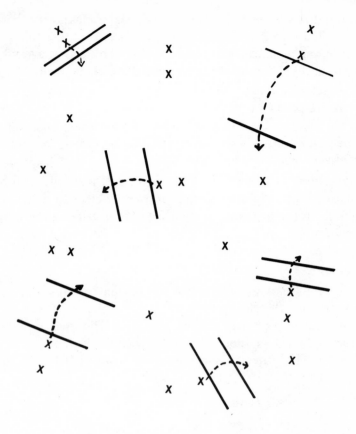

Figure 3 JUMPING BROOKS

Place each set of ropes so that the two ropes in each set are parallel and various distances apart, as shown in Figure 3. The distance will vary according to grade levels. Each set represents a brook—some are wider than others. Ask the children to start at a brook that they think they can run and jump over and then progress as they are successful to wider brooks. If they get their feet "wet," they simply dry them and try again.

Points to Ponder

Discuss such things as watching for others and sharing turns.

Place the brooks approximately 15' away from each other so that there will be plenty of room in which to run. Encourage jumping from one foot and landing on two feet.

The use of ropes was only a suggestion; anything that can be

easily seen and is safe may be substituted. Many classes use cord or newspaper rolled into the shape of a short rope.

The jumping distances will vary. Adjust them so that every child can progress, and yet the most highly skilled are challenged.

WALKIE-TALKIE (K-6)

Highlights—free play, creativity and self-expression; *Equipment*—choice of any—none required; *Area*—playground, paved area, activity room, or classroom; *Number of players*—suited best for 2-6 per group.

Walkie-Talkie is a favorite of all children. It is simply a glorified version of free play. Children in the group may elect to sit and chat, walk around, create a game, or play a familiar game—they may do anything *within reason*.

Points to Ponder

Use *Walkie-Talkie* as a station to which small groups rotate for a few minutes during the class period.

Equipment may or may not be provided. The idea is that each child is free to do as he chooses—alone or with the group.

There may be a need for a brief discussion of behavior that is considered *within reason*.

September LESSON PLAN GUIDE Grades K-2

WEEK	MONDAY	TUESDAY	WEDNESDAY	THURSDAY	FRIDAY
1	Ball-handling skills Explosion	Explosion Touché Turtle I See	Ball-handling skills Moon Man Touché Turtle	Classroom: Sock It to Me Stride Ball	(Long) rope jumping (Short) rope jumping
2	Explosion Touché Turtle Moon Man	Sock It to Me Stride Ball Jumping Brooks Moon Man	Stations: 1. (Long) rope jumping 2. Stride Ball 3. Jumping Brooks 4. Walkie-Talkie	Classroom: I See Stride Ball	(Short) rope jumping Jumping Brooks
3	I See Ball-handling skills Back Away	Stations: 1. (Short) rope jumping 2. (Long) rope jumping 3. Ball-handling skills 4. Walkie-Talkie	Stations: 1. Jumping Brooks 2. (Short) rope jumping 3. Back Away 4. Walkie-Talkie	Classroom: Sock It to Me I See	Choice of Activities
4	V-r-r-room Touché Turtle Stride Ball Jumping Brooks	Stations: 1. Ball-handling skills 2. Back Away 3. (Short) rope jumping 4. Walkie-Talkie	Moon Man I See V-r-r-room	Classroom Stations: 1. Ball handling 2. Stride Ball 3. (Long) rope jumping 4. Walkie-Talkie	Choice of Activities

September   LESSON PLAN GUIDE   Grades 3-6

WEEK	MONDAY	TUESDAY	WEDNESDAY	THURSDAY	FRIDAY
1	Ball-handling skills Explosion	Sock It to Me True or False Jumping Brooks	Ball-handling skills Defrost (3) Capture the Flag (4-6)	Classroom: Sock It to Me True or False	(Long) rope jumping Stride Ball (Short) rope jumping
2	Explosion Defrost Jumping Brooks	Defrost (3) Capture the Flag (4-6) Spud	Stations: 1. (Long) rope jumping 2. Stride Ball 3. Spud 4. Walkie-Talkie	Classroom: True or False Stride Ball	Ball-handling skills Spud
3	Ball-handling skills Back Away Spud	Stations: 1. (Short) rope jumping 2. (Long) rope jumping 3. Ball-handling skills 4. Walkie-Talkie	Stations: 1. Spud 2. (Short) rope jumping 3. Back Away 4. Walkie-Talkie	Classroom: Stride Ball Sock It to Me	Ball-handling skills
4	Jumping Brooks (3) Capture the Flag (4-6) Defrost	Stations: 1. Spud 2. Ball handling 3. Back Away 4. Walkie-Talkie	Explosion Defrost (3) Capture the Flag (4-6)	Classroom Stations: 1. (Short) rope jumping 2. Ball handling 3. Stride Ball 4. Walkie-Talkie	Choice of Activities

THUS A CHILD LEARNS . . .

Thus a child learns: by wiggling skills through his fingers and toes into himself; by soaking up habits and attitudes of those around him; by pushing and pulling his own world. Thus a child learns: more through trial than error, more through pleasure than pain, more through experience than suggestion, more through suggestion than direction. Thus a child learns: through affection, through love, through patience, through understanding, through belonging, through doing, through being. Day by day the child comes to know a little bit of what you know; to think a little bit of what you think; to understand your understanding. That which you dream and believe and are, in truth, becomes that child. As you perceive dully or clearly; as you think fuzzily or sharply; as you believe foolishly or wisely; as you dream drably or goldenly; as you bear false witness or tell the truth . . . thus a child learns.

——Frederick J. Moffitt

October

TO THE TEACHER—On Communication

It is extremely rewarding to feel that you have truly communicated yourself to another person—even for a moment in time. It is also a precious moment when you have truly *heard* someone else—not just the spoken words, but also the thoughts, the feelings, the personal meaning, and even the meaning that may be in the subconscious mind of the speaker.

In the classroom, many a child has asked a question and received a perfectly reasonable answer to an entirely different question—the kind that makes you want to say, "But you didn't even hear him!" And there are those who say things that on the surface do not seem very important; yet, there is a deep silent scream lying buried and unknown far beneath the surface of the person.

Hearing has consequences! When a child feels that he is heard—not simply his words, but him—often there is a grateful look, a feeling of being released, and a desire to share his world. He seems to come alive in a new sense of freedom—perhaps one that frees him to learn.

SOCCER SKILLS (K-6)

For a more complete understanding of the skills involved in soccer, children should first have many experiences in learning to control the ball with their feet. There is no set, step-by-step approach to provide these experiences because each step depends on the understanding of and progress in the preceding one.

Assuming that this is clearly understood, the following examples are intended only to establish the style of thinking. The degree to which a class explores the movements in depth should depend entirely on the children's physical, intellectual, and emotional stages of development.

Although suggested grade levels are given, each child should be allowed to progress at his individual level of readiness.

(1) *Control ball while moving (K-6).*   Give each child a ball and have him carry the ball with him as he moves around in the area

assigned to the class. He may use *only his feet* to move the ball, and must try at all times to keep the ball near him, on the floor, and *under control.* This is called *dribbling.* (Stress using the sides of the feet.)

Watch each child as much as possible, and offer challenges as needed such as, "What can you do to keep the ball from rising? Why do you think you are losing control of the ball? What must you do to avoid bumping into others?" Other suggestions will be apparent as the need arises.

(2) *Control ball while alternating between moving and stopping (K-6).* When the children show some degree of skill in dribbling, let them experiment with ways to bring the ball to a complete stop with their feet before moving it again. This is called *trapping.* (Stress placing one foot on top of the ball.)

If feasible, they may either experiment on their own or follow specific instructions, such as, "Trap the ball each time you feel that you're losing control of it; each time you meet another player; each time you want to change direction."

(3) *Control ball while being attacked (3-6).* At a later time—when the children are more skillful in dribbling and trapping with their feet—let them choose partners and get one ball for each pair. One player tries to get the ball and keep it moving under control as his partner tries to get it away from him and do the same. Only the feet may be used, and players may not touch each other with their hands.

Controlling the ball while being attacked is called *feinting*—that is, dribbling and trying to throw off pursuers by pretending to move in one direction and then suddenly moving in another. It is a very difficult skill to learn because it requires the dribbler to take his eyes off the ball to watch his attackers. (Stay between the ball and the attacker.)

(4) *Receiving and sending the ball while moving (3-6).* Let children choose partners and get one ball for each pair. While constantly moving in the same direction (down the field) parallel to the other, each one receives and traps the ball, controls it while dribbling, and sends it back to his partner. Sending the ball to someone else is called *passing,* and only the feet are used.

Some children may need assistance in finding the right parts of the feet to use in passing the ball so that it stays on the ground. Many may try to use their toes in a kick that causes the ball to rise. (Stress using the sides of the feet.)

As individuals appear ready, group them in four's with three traveling parallel to each other. Three dribble, feint, pass, and trap the ball while the fourth one attempts to intercept it and gain control. Because of the added competitive element, they will probably lose some of their skills and ease of movement temporarily.

Points to Ponder

In some of the examples above of ball-control learning experiences, the following suggestions may be helpful:

1. Before the children work with a ball, let them experience moving around in a given area without touching anyone else. This may begin with walking, and progress to running—with the emphasis on how to avoid bumping into anyone.
2. Balls may be made easily, if there are not enough for each child to have one. Roll sheets of newspaper into a light, firm ball, adding enough paper to make the ball about the size of a soccer ball (8"-10"), and secure by wrapping with masking tape or a nylon stocking (see Everyday Hints). However, if utility, soccer, volley, or playground balls are used, deflate them enough so that they do not roll too easily. Colorful vinyl balls may be purchased in many discount stores for as little as fifty cents.
3. Although many of the suggested activities involving soccer skills could be done in an activity room or gymnasium, they are best suited for the playground, preferably a grassy area.
4. For all grades, especially the primary, there may be a need for a brief discussion on the meaning of the word *control*. Ball control covers *all* aspects of ball handling, including dribbling, trapping, feinting, and passing. However, you might mention self-control, too.
5. Two keys to successful learning experiences are:
   (1) the teacher must *really see* how each child is responding through movement to the given task, and
   (2) the teacher must keep in mind the final objectives in order to start the next task.
6. After instructions or directions are given, look closely at the responses made. Don't accept just anything. If the directions were to keep the ball close and under control, keep working toward that end.
7. In situations that require trapping a ball that is not coming directly at the receiver, help children understand where they should try to position themselves in order to receive it best. Soon they will be making every effort to place themselves in line with the ball for better control.
8. Most important, *don't rush!* Many lessons may be built around any of the suggested experiences. Each could go on and on as ideas develop. At the end of several months of periodic lessons spent in this area, the need for new experiences will become apparent. The teacher who inspires children to think and work both independently and in groups should be quite successful.

9. If a game situation is desired, by far the most suitable and enjoyable games are those created by the students; they can make up and add rules as needed. However, if the following games are taught, feel free to change or add anything that will make for a better game in a particular situation.

SOCCER STEAL (K-6)

Highlights—controlling a ball with the feet, stealing an uncontrolled ball, moving cautiously and safely in relation to others; *Equipment*—several markers or lines, and four paper balls for every five players; *Area*—playground or activity room; *Number of players*—unlimited.

Divide the class into groups of five players, with four balls per group. Use markers to confine play for each group to a specific area. Each player with a ball moves it with his feet anywhere within the area while attempting to keep it under control. Players may not touch the balls (or other players) with their hands. Each player without a ball attempts to gain possession of any uncontrolled ball within his group. Any player who loses his ball attempts to steal another. Play is constant, and no one is eliminated.

Points to Ponder

Help children realize the advantages of keeping the body between the ball and the attacker. Encourage attackers to try to gain possession of a ball not under control.

If soccer or utility balls are available, they may be used instead of paper balls. Deflating them slightly makes for better control.

SOCCER TOUCH (K-6)

Highlights—defense tactics, quick movements, individual challenge; *Equipment*—one ball—6"-8" in diameter—per two players; *Area*—playground, activity room, or paved area; *Number of players*—unlimited sets of two players.

The object of the game is for one player (the guard) to try to keep the other player (the opponent) from touching the ball (with his foot). The guard protects the ball by positioning himself between it and his opponent. Players may *not* touch each other, and they may *not* kick the ball. The ball remains *still* throughout the game. When the opponent touches the ball (with his foot), the two players exchange roles and play again.

Explain the game, and give every two children a ball. Let them find a good space and decide which one will be the guard first. Ask all guards to face the ball and take a giant step backward; then, ask the

opponents to stand a giant step behind their guards. Each game begins when the guard looks at his opponent and says, "Ready? Go!"

Points to Ponder

The ball may be one made of paper, or other objects may be substituted for balls.

The game is very active. It may be used for a short time with the whole class participating, or for a station activity to which small groups rotate.

If there is an uneven number of players, let one group of three alternate turns.

Call attention to the concept of always positioning oneself between the opponent and the ball in many sports—football, basketball, and so on.

LANE SOCCER (4-6)

Highlights—controlling the ball with the feet during competitive play, teamwork, basic knowledge of the game of soccer; *Equipment*—one soccer or paper ball; and 6 markers to outline the field; *Area*—playground; *Number of players*—20-30 players.

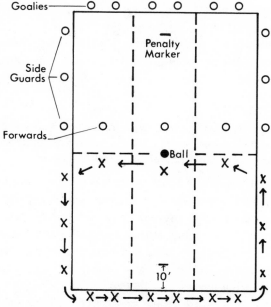

Figure 1 LANE SOCCER

Before children become involved in the game of *Lane Soccer*, they should be well skilled in controlling the ball. The preceding suggestions under Soccer Skills may be used to accomplish this.

Explain the game by drawing a diagram of the game on the chalkboard. The game begins with the flip of a coin to determine which team has possession of the ball. The ball is placed as shown in Figure 1. The Center Forward of the team in possession of the ball moves forward, and passes the ball to either of his Side Forwards. Once the Side Forward *contacts* the ball, the Forward opposing him may attack.

Each Forward tries to gain possession of the ball and dribble it (within his approximate area of the field) toward the opponents' goal line, passing it to a teammate when attacked. Forwards should try to stay within their lanes, and move up and down the field rather than into another lane. The object of the game is to kick the ball through the opposing line of Goalies to make a goal. Forwards may not play the ball with their hands, or push, or hold an opponent.

Side Guards should be *constantly* shifting up and down the sides of their half of the field to position themselves parallel with the ball whenever it is in their area. Their job is to push the ball (with side of foot) back into the playing area when necessary. They may *not* kick the ball. If the ball escapes the Side Guards, they may pick it up with their hands, and roll it back into the playing field.

Goalies should form a "chain," or "wall of players," that moves like a sliding door. They should always be shifting sideways to position themselves in line with the ball, because their job is to keep the ball from passing through their line. They may stop it with any part of their bodies, and they may kick, throw, or roll it to a teammate.

For each goal made, 2 points are given to the scoring team, and *both* teams rotate three positions counterclockwise. To score 2 points, the ball must pass over the Goalies' line *below* shoulder level; otherwise 1 point is given to the *defending* team. Play continues after each score with the Center Forward of the team that did *not* score passing the ball to one of his Side Forwards.

The penalty for violating any rule is a *free kick* (from the penalty marker) for a player from the opposing team. Only Goalies may defend the goal on a penalty kick. If the free kick is good, 1 point is scored; if not, the ball remains in play. In order to keep the game moving, rotate players if the Forwards kick the ball out-of-bounds three times, or if they fail to score within a reasonable time.

Use the penalty kick sparingly to avoid slowing down the game, but sufficiently to prevent roughness.

Points to Ponder

The ideal playing area would be a field with appropriate markings as shown in Figure 1. However, a field may be easily outlined by placing a large plastic bottle in each corner, and a bottle or base on each sideline to indicate half lines. Ropes spread to indicate approximate lanes also help in the initial learning of the game.

When players are able to keep their positions during play, these lane indicators may be removed; the only purpose of lanes is to keep all six Forwards spread out so that only two play the ball at one time. The ultimate aim is for Forwards to "cover" for each other when necessary, even if it means being out of one's own lane.

When assigning positions to begin the game, place three players from each team as Forwards, three on each side for Side Guards, and all remaining players at the ends as Goalies.

The size of the field is very important for a successful game. If at all possible, make it at least 60' x 120'

ONE AGAINST THREE (3-6)

Highlights—vigorous activity, anticipating and reacting to movements of others, teamwork, quick movements from side to side; *Equipment*—none; *Area*—playground or activity room; *Number of players*—4 players per group.

Three of the four players in each group join hands, forming a circle. The fourth player is IT. He walks around the circle of players until he is facing (across from) the player he wishes to tag. He calls the name of that player and attempts to tag him. At the same time, the other two players assist the one called in his effort to avoid being tagged.

All three must continue to hold hands throughout the game. If their circle breaks, IT chooses a replacement and the game continues. However, if IT is successful, the tagged player becomes the new IT.

Points to Ponder

At first the players will attempt to go around and around in a circle in an effort to outrun IT (or vice-versa). Soon they will develop some skill in shifting from side to side as they are able to anticipate each other's moves.

An entire class may play in groups of four, or the game may be played as one of several different stations to which groups rotate.

If the number of players in a group is one less or one more than four, the game may be played successfully with one against two or one against four.

Because it is quite an active game, children will not be able to continue this activity for a long period of time.

BRIDGE (3-6)

Highlights—cooperation during competition, quick reaction to a called number; *Equipment*—none; *Area*—activity room or playground; *Number of players*— suited best for 8-12 players per team; the number of teams is unlimited.

At least two teams of equal size are needed for this competitive game. The teams are in relay formation, one player behind the other and numbered consecutively as shown in Figure 2. The leader calls any two consecutive numbers, such as 4 and 5. Players 4 and 5 on each team step out of line—one on each side—face each other, and join hands to form an arch through which their team can pass (as in "London Bridge").

All players in front of the arch (1, 2, and 3) turn to the right (or the left—but all go the same way), go to the end of the line, go under the arch, and stop in their original positions. Those players behind the arch (6, 7, and so on) go under the arch and follow the front players until they have returned to their original positions. Players 4 and 5 release hands and step back in place.

The first team to successfully go under the arch and resume its original formation is the winner.

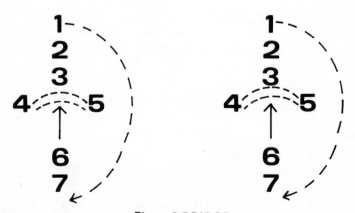

Figure 2 BRIDGE

Points to Ponder

Use extra or handicapped players to be the caller, judge the winner, watch for mistakes, or in any other such capacity. Always include everyone, even if it means they must take turns being the caller or the judge, and even if it means you must be a player, too. Each child needs to feel that he is involved and making a contribution.

Encourage lining up without touching.

GIVE ME TEN (3-6)

Highlights—teasing an opponent, running/chasing on a given signal; *Equipment*—none; *Area*—playground; *Number of players*—suited best for 6-12 per game.

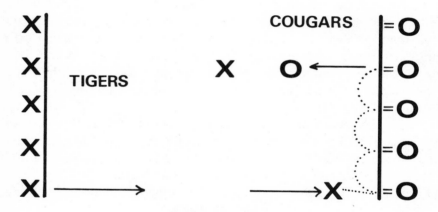

Figure 3 GIVE ME TEN

Players select the names of two teams and stand behind parallel lines as shown in Figure 3. Vary the distance according to the group, but have it far enough for a good chase. In the following example, the teams are Cougars and Tigers, and one of the Tigers in this example is named Ashlie.

The Cougars call to the Tigers, "Ashlie, Ashlie, where've you been? Come over here and give me ten." While Ashlie is running over, all Cougars extend both hands (10 fingers) side by side. With a downward movement, Ashlie slaps each set of hands in turn. When she slaps the hands of a player with a downward *and* an upward movement, that player chases her home. If caught, Ashlie returns with the Cougar to be a member of his team. If uncaught, Ashlie remains a Tiger. Then, the Tigers call the name of a Cougar to come over, and the game continues with the teams alternating turns.

The winning team is the one to get all players on its side or to have more players at the end of a given time.

Points to Ponder

Because there is opportunity for only two players to run at a time, this game is more suitable as a station or small-group activity. The entire class can play, of course, but there should be several games instead of one.

Let children choose names for their teams according to their interests.

The game may be played with names being called at random as written; or there may be a definite order established (as shown).

The fun in this type of game usually outweighs the winning-losing element. However, teams should begin with an equal number of players if a winner is to be declared.

Note: This game is fast replacing the game of *Red Rover* because it offers the same type of challenge without the safety hazard of breaking through joined hands.

OLD MOTHER WITCH (K-2)

Highlights—running and chanting with a large group, capitalizing on the Halloween spirit of fun, choosing replacements, admitting when tagged; *Equipment*—two plastic bottles; *Area*—playground; *Number of players*—suited best for 6-40 per game.

"Have you ever heard of an old witch? I'll bet you also know what witches ride . . . That's right—they ride across the sky on a broom. What time of the year do we usually think of witches?. . . Yes, of course, at Halloween! We think of lots of other things at Halloween, too. Today we're going to play a fun game that some other boys and girls made up because of a story they heard about an old, old witch. Would you like to hear the story?

"Once there was an old witch. She had so many children that by the time each day ended and she had them tucked in bed, she was very, very tired. Because she found it so relaxing to ride her broom, she usually went for a ride after putting her children to sleep. One night, her children began to wonder where the old witch went every night. So, they decided to fool her that night. She came to get them ready for bed, and was quite shocked to find them sound asleep. Of course, they were only pretending to be asleep. They were fully dressed and waiting for her to tiptoe out so that they could follow.

They got in a huddle, and made up a little chant to tease her as they followed, and they also decided whose children they would pretend to be in case she asked."

While the children are in the huddle, teach them the chant: "Old Mother Witch, fell in a ditch, picked up a penny, and thought she was rich." Then select one child to be the witch; explain to all that the witch will stand just far enough from the group so that she will not be able to hear them plan whose children they will pretend to be. Explain that they will chant as they follow her. After the last word of the chant ("rich"), everyone stops, the witch turns around, strains to see the children in the dark, and says, "Whose children are you?" They reply whatever they decided together. (A current hero, their teacher, their principal, Mickey Mouse, etc.) If they do not answer "Yours!," the witch says, "Whew, you're not mine," and the game continues until the children's answer is "Yours!" At this time, she chases them back "home" trying to tag as many as possible. All of those who are tagged stand to the side while the witch chooses a replacement from those *not* tagged before the group can slowly count to three. Those tagged re-enter the game, the children go into their huddle to decide whose children they will be while the new witch waits, and the game continues. When a boy is chosen, use "Father Witch." (Although a male witch is often called a warlock, children may prefer to say "witch" to keep the same rhyme in the chant.)

Points to Ponder

Before playing the game, discuss with the children important things to remember when running close together. After they have given their ideas, let them test their ideas by running to a designated area. Discuss some things like: "How did you keep from falling or from bumping into someone? How do you think the witch should tag you? . . . That's right, just a tap on the shoulder. She doesn't need to pull your shirt or hold onto you, does she? Besides, she needs to hurry and chase others. How will we know who was tagged? . . . Do you think you would know if *you* were tagged? . . . Yes, surely you would, and *you* would know better than anyone else. It will not be necessary to tell anyone when you are tagged because each of us will be honest." Ask if they like this idea and if they think they can do it. This kind of self-discipline does not come easily for young children. They will need constant help and guidance in this and in developing a feeling of responsibility for their own safety as well as that of others.

One of the simplest ways to make "home" is to use an imaginary line between two plastic bleach or milk bottles. It should be wide enough for them to avoid bumping into others, and far enough away from fences, walls, and so forth to allow the children to run past it rather than coming to an abrupt stop on the line.

Consider the weather when planning this activity because it involves lots of running and makes an ideal game for cool days.

The older the children, the more names they will be able to remember in teasing the witch before they say, "Yours!" The younger children may not progress beyond one or two names. It is not necessary to play long enough for each child to be the witch because there is constant activity. After the children know the game, it is a good one to play for a few minutes at the beginning or end of a class period. Children enjoy repetition, and will probably choose this game to play often during the year.

THINK AND DO (K-2)

Highlights—understanding directional words and their relationships, listening and responding through movement; *Equipment*—a box approximately 4"-12" high and 12"-18" wide for each child. (Improvised boxes and their substitutions are given in Points to Ponder); *Area*—classroom or activity room; *Number of players*—unlimited.

These activities are designed to help young children better understand meanings of certain words (such as *slow, fast, behind, in front of, beside, on top of, softly, forward, sideways, backward, greater than, less than*, etc.) and their relationships to each other and to other things.

They are not intended for "one-shot" lessons, but rather for beginning the kinds of experiences that very young children need throughout the year. As you see the need to develop other concepts, simply add the movements involved. Children should be barefoot or wear sneakers.

—"Place your box so that you have enough space in which to work. I am going to give you some fun things to do; but you must *listen, think,* and then *do* what I ask. Everyone ready? . . . Here we go.

—Face me and stand *beside* your box.

—Face the chalkboard [or a quarter turn to face a different direction] and stand *beside* your box.

—Face the flag [another quarter turn] and stand *beside* your box.

—Face the windows [or a direction that calls for a half turn]. Do you need to move, or are you still *beside* your box?

—Face any direction and very *slowly* get *on top of* your box.
—Can you get off your box very, very *slowly?*
—This time, go even more *slowly* when getting on and off your box.
—Without losing your balance, get *on top of* your box as *quickly* as you can.
—As *softly* [gently] as you can, jump off your box.
—Can you try that again, and land even more *softly*—so that I don't hear your feet hitting the floor?
—Marie landed very *softly*. Let's watch her to see what she did that helped her. [Discuss landing on the balls of the feet with knees and ankles "giving" to absorb the force. Let everyone try several times.]
—From the *top* of your box, can you jump so that you land *softly*, but also jump a distance *greater than* you did before? Work on it until you can do it with good body control.
—Can you jump a distance *less than* your last jump?
—Face me and stand *in front of* your box.
—Face the chalkboard and stand *in front of* your box.
—Face the flag and stand *in front of* your box.
—Face the flag and stand *behind* your box.
—From the top of your box, jump *forward* and land *softly*.
—From the top of your box, jump *sideways* and land *softly*.
—From the top of your box, jump *backward* and land *softly*."

Many other movement experiences may be developed in addition to various combinations of any of the above suggestions.

Points to Ponder

Many teachers have asked parents or industrial arts classes in a local high school to construct wooden boxes. Others have used regular classroom chairs, wooden soft-drink crates, newspapers or cardboard stacked and tied into the shape of a box. (If wooden crates are used, they should be covered with some type of material to prevent splintering.) The height of the box is relatively unimportant in developing the particular concepts suggested. In fact, a beanbag, a sheet of paper, a piece of cardboard, or any similar object could be used.

Most children will need to be reminded to listen to the *whole* task or instruction given before attempting to give a movement response. They will also need help in responding through action or movement rather than responding verbally. Keep working toward that end.

Make sure their responses are correct and that they understand *why* before going on to the next problem.

There are indications that once children clearly understand the

relationships involved in the given movement responses, there is considerable progress apparent in their readiness to read.

Remember that what may be easy for one child may require tremendous effort and concentration for another. Give sincere praise to the class and to individuals as often as possible.

RIGHT ON/LEFT OFF (K-6)

Highlights—accuracy in judging short distances, accuracy in tossing a small object, cooperating with a partner; *Equipment*—a beanbag or small paper ball and a sheet of newspaper for every two people; *Area*—activity room or as a station in the classroom; *Number of players*—2 per game.

One partner spreads the sheet of paper on the floor in front of him as the other one stands as close (or as far) as he wishes to toss the beanbag (or paper ball). Each time he tosses the beanbag and hits the paper, his partner says, "Right on!" and tosses the bag back to him.

The next toss (or throw) must be from a little farther. This continues until the beanbag fails to hit the target. The partner then says, "Left off!" and the two change places and roles. Each time there is a miss, the next toss may begin at any desired distance.

Points to Ponder

Beanbags work better; but, if a paper ball is used, roll only one sheet of newspaper or several paper towels into a loose round shape and secure with tape.

Substitutes for a sheet of newspaper for the target are: cardboard boxes; flat cardboard; rope in the shape of a circle, square, or rectangle; and the like. The size would depend on the abilities of the students.

Other ideas may be incorporated according to individual class interests, abilities, ages, space, and maturity. Some of these are:

—the tosser calls the area he will attempt to hit (right side, left side, top of sheet, bottom of sheet, top-right, bottom-left, etc.).
—the one tossing must use one hand, then the other.
—the toss must be from a low position; from a high position; from a side position; and so on.

October   LESSON PLAN GUIDE   Grades K-2

WEEK	MONDAY	TUESDAY	WEDNESDAY	THURSDAY	FRIDAY
1	Soccer skills Soccer Touch	Stations: 1. Soccer skills 2. (Short) rope jumping 3. Soccer Steal 4. Walkie-Talkie	Stations: 1. (Long) rope jumping 2. V-r-r-room 3. Soccer Steal 4. Back Away	Classroom: I See Sock It to Me	Choice of Activities
2	Explosion Jumping Brooks I See	Stations: 1. Jumping Brooks 2. Right On/Left Off 3. Soccer skills 4. Walkie-Talkie	Explosion Moon Man Touché Turtle I See	Classroom: Think and Do Stride Ball	Choice of Activities
3	Ball handling (K) Back Away (1-2) Old Mother Witch Jumping Brooks	Old Mother Witch Touché Turtle I See	Ball handling (K) Back Away (1-2) Soccer Touch Stride Ball	Classroom Stations: 1. Stride Ball 2. Ball-handling 3. Right On/Left Off 4. Walkie-Talkie	Choice of Activities
4	Right On/Left Off Old Mother Witch Sock It to Me	Stations: 1. (Short) rope jumping 2. Right On/Left Off 3. Moon Man 4. Walkie-Talkie	Stations: 1. Soccer Touch 2. (Long) rope jumping 3. Ball handling 4. (Short) rope jumping	Classroom: Sock It to Me Think and Do	Choice of Activities

October

LESSON PLAN GUIDE

Grades 3-6

WEEK	MONDAY	TUESDAY	WEDNESDAY	THURSDAY	FRIDAY
1	Soccer skills Soccer Touch	Stations: 1. Soccer skills 2. Soccer skills (with partner) 3. Soccer Steal 4. Walkie-Talkie	Stations: 1. Soccer skills 2. Soccer Touch 3. Spud 4. Back Away	Classroom: True or False Sock It to Me	Choice of Activities
2	Soccer skills (3) (creative game) Lane Soccer (4-6)	Explosion Defrost (3) Capture the Flag (4-6) Bridge	Soccer skills (3) (creative game) Lane Soccer (4-6)	Classroom: Stride Ball True or False Sock It to Me	Choice of Activities
3	Soccer skills (3) (creative game) Lane Soccer (4-6)	One Against Three Bridge Give Me Ten	One Against Three (3) Lane Soccer (4-6) Bridge	Classroom Stations: 1. (Long) rope jumping 2. Ball handling 3. Stride Ball 4. Walkie-Talkie	Choice of Activities
4	Explosion Spud (3) Capture the Flag (4-6) Defrost	Soccer Steal (3) Lane Soccer (4-6)	Stations: 1. (Long) rope jumping 2. Spud 3. (Short) rope jumping 4. Give Me Ten	Classroom: Sock It to Me Stride Ball	Choice of Activities

A CHINESE PROVERB

I hear . . . and I forget . . .
I see . . . and I remember . . .
I do . . . and I understand.

November

TO THE TEACHER—On Self-image

Most of us desire to help children learn the skills they will need when they go out into the world on their own. However, because of rapid changes, it is almost impossible to predict the kind of world they will inherit. Some skills, now considered essential, may become useless. Yet, man has always been confronted by change; in fact, the only sure thing we know about the future is that it will bring more rapid change. Certain individuals meet the demands of change and are able to function as happy, effective people. Others are unable to adjust their thinking and behavior, and are faced with insurmountable problems.

Because one thing held in common by all truly effective and happy people is a *positive* self-image—and because the strength of an individual's self-image has a direct influence on his ability to cope with change—the top priority of teaching would seem to be the cultivation and reinforcement of the child's self-image. It is true that the home has the first responsibility for installing and consistently promoting these feelings of love, security, and self-worth. However, the school shares the responsibility by supplementing, reinforcing, and in some instances, replacing the efforts of the home.

Opportunities arise every day to help each child develop self-confidence, self-value, interpersonal relationships, responsibility, and concern for others. Once a child begins to feel good about himself—in even the smallest way—his whole world seems happier. His attitude toward others seems to change, as does his incentive for self-improvement. There may be many times, however, when he takes one step forward and two back. The effort to promote a positive self-image must be constant. Once progress is apparent, it must, like any beautiful, living thing, be nourished daily if it is to survive.

It is not impossible to believe that we can help children develop internal feelings of adequacy that are so stong that they need never escape behind the false wall of security produced by drugs.

TOUCHDOWN (3-6)

Highlights—teamwork and strategy, highlighting elements in the game of foot-

ball, girls competing against boys; *Equipment*—one object small enough to conceal in one hand (miniature football, marble, stone, piece of chalk, button, etc.); *Area*—playground; *Number of players*—unlimited.

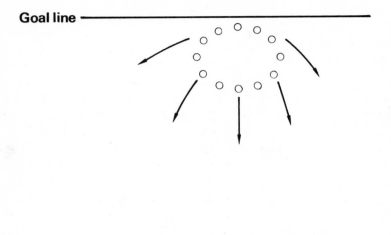

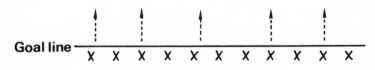

Figure 1 TOUCHDOWN

With all players together, explain the entire game before getting into teams. The game begins with a flip of the coin to decide which team has first possession of the "ball" (marble, stone, etc.). Each team goes to its own goal line. The team with the ball goes into a huddle and their opponents space themselves as shown in Figure 1. The team in the huddle gives the ball to one player who closes both hands, concealing it in one. *All* players on that team pretend to have the ball by closing both hands. The object of the game is to *carry* the ball across the opponents' goal line without being tagged. As soon as the team with the ball comes out of its huddle to attempt to score, the opposing team advances toward them and tries to tag as many of them as possible. Each person tagged must stop and show both opened hands to the one who tagged him *before* either can rejoin the game. If the player with the ball is tagged, the next game continues with the opposing team in possession of the ball. If, however, the player with the ball crosses the opponents' goal line without being

tagged, he scores a touchdown, earning six points for his team. The game continues as in the beginning with the teams taking turns at attempting to score.

When everyone understands, divide the class into two teams—boys versus girls.

Points to Ponder

Stress the importance of both players—the one tagged and the one who tagged him—stopping momentarily each time one is tagged. The one tagged must open both hands immediately so that his opponent can see whether or not he possesses the ball.

In their efforts to tag as many as possible, taggers often do not wait to see if those tagged possess the ball. If this becomes a problem, make the rule to the effect that a tagged player may continue in the game if the one who tagged him does not wait to see his opened hands—even if he has the ball.

At first, players will tend to choose the fastest runner to carry the ball. Without much guidance, they will soon realize that more strategy is needed to deceive the opponents.

In the upper grades, the try for an extra point after a score may be added. Students may be challenged to find a way to do this. It may be done by having the player who scored face the opponents on their goal line, count to three, and toss the ball so that it is *possible* for them to catch. If no one catches it, one point is scored. If it is caught or thrown out of reach (in the opinion of the teacher or student official), no point is scored.

The game involves strategy, teamwork, and maneuvering to deceive the opponent. There is *no* body contact except a tag (touch on the shoulders, arms, etc.).

JACK BE NIMBLE (1-2)

Highlights—quick thinking, chanting with a group, racing against another person; *Equipment*—none; *Area*—playground or activity room; *Number of players*—best suited for 6-8 players per game.

Most children know the rhyme: "Jack be nimble, Jack be quick; Jack jump over the candlestick." With all players together, go over the rhyme and choose someone to be *Jack*. Ask the remainder of the class to form a circle around Jack. Explain that everyone will jump in place and say the rhyme together. On the word "candlestick," all will stoop as Jack jumps (passing between any two players) to the outside

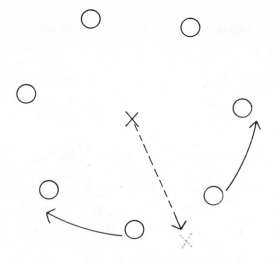

Figure 2 JACK BE NIMBLE

of the circle and holds his arms out to the sides as shown in Figure 2. Have the children stoop, and ask Jack to practice that part. Explain that the player on each side of Jack—the two he passed between—run (away from each other) in the opposite direction around the outside of the circle in an attempt to be the first one back to touch one of Jack's outstretched hands. The first one to touch is the new Jack for the next game. For complete understanding, walk through the whole game once. If there are no questions, begin with the original Jack, and play the game a few times; then, divide the class into small groups of 6-8 players to play separate games—so that each child will be more active.

Points to Ponder

Having each player jump during the rhyme increases the amount of exercise. After the game is completely understood, however, you may wish to let each Jack initiate some other movement that the group will do while he is IT. Players should not have to wait for Jack to decide what to do. Let them continue jumping until Jack does something different (hop, hop and turn, jumping jacks).

Because of the small number of players, children may need help at first in keeping the circle large enough for a good run. Speak with them about reminding each other when the circle gets too small.

Each time two players run, they will meet each other somewhere around the circle. Discuss the importance of each keeping to

the right (so that left shoulders pass) when meeting an oncoming player.

If there is a doubt about which player touches Jack first, Jack knows better than anyone else. If it is a tie, Jack gets another turn.

MONKEY TAG (K-2)

Highlights—daring to take chances, teasing and chanting, leisure-time activity; *Equipment*—a rope approximately 8' long attached to a plastic bottle or a tree; *Area*—playground or activity room; *Number of players*—suited best for 6-8 per game.

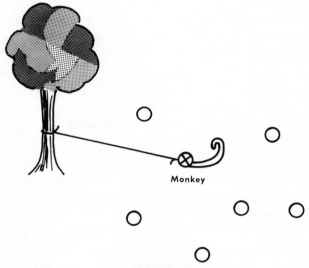

Monkey

Figure 3 MONKEY TAG

Monkey Tag is an active game that provides the teasing element enjoyed by young children. IT holds the end of a rope attached to a weighted plastic bottle or a tree as shown in Figure 3. He is the *Monkey*, and he may not release the rope. The Monkey attempts to tag the other players who dart back and forth across his path, getting as close to him as possible without being caught. During this time, they are teasing and taunting him, chanting: "Monkey, Monkey tied to a tree; Monkey, Monkey can't catch me!" The chant need not be said in unison and may be varied with any creative thought: "Poor Monkey, I feel sorry for you." "Aw, Monkey, can't you catch anybody?" "Here Mister Monkey, touch my hand." The first players caught are eliminated briefly, and keep out of the way. When three players (or any designated number) have been caught, the Monkey chooses a replacement from those *not* caught. The ones who were

caught rejoin the game, and the game continues with the new Monkey holding onto the rope.

Points to Ponder

At the primary level, there must be deliberate planning in not letting the first one tagged be IT. Otherwise, all of the children would clamor to be the first one tagged. At this age level, the pleasure and enjoyment of being IT supersede the prestige of not getting caught.

If any problems develop, such as the Monkey's releasing the rope or overturning and dragging the bottle, let the children decide on a solution. Some groups may decide that he must choose a replacement before the count of 3.

BICYCLE RACE (K-6)

Highlights—individual competition, use of arm and shoulder strength; *Equipment*—classroom desks or chairs; *Area*—classroom; *Number of players*—unlimited.

Use three children to demonstrate the activity while the others remain seated. One child stands between two desks (or two chairs, back to back), and the other two sit on the desks (or in the chairs). On a signal, the one in the center places a hand on each desk, lifts his feet off the floor, and moves his legs as if he were peddling a bicycle. He may peddle quickly or slowly, but he must keep peddling as long as he can keep either foot from touching the floor. (Let him demonstrate only long enough for understanding.)

Have the class count off by 3's, and explain that the 1's are a team, the 2's are a team, and the 3's are a team. Each team will take a turn to see which one of its players can peddle the bike the longest. Then the winner from each team will compete against the other winners.

Let the 2's and 3's sit to anchor the desks or chairs for the 1's, the 1's and 3's anchor for the 2's, and so on until all three teams have a winner. However, before letting the winners compete, play some other game, or wait until another time so that all of them (especially the last one) have a chance to rest.

EXCHANGE TAG (3-6)

Highlights—moving quickly but safely in the classroom, highlighting a special occasion or area of study; *Equipment*—none; *Area*—classroom; *Number of players*—entire class.

Place the names of several holiday-related things on the chalkboard, and let each student decide which one he would like to be. *Examples:* Indians, turkeys, pumpkins, Pilgrims. Choose someone to be IT, and have him stand at the front of the classroom. Move all vacant desks or chairs from the playing area; or place something in them to indicate that they may not be used. IT calls, loudly and clearly, one name (turkeys), or two names (Pilgrims and Indians), or three names (turkeys, pumpkins, and Indians). All those whose names are called get up, and quickly sit in a different seat while IT also attempts to find a seat. The person left standing is IT for the next game. IT may also call, "Thanksgiving!" at anytime, in which case *all* players find different seats.

Points to Ponder

Players may need to be reminded to walk quickly (rather than to run) and not to touch anything while moving. Those who are not changing seats should keep their feet out of the path of others.

BOWLING (K-6)

Highlights—rolling a ball at a stationary target, hand-eye coordination, leisuretime activity; *Equipment*—one ball—6"-10" in diameter—and one plastic bottle; *Area*—playground, activity room, paved area, or classroom; *Number of players*—suited best for 3-6 per game.

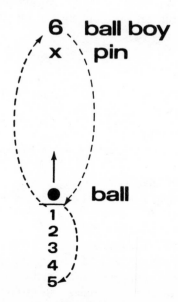

Figure 4 BOWLING

Discuss with your class whether or not any of them have ever bowled or seen the game on television. Discuss the weight of the balls, size and number of pins, automatic "pin boys," size of a lane, etc. However, keep the discussion brief.

Bowling is a game that can be enjoyed by people of all ages. Children can learn the skills involved without actually being at a real bowling lane.

As shown in Figure 4, player 1 rolls the ball in an attempt to hit the pin and cause it to fall over. Immediately, he runs to set up the pin, if necessary, and becomes the next ball boy. Player 6, the ball boy, gets the ball (he does *not* set up the pin) and brings it to player 2, who is next in line. Player 6 goes to the end of the line, and the game continues (with player 2 bowling and running to set up the pin; player 1 getting the ball, giving it to player 3, and going to the end of the line). One point is scored for each pin knocked down, and points are accumulated for a team score.

Note: The rule of having the ball boy *hand*, rather than *throw*, the ball to the waiting player may become essential from the standpoint of safety and to avoid time lost by chasing missed balls. The distance to the pin should be challenging, but not too difficult to allow success. The sizes of the balls and pins used should also be considered (the larger they are, the greater the distance). As a starting point, 10'-15' is generally used. Make definite areas (using chalk, tape, rope, or other appropriate material), designating a specific spot on which to set the pin and indicating the line over which they may *not* step when rolling the ball.

Variations for Grades 4-6

The basic game remains the same. Some of the possible variations include such things as:

—increasing the distance to the pin.
—teaching the 3-, 4-, or 5-step approach, and releasing the ball using opposite hand and footwork.
—keeping individual rather than team scores.
—using 3 pins in a triangular arrangement representing pins 1, 2, and 3 in official bowling. Right-handers aim for the "pocket" between 1 and 3, and left-handers aim between 1 and 2.
—depending on your individual situation, obtain official bowling score sheets from a local bowling lane and teach official scoring using 10 pins (see Figure 5). Your class probably could be quite creative in constructing a suitable numbered mat (made of plastic or similar material) on which to set the pins so that their arrangement is constant as shown. Playing near a wall will aid in keeping the pins from scattering when hit.

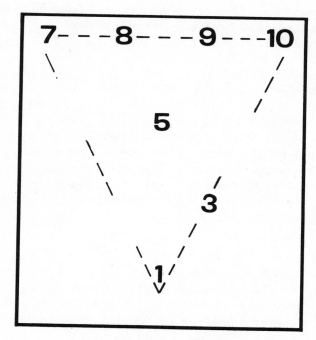

Figure 5 VARIATION (4-6)

Points to Ponder

Let children explore ways to make a ball roll smoothly from the hand toward a designated target. This may be to another person (in partners) or to a wall. Discover what happens to your feet, knees, and hands as the ball is released.

Discuss where the body weight is when a right-handed person releases the ball and when a left-handed person releases it. With lower grades, the emphasis probably would be best placed on finding a way to hit the target using any ball-rolling method with which each child feels comfortable. In the upper grades, the children probably could analyze a balanced position well enough to feel that the opposite hand and foot are forward at the point of release.

To save time and promote understanding of the game, diagram and explain the basic game indoors on a chalkboard or use a few students to walk through the movements.

Because of the number of balls and pins required for *Bowling,* we offer the following hints:

—Balls may be made by rolling single sheets of newspaper into a round shape, adding sheets as needed to make the desired size. The tighter the paper is packed, the harder the ball will be. Use masking tape or a nylon hose to cover the ball (see Everyday Hints).

—Punctured balls not useful for some other games may be used since inflation is not required. Upper grades may cut 2 or 3 finger holes into balls that are damaged beyond repair (volleyballs, soccer balls, playground balls, etc.) and use them as in official bowling. Once the holes are cut, even a flat ball will self-inflate enough to be used. If additional weight is desired, newspaper or a similar material may be twisted and stuffed through the holes into the ball.

—Various kinds of plastic bottles may be used or any wooden or cardboard objects that will stand alone, such as spindles from a mill. Plastic is suggested because of the noise and breakage factors. To prevent the wind from blowing the bottles over, pour a small amount of gravel or similar material in them.

—This game is recommended for small numbers of players per game to eliminate players waiting in line for a turn. Depending upon the age and readiness of your class, *Bowling* could be one of three or four other stations to which small groups rotate after several minutes of play at each.

SMUSH (3-6)

Highlights—alertness and agility, accuracy in hitting a moving target; *Equipment*—two soft balls of the same size (approximately 8''-10'' in diameter) that can be distinguished from each other; *Area*—playground, activity room, or paved area; *Number of players*—suited best for 8-12 players per game.

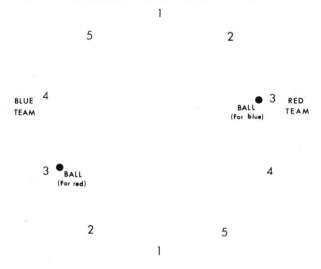

Figure 6 SMUSH

Depending upon individual situations, *Smush* may be explained using a diagram on a chalkboard or with the others watching while part of the class demonstrate the game.

With players standing in a circle (approximately 20' in diameter), number them so that each player is across from his opponent as shown in Figure 6. Designate a captain from each team; the two captains will alternate turns calling a number. Assign one ball to each

team, and place it just inside the circle, but near the *opposing* team. When a number is called, the player with that number (one from each team) runs to get the ball assigned to *his* team and throws it at his opponent (inside the circle) in an attempt to hit him below the head. Each of the two will also be trying to avoid being hit by the other. All other players making the circle are kept active by *gently* tapping the balls back into the circle for their teammate to continue play. The first player to hit his opponent (below the head) with the ball scores one point for his team. Balls are replaced, and the game continues with the other captain calling a number.

Points to Ponder

The balls should be very soft and distinguishable from each other. You and your students may think of ways to improvise other than those that follow:

—Make two different colored yarn balls.
—Make balls of newspaper, using differently colored tape or old nylon stockings to secure them.
—Deflate two balls that are not alike.
—Use worn-out or discarded volley or soccer balls and cut several quarter-size holes in them.
—If balls are of the same color and size, decorate or mark one of them with magic marker, tape, or textile paint.

The softer ball (paper or yarn) is less likely to roll far from the circle when it passes between two players making the circle and neither can keep it "in play."

Discuss saving time in getting a ball that does go out of the circle: "How many people does it take to go after one ball? [Usually they will decide that only one is necessary.] How will you decide who goes? One of the two it passes between? . . . Which *one* of the two?" [It can be the one the ball passes to the right of, or one of the two could say, "I've got it," but use their suggestions. Whoever gets the ball places it just inside the circle and play continues.]

It may become necessary to eliminate the "gentle tapping" of the ball by outside players, and have them *catch* balls and place them just inside the circle. This would be necessary if, rather than simply letting the ball rebound from their hands or any part of their bodies, they began hitting or kicking it, which would only cause confusion.

It may also become necessary to have a rule-making session on what should be done when circle players are deliberately letting the opposing team's ball go outside the circle and taking their time in

getting it back into play. Some classes will probably decide that when either of the balls gets past the circle players, the opponent (in the center) is not allowed to throw until the other ball is back in the hands of his opponent. (This might be a rule that should be included from the beginning.)

According to the abilities of the students, rules should be changed or added as necessary to make for more interesting and challenging play.

Note: Some groups prefer to use two lines of numbered players facing each other (rather than a circle).

INDIAN BALL (5-6)

Highlights—self-discipline, accuracy in hitting a moving target, decision-making and judgment, simultaneous offensive and defensive play, throwing, catching, and dodging balls, regard for safety of oneself and others; *Equipment*—six balls—6"-10" in diameter; *Area*—activity room, paved area, or playground; *Number of players*—suited best for 20-40 players per game.

Arrange players in two teams, and place the balls on center lines as shown in Figure 7.

This is a type of dodgeball game, and the objective is to eliminate all players on the opposing team. The differences in this game and other types of dodgeball games are in the way by which a player can be eliminated. They are as follows:

—If a ball thrown by an opponent hits him below the head *before* the ball touches anyone else, the floor, the wall, or anything else.
—If the ball he throws is *caught* by an opponent.
—If the ball he throws hits an opponent on the *head* before the ball touches anything else.
—If he steps on or across the center line.
—If he attempts to catch a ball thrown at him and drops the ball.
—If he throws a ball (indoors) that hits a wall before hitting anything else.
—If, in the leader's judgment, he throws a ball too hard (safety).

When the starting signal is given, any player from both teams is free to get a ball from the center line. At the same time, he must exercise caution to avoid being hit by a ball thrown by an opponent who gets there first. From the time the starting signal is given, the game continues with each team moving anywhere within its half of the area to retrieve and throw balls at opponents until everyone on one team is eliminated.

There are two additional rules that make the game even more exciting and challenging. Add these if and when you feel your class is

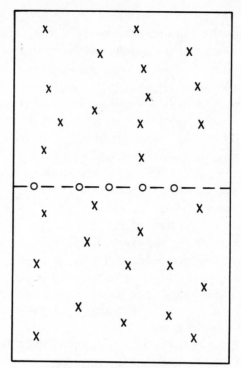

Figure 7 INDIAN BALL

ready for them. One is that if a player being thrown at has a ball in his hands, he may use if for protection by letting the thrown ball rebound from the one he is holding. If, however, in the process, he drops his own ball or the thrown ball rebounds from his ball and touches him, he is eliminated. The second one is that when *each* team has three or less players remaining in the game, all eliminated players begin chanting, "Wild, wild, wild." This means that all remaining players may cross the center line and play within the complete playing area.

Points to Ponder

Stress the importance of honesty in being eliminated. No one should have to tell anyone else when he is out.

Discuss the importance of accuracy and control of the ball versus hard, uncontrolled throws.

If the game is played indoors (activity room, multipurpose room, gymnasium, etc.), enjoyment of the game is heightened because of balls rebounding from the walls. This also eliminates having to chase balls thrown out-of-bounds.

If played outdoors, the boundary lines should be clearly

understood, and the eliminated players should stand outside the playing area to place out-of-bounds balls back into the playing area. Paper balls should be considered for outdoor play. Some of the fun of the game would be taken away because they will not bounce, but, at the same time, they will not roll as far when missed. Also, if you do not have enough volley or playground balls, paper balls make good substitutes. Let your situation and class make this decision.

When learning the game, it is not unusual for all players to rush to the center line to get a ball when the starting signal is given, but soon they will exercise more caution.

Very few games offer as much opportunity for promoting sportsmanship, honesty, fair play, wise judgment, alertness, self-discipline, and concern for the safety of all.

Watch for things like holding the ball too long (monopolizing a ball for self-protection), throwing too hard at a player at close range, and arguing over whether or not someone is eliminated. If any or all of these happen, discuss with the class how these can be corrected for a better and/or safer game.

Although the rules are different from other types of dodging games, actually they are simple; for "in a nutshell" with few exceptions, it is what the ball hits *first* that determines whether or not a player is out. It must hit him *before* it touches anyone or anything else. The big exception is that the *one who threw the ball is eliminated* if the ball he threw is caught by an opponent *before* it bounces or touches anything else.

This game will quickly become one of the favorites of your class, but it should not monopolize the entire physical education program any more than any other one activity. However, it is a good one to play at the end of a class period.

MOUSETRAP (K-6)

Highlights—quick response to an unexpected signal, regard for the safety of oneself and others, rhythmic movement; *Equipment*—preferably a record suitable for marching, running, or skipping and a record player; however, a drum may be used; *Area*—classroom or activity room; *Number of players*—suited best for 20-40 players per game.

Have the students stand around the outer edges of the room (desks, tables, etc., toward center), to form one large circle. Ask two players to be the first "mousetrap." They stand facing each other (one has his back toward the center of the room) with hands joined and held high to form an arch as in "London Bridge." Let the two

demonstrate this and then drop hands while you explain the game. When the music starts, everyone walks in a counterclockwise direction passing through the mousetrap (under the arch), and keeping time with the music. The instant the music stops, the trap will close (bring arms down), and any person in the trap when it closes goes to the center of the room, and the game continues as before. When there are two players in the center, they will form another trap in another part of the circle. This continues with traps being formed as players are eliminated. The last one is the winner.

Points to Ponder

The person operating the record player need not pick the needle up each time to signal players to stop. He may quickly turn the volume down to give the same effect as lifting the needle. Turning the volume up would be the signal to start again. He should turn his back to the group before stopping the music so that he cannot be accused of playing favorites. He should also vary the length of time he allows the record to play between stops.

If a drum is used, beat it softly while players move. *One loud* beat is the signal for players to stop and the trap(s) to close.

Marching, skipping, galloping, or light running may be used instead of walking. To add variety, use combinations—march until the music stops, and skip when it starts again, then march, etc.

To provide more activity for everyone, ask the players forming the traps to walk, skip, march, etc. *in place* as the others are moving around the circle.

Discuss any rules for safety—especially for closing the traps without hurting anyone.

HOT POTATO(K-6)

Highlights—hand-eye coordination, alertness, fun and excitement; *Equipment*—one ball, a record suitable for marching, and a record player; *Area*—classroom; *Number of players*—suited best for 10-40 per game.

Have children form one large circle around the outer edges of the room. Let them practice marching in place to the music. Stop the music and let them practice jumping in place to the same music. Repeat marching, jumping, marching, jumping, and so on until they understand that each time the music plays, they alternate marching or jumping until the music stops.

Explain that as they are marching or jumping, they will be handing a ball to the next person (counterclockwise) around the

circle. When the music is stopped, the person with the ball in his hands, or the last person to touch the ball, is elinimated. Each eliminated player stands beside his desk and must continue to jump (or march) to the music. Play until only 5 or 6 children remain. Let them come to the front of the room (or largest space) while all eliminated players sit to watch the finish of the game. Play until 1 player remains—the winner.

Points to Ponder

Any object that can be handled easily may be used, such as a beanbag, eraser, or a ball (deflated, punctured, made of paper, plastic, or yarn). You and your class can think of other items.

If your class is large in number, 2 or 3 balls may be used to begin the game—eliminate all except 1 ball as needed.

Let the whole class practice a few times before beginning.

Whoever operates the record player may watch to see when it is time to start the music, but he should have his back to the players before stopping the music. He should be quick and precise in lifting the needle from or placing it on the record to keep the game moving and to avoid damaging the record or needle. He may quickly turn the volume up and down rather than lifting the needle because it is not necessary to start the music from the beginning each time. However, the length of time the music plays should be varied each time.

When situations occur in which it is difficult to determine which player should be eliminated, eliminate no one; but let the class make a rule for the situation should it happen again.

SEVENS AND THREES (K-2)

Highlights—listening, creative thinking, rhythmic movement; *Equipment*—a record player and a recording of "Sevens and Threes" (Ruth Evans, Childhood Rhythms, Series VI); *Area*—activity room or classroom; *Formation*—a single circle.

Walk seven steps clockwise; turn and repeat the steps walking counterclockwise. Clap hands three times and pause. Repeat three claps. Jump seven times while turning once around in place.

Points to Ponder

Although a specific recording is listed, other music with a *distinct* beat may be substituted. There does not have to be any particular combination of beats to walk, clap, and turn. You may

prefer to use a drum and beat other combinations of numbers. The suggested record uses 7-7-3-3-7, but if the children understand, any combination may be used.

Let the class create other movements and explore directions to move in creating new patterns.

JUMP JIM JO (2-3)—American Singing Game

Highlights—timing, coordination, and rhythm, listening and following directions, cooperating and moving with a partner; *Equipment*—a record player and a recording of "Jump Jim Jo" (*Folkraft* #1180); *Area*—activity room, classroom, or playground; *Formation*—double circle of partners facing each other—boys on the inside, girls on the outside—hands on hips.

Song and Actions

"Jump, jump, jump, Jim Jo" [jump in place five times—two slow and three fast] . . . "Take a little whirl and away you go" [each turns toward his left and walks four strolling steps in a counterclockwise direction behind his own space back to his partner; these are four bouncy steps taking eight beats of the music] . . . "Slide, slide, and point your toe" [partners join both hands and take two sliding steps—entire circle moves counterclockwise—ending with partners pointing toe of leading foot on floor in the direction they were sliding] . . . "And you take another partner and you jump Jim Jo" [girls move counterclockwise to next boy, and all jump in place on the last three words]. Repeat all, ending with new partner each time.

Points to Ponder

Be sure the children learn the song before introducing the footwork. Consider teaching all of the steps before getting partners. This can be done with the children in a single circle or informally spaced. The only things to add, after each has a partner in a double circle, are that partners slide in the same direction (boy left, girl right) and that the girls move up (counterclockwise) to change partners. Let them *listen* to the music first as you call or demonstrate the footwork. On the part when they "take a little stroll," often they choose to snap their fingers in time to the music.

For variety, let each child get a partner of his choice and find an available space. The boy would remain in place on the last part while the girl finds another boy nearby. This is a challenging suggestion and should be pursued only if your class has reached the point in self-discipline that you feel is necessary.

Other movements may be added to the jumps. One suggestion is to alternate twisting slightly toward the right and then the left on the jumps. This increases the amount of balance and coordination required.

If you are using the classroom for this activity, more space is made available by moving desks, tables, or chairs to the outer edges of the room. This arrangement also makes it possible for you to see the footwork and help those having difficulty.

Although a record is suggested, once the class knows the song, they may sometimes wish to use it outdoors without a record.

STUNTS (K-6)

Endurance Hop: The object of this stunt is to see how long a person can hop on one foot without losing his balance or touching anything with his hands. He may not rest, change feet, or let his free foot touch the floor.

Challenge children to see how few times they miss in a short period of time before letting them try hopping on the other foot.

This activity is good as a break between long periods of sitting.

Crane Dive: This individual stunt is also a good refresher break in the classroom. Each child folds a sheet of notebook paper in half lengthwise so that it will stand on end when placed on the floor. Standing on one foot, each child attempts to pick up his paper using only his mouth and without touching anything with his hands.

Points to Ponder

These stunts may be used as stations in the classroom or on the playground. Competition may be against oneself or others in the group. Usually, excellent opportunities arise to discuss honesty. Sometimes a child's desire to succeed blinds him to "lesser" points of importance: "Did my foot really touch the floor?"

LUMMI STICKS (K-6)

Highlights—coordinating objects that are extensions of the hands, creative and rhythmical responses, hand-eye coordination, concentration; *Equipment*—a recording in 3/4 or 4/4 time in moderate tempo (optional), and two lummi sticks (see Points to Ponder) per child; *Area*—classroom or activity room; *Number of players*—unlimited.

Lummi (rhymes with mummy) *Sticks* is a favorite, practical, and challenging rhythmical activity. Children love to beat two sticks

rhythmically. This activity originated with the Lummi Indians who used sticks for rhythmical games.

Give each child two sticks—one for each hand. Children may sit Indian style or in any comfortable position that does not restrict movements of their hands and arms. They may be informally spaced or in a circle to learn the basic skills. However, before teaching any specific skills, let them explore ways to use the sticks to produce different sounds and movements.

Teach the basic skills as follows, repeating each one several times.

Basic Skills (K-6)

Down: Hold sticks vertically in front, approximately 8" apart; tap bottoms of both sticks on floor at the same time.

Together: Hold sticks vertically in front, and tap sides together.

Right: Hold sticks at an angle so that the top ends slant away from the body, sticks remain parallel; tap the top ends of the sticks on the floor diagonally to the right.

Left: Reverse actions for *Right.*

Front: Hold sticks in front with top ends slanted away from the body and tap the top ends of the sticks on the floor in front.

Cross: Hold sticks in front with top ends slanted forward as in *Front;* cross hands and tap the top ends of sticks on floor in front.

Side: Hold one stick to the right side, slanted away from the body; hold the other stick to the left side and tap the top ends of both sticks on the floor simultaneously.

Shoulder: Tap top of both shoulders simultaneously with top ends of the sticks.

Brush: Hold sticks vertically in front; with an upward motion of one stick and a downward motion of the other, brush their sides together.

Extend: Hold sticks vertically and extend one hand (right or left) forward; this movement is generally preceded by *Down, Together.* [*Down, Together, Extend* (right), *Down, Together, Extend* (left)]

Combine several of the basic skills into a rhythmical pattern.

Sample Rhythmical Patterns (K-6)

        (1)   (2)   (3)   (1)   (2)   (3)

3/4 time—Down, Together, Extend (right); Down Together, Extend (left)
        [Repeat three times]

        (1) (2) (3) (4) (1) (2) (3) (4)

4/4 time—Front, Front, Front, Front; Side, Side, Side, Side [Repeat]

    (1) (2) (3) (4)
4/4 time—Down, Brush, Brush, Brush [Repeat three times]
    (1) (2) (3) (4)
4/4 time—Front, Cross, Front, Shoulder [Repeat three times]
    (1) (2) (3) (4)
4/4 time—Front, Side, Front, Together [Repeat three times]

After the children can manipulate the sticks, play a recording of moderate tempo, and see if they can beat their patterns to the music. Depending on their abilities and interest, let them try combining patterns. In the upper grades, they should be able to combine as many as four patterns to repeat throughout the music.

Advanced Skills (3-6)

Pass-Pick Up: Sit facing a partner. Each person places his right stick on the floor *in front of* his right hand so that it is perpendicular to his body and parallel to his partner's stick; he then picks up his partner's stick with his right hand. This skill is usually preceded by *Down, Together* [*Down, Together, Pass-Pick Up*]. To simplify the passing, the right-hand stick is always the one that is passed.

Flip: This skill is generally preceded by *Front, Cross,* or *Side.* The top end of the stick touches the floor (*Front*) and, keeping the hand almost stationary, a slight wrist action is used to flip the top end of the stick up and toward the body, and into the hand. (The stick makes only a half turn.)

Toss: The toss is generally preceded by *Down, Together.* This is the most difficult of all the skills because, in one motion, one stick is tossed and the partner's stick is caught. (*Down, Together, Toss, Down, Together, Toss.*) Usually the right stick is tossed the first time and the left stick the next time [*Down, Together, Toss* (right), *Down, Together, Toss* (left)]. There is only one beat for the toss *and* the catch. Players toss straight ahead—the right stick travels toward the partner's *left* hand; each reaches to his left to catch his partner's stick.

Combine some of the basic skills and advanced skills into a rhythmical pattern.

Sample Rhythmical Patterns (3-6)

   (1) (2)   (3)   (4) (1) (2) (3) (4)
4/4 time—Down, Down, Together, Together; Front, Front, Front, Flip [Repeat three times]
   (1) (2) (3) (4) (1) (2) (3) (4) (1) (2) (3) (4)
4/4 time—Side, Side, Side, Flip; Side, Side, Side, Flip. Front, Front, Front, Flip;
   (1) (2) (3) (4)
   Front, Front, Front, Flip.

   (1) (2)   (3)   (4)   (1) (2)   (3)   (4)

4/4 time—Down, Down, Together, Toss (right); Down, Down, Together, Toss
   (left) [Repeat]

   (1) (2)   (3)   (1) (2)   (3)

3/4 time—Down, Together, Toss (right); Down, Together, Toss (left) [Repeat
   three times]
    (1)   (2)   (3)   (4)

4/4 time*—Down, Together, Toss (right), Toss (left) [Repeat three times]
    (1) (2) (3) (1) (2) (3) (1) (2) (3)   (1)

3/4 time*—Front, Flip, Front; Side, Flip, Side; Front, Flip, Down; Together,
   (2)   (3)
   Toss (right) Toss (left)
    (1) (2) (3) (1) (2) (3) (1) (2) (3)   (1)

3/4 time*—Cross, Flip, Cross; Side, Flip, Side; Front, Flip, Down; Together,
   (2)   (3)
   Toss (right) Toss (left)

Again, when they are successful, add music. Use their selections if possible. Also let them combine patterns to repeat in order to make a routine.

Points to Ponder

The sticks are round, 12"-13" long, and 1/2"-5/8" in diameter. Those made of wood are fun to use *after* the children learn the skills. They may be easily made by cutting broom or mop handles. However, those made of paper are most practical for beginners; they are inexpensive and make less noise. (1. Open two double sheets of newspaper and lay them flat. Fold them along the crease in the center; bring the top to the bottom and crease; bring each side to the center and crease; roll it from one side to form a round, 12" stick—approximately—and secure with rubber bands or tape. 2. Roll thin magazines and secure with tape.)

Sticks can be made attractive by covering them with colored tape, wrapping paper, paint, or adhesive-backed paper.

Lummi Sticks is suitable for large groups, small groups, partners, or individuals.

Interesting patterns are often determined by the seating arrangement of the group.

---

*Recommended for grades 5 and 6 only.

November LESSON PLAN GUIDE Grades K-2

WEEK	MONDAY	TUESDAY	WEDNESDAY	THURSDAY	FRIDAY
1	Monkey Tag Old Mother Witch (K) Jack Be Nimble (1-2) I See	Stations: 1. Monkey Tag 2. (Long) rope jumping 3. (Short) rope jumping 4. Walkie-Talkie	Classroom: Sock It to Me Sevens and Threes Hot Potato	Classroom: Mousetrap Endurance Hop Crane Dive Bicycle Race	Favorite Activities or Soccer Touch Right On/Left Off
2	Classroom: Hot Potato Lummi Sticks	Explosion Jumping Brooks Touché Turtle	Stations: 1. Monkey Tag 2. Moon Man (K) Jack Be Nimble (1-2) 3. Soccer Steal 4. Walkie-Talkie	Classroom: Mousetrap Sevens and Threes Lummi Sticks	Favorite Activities
3	Classroom: Sevens and Threes Mousetrap (K-1) Jump Jim Jo (2)	Stations: 1. Touché Turtle 2. Soccer Touch 3. Soccer Steal 4. Walkie-Talkie	Classroom: I See Lummi Sticks	Classroom: Hot Potato Stride Ball Sock It to Me	Favorite Activities or Monkey Tag Moon Man
4	Explosion Bowling Old Mother Witch	Stations: 1. Bowling 2. Back Away 3. V-r-r-room (K) Jack Be Nimble (1-2) 4. Walkie-Talkie	Ball-handling skills	Classroom Stations: 1. Bicycle Race 2. Bowling 3. Lummi Sticks 4. Walkie-Talkie	Favorite Activities

November LESSON PLAN GUIDE Grades 3-6

WEEK	MONDAY	TUESDAY	WEDNESDAY	THURSDAY	FRIDAY
1	Touchdown One Against Three Ball-handling skills	Bowling Smush	Soccer Touch (3) (creative) soccer game (3) Lane Soccer (4-6)	Classroom: Mousetrap Endurance Hop Crane Dive Bicycle Race	Favorite Activities or Ball-handling skills
2	Explosion (3-4) One Against Three (3-4) Spud (3-4) Indian Ball (5-6)	Touchdown Defrost (3) Capture the Flag (4-6)	Ball-handling skills One Against Three	Classroom: Jump Jim Jo (3) Exchange Tag Hot Potato True or False (4-6)	Favorite Activities or Give Me Ten (3-4) Spud (3-4) Indian Ball (5-6)
3	Classroom: Sock It to Me Lummi Sticks	Stations: 1. Right On/Left Off 2. (Long) rope jumping 3. Bowling 4. Soccer Touch	Classroom: Hot Potato Exchange Tag Mousetrap	Classroom: Jump Jim Jo (3) Bicycle Race Exchange Tag Sock It to Me (4-6)	Favorite Activities or Bridge Touchdown Smush
4	Stations: 1. Back Away 2. One Against Three 3. Rope jumping 4. Walkie-Talkie	Soccer Steal (3) (creative) soccer game (3) Lane Soccer (4-6)	Touchdown (3-4) Smush (3-4) Indian Ball (5-6)	Classroom Stations: 1. Target 2. Lummi Sticks 3. Bowling 4. Walkie-Talkie	Favorite Activities or Smush Stride Ball Rope jumping

A FEW DON'TS

—Don't be afraid to be firm with me. I prefer it. It makes me feel more secure.

—Don't correct me in front of others if you can help it. I'll take much more notice if you talk quietly with me in private.

—Don't try to discuss my behavior in the heat of the situation. For some reason my hearing is not very good at this time and my cooperation is even worse. It is all right to take the action required, but let's not talk about it until later.

—Don't make me feel that my mistakes are sins. It upsets my sense of values.

—Don't pay too much attention to my small ailments. Sometimes they get me the attention I need.

—Don't tax my honesty too much. I am easily frightened into telling lies.

—Don't be inconsistent. That completely confuses me and makes me lose faith in your guidance.

—Don't put me off when I ask questions for information. If you do, you will find that I stop asking and seek my information elsewhere. If I ask questions for attention, this is a different matter.

—Don't ever suggest that you are perfect or infallible. It gives me too great a shock when I discover that you are neither.

—Don't ever think that it is beneath your dignity to apologize to me. An honest apology makes me feel surprisingly warm toward you.

—Don't forget I love experimenting. I couldn't get on without it, so please put up with it.

—Don't use force with me. I will respond more readily to being led.

Author unknown

December

In today's world of *do your own thing, say what you feel,* and *question anything,* surely children are able to rid themselves of many potential hang-ups. To a degree, this kind of atmosphere is most conducive for learning. Most educators agree that real learning occurs best when there is no intimidation—when a child is free to learn.

Children need many different kinds of opportunities to feel free to express themselves, perhaps through movement, art, music, language, and combinations of all areas. They also need encouragement to question things, probe deeper, and find their own answers.

However, living involves a lot more than being able to freely express individuality. Living involves, among other things, consideration of the rights and feelings of other people, abiding by the laws of the land, and sharing oneself. It can be quite difficult for a child to comprehend that his individual rights exist only to the point that they do not infringe upon the rights of another or are not detrimental to the group.

As teachers, we need to capitalize upon some of the countless opportunities that occur every day in order to help children realize their rights as individuals, as well as their responsibilities for working together for the good of all.

ABOUT DANCE

No other phase of physical education offers more opportunity for the development of endurance, coordination, agility, timing, balance, self-control, and creative expression than dance.

Too often, dance is thought of in such narrow terms as: boy-girl partners, predetermined sets of steps and patterns, and adult-selected recordings. Little or no thought is given to involving children in a way to make learning more meaningful and dance more fun.

In planning dance experiences, determine the main objectives. For example, if the objective is to learn a traditional folk dance from a specific country, then set the stage by involving the children in a study of the customs and mores of its people. Thus, the dance

becomes more meaningful, and it is learned as it is performed traditionally (specific boy-girl partners, special music, and so forth). However, if the objective is to learn various patterns of movements involving a partner, then partner selection can be rather free. In most partner dances, a time to change partners can be worked into a section of the music, and it is wise to do so whenever possible. If the objective is to promote creativity and self-expression, provide times when children work alone, and times for creative expression in relation to another person, or two or three other people. In the latter case, boys may prefer to work with other boys, and girls with other girls. Let *them* decide. Music may or may not be used.

If the number of boys and girls is uneven and the occasion calls for boy-girl partners, let a girl take the boy's part or a boy the girl's part. Make this an important and interesting challenge. *Never* make statements such as: "Johnny will be a girl."

When performing specific movements to music, give the children adequate time to master the steps before adding the music and partners, if used. Let the children listen to the music before attempting to move to it. Make sure that everyone understands the phrases of the music and how they relate to the movements being performed. Emphasize listening to and moving with the music rather than concentrating on a specific number of steps.

Lower the volume on the record player before lifting the needle from or placing it on the record. This touch of thoughtfulness is greatly appreciated by the children. If there is an occasion to perform to music for an audience, this gesture also adds to the smoothness and enjoyment of the performance.

TARGET (K-6)

Highlights—accuracy in hitting a stationary target, hand-eye coordination, leisure-time activity; *Equipment*—one ball—6"-8" in diameter; a circular target—3'-4' in diameter; a starting line—12'-20' from the target; *Area*—playground, paved area, activity room, or classroom; *Number of players*—suited best for 3-6 per game.

Following the diagram in Figure 1, player 1 throws the ball in an attempt to cause it to land inside the circle (target). Immediately, he runs to stand behind the target and becomes the ball boy for player 2. Player 6 retrieves the ball thrown by player 1, brings it to player 2, and goes to the end of the waiting line. The game continues with player 2 throwing the ball at the target, etc. One point is scored

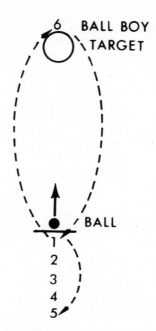

Figure 1 TARGET

for each ball landing inside the target. The team having the most points within a given time period wins.

Points to Ponder

Let a few children walk through the game to make sure everyone understands it before playing.

Make as few rules as possible, letting the children add others they feel necessary. For example, if much time is spent chasing balls thrown by the ball boy to the next player in line, call the group together and get their suggestions on solving that problem. When they decide what can be done (take more time in throwing, *hand* the ball to the next player, or whatever), *use their suggestion.* (Even if you know it will not work, let them figure out why it didn't, and let them try again.) This is how real learning takes place. Let them decide, too, when the distance from the foul line to the target is too great for success or too short for challenge, and whether or not balls hitting on lines are good.

Balls may be made of paper (see Everyday Hints), or beanbags may be used instead of balls.

Target may be set up as a station to which small groups rotate

from other stations. Having only three players per game allows for more activity.

The only directions needed are (1) to stay behind the foul line and (2) to throw the ball so that it lands inside the circle. Stress *control,* and encourage finding different ways to throw the ball.

In the upper grades, definite types of skills (throwing, passing, shooting) may be used: overhand, overhead, shoulder, underhand, chest pass, bounce pass so that the second bounce falls inside target, etc. It is not necessary for each child to use the same skill *unless* one of your objectives is to teach a particular skill.

Foul lines and targets may be made by using chalk, ropes, cloth tape, bases, etc. on the ground or floor. Let the children decide the penalty for stepping on or over the foul line when throwing at the target.

If there is a wall on which the target can be placed, use it for additional challenge. This requires much more skill in control and accuracy in throwing. If a wall target is used, any size ball may be used, but the distance to the wall and the height of the target will vary with the size of the ball and the skill involved. Let the children experiment with different balls and skills.

Many shapes other than circles may be used as targets: for Halloween—a cat, for Christmas—a Santa Claus, for Easter—a bunny, and so on.

KEEP AWAY (4-6)

Highlights—throwing/catching skills, alertness and quick reaction, competitive play in a small group; *Equipment*—one ball—6"-10" in diameter—per game; *Area*—playground or activity room; *Number of players*—suited best for 6-8 players per game.

Within a designated area, arrange players so that there are two teams of 3-4 players each. The object of the game is for one team to pass the ball five consecutive times among themselves without having it intercepted by the opposing team. The team with the ball may use any type of pass. The opposing team may guard, but may *not* touch the ball while it is in the hands of a player. All members of the team possessing the ball call out the number of each pass. Once the ball is intercepted, the count goes back to "One." Each time a team completes five consecutive passes, all of its members stoop to indicate the end of that play. The ball is then given to the opposing team, and play resumes as before.

A flip of the coin decides which team has first possession of the ball.

Points to Ponder

Before introducing the game, let the children practice quickly passing and receiving the ball among themselves (in groups of 3 or 4) while constantly moving within the designated area.

The size of the area should be relatively small for each group. Usually an area approximately 25' x 25' is sufficient.

When players understand the game and demonstrate proficiency in the skills, add the restrictions of being allowed only one step when in possession of the ball and being allowed to hold the ball no longer than 3 seconds. For any violation, the ball is given to the opposing team.

Because there is no need to have a ball that bounces, balls made of sheets of newspaper and secured with tape work well.

When properly played, the game is physically tiring. For this reason, use the activity for a part of a class period or as a station to which groups rotate from other small-group activities.

PAR THREE (5-6)

Highlights—accuracy in hitting a target, knowledge of rebound play, individual challenge, leisure-time activity; *Equipment*—one to three basketballs or similar balls, three bases (or tape or chalk marks), and one basketball goal; *Area*—activity room or playground; *Number of players*—suited best for 1-8 players.

Par Three is a basketball lead-up game designed for individual challenge. Place three bases (or mark three spots) at random in front of a basketball goal; place a ball on each base. The object of the game, as in golf, is to score from each base in as few shots as possible. A running score is kept, and "par for the course" is three.

Players start at the base of their choice, and three players (if three balls are used) can start at the same time. Each shoots; if he makes the shot, his score is 1; if he misses, he continues to shoot, counting 1 for each shot. When it is successful, he gives the ball to the next player at his base and goes to either of the other two bases to await his turn. (Thus, if his score were 4 at the first base, his first shot from the next base would make 5.)

Points to Ponder

The number of players determines how many balls are needed; avoid having players wait too long for a turn.

This game is challenging even for one player (and is a good leisure-time activity). It also makes a good station activity.

Wishful thinking sometimes makes a child "forget" his score.

(His elders often have the same trouble on the golf course.) If the opportunity arises, have a discussion on the merits of "remembering." Keep in mind that an embarrassed child is not likely to be motivated toward honesty.

When a player is shooting, encourage others to let him get his own rebounds.

Players may prefer to keep score for each base (hole) separately as in golf, then total the three scores.

ROTATION DRIBBLE (5-6)

Highlights—dribbling/shooting/rebounding, accuracy in quickly passing a ball, competitive play; *Equipment*—two basketballs (or similar balls) and one basketball goal; *Area*—activity room or playground; *Number of players*—suited best for two teams of 6-8 players each.

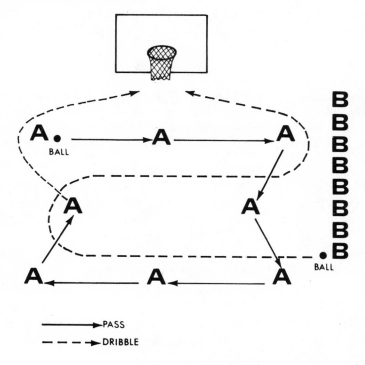

Figure 2 ROTATION DRIBBLE

In the game of *Rotation Dribble,* A is the passing team, and B is the dribbling team. Balls and players are arranged as shown in Figure 2. The left corner player on A and the first player on B start the game by looking at each other. Either of them says: "Go!"

Players on A pass the ball as indicated by the arrows; when the last team member receives the ball, he dribbles it (as shown) and shoots. At the same time, the first B player dribbles the ball (as shown); when he completes his run, he also shoots. Both players continue to shoot until *one* of them scores. The first ball in the basket counts two points for that team, and the play is over (the other player does not continue to shoot). The A player keeps the ball, and takes the place of the left-corner player as all other A players rotate to the spot where they passed the ball. (This is called *circle rotation* in net games.) The B player throws the ball to the next player in his line and goes to the end of the line. Play resumes as in the beginning. When all players on both teams have had a turn, the teams change places.

Points to Ponder

In dribbling a basketball, push it with either hand, or one hand and then the other, but never with both hands at the same time (double dribbling).

Precede this game with passing, receiving, shooting, and dribbling experiences. (See Ball-handling Skills.) Work toward the understanding that a dribble is not hitting or spanking the ball, but rather a push. To travel, encourage children to use a forward push so that the ball will stay ahead of them and not impede their speed.

Also, help them understand that a pass to a teammate should be easy to catch.

When starting the game, be sure that *both* players are looking at each other before one of them says: "Go!"

Interest is added to the game if the teams choose team names.

The two players generally arrive at the basket at the same time; however *if* one team is *consistently* late in arrival, adjust the distance that the players pass (or dribble) the ball.

If there are only 6 members on a team, use only two rows of players on the passing team; have B dribble *behind* the back line of players, behind the front line, and around to shoot.

PARACHUTE ACTIVITIES (K-6)

Highlights—endurance and arm and leg strength, fun working with a group; *Equipment*—one personnel parachute (cargo chutes are too large); *Area*— playground, paved area, or activity room; *Number of players*—unlimited.

"Guess what's in this box . . . It is something you may never

have seen. It opens out big and round. It is used in the sky. Yes! . . . a parachute. This is one that was really used. We bought it at the Army-Navy store. When we unroll the parachute on the floor, it will lie flat like a giant pancake because I cut off all the cords. (Let the children help unroll it slowly and then spread around it so that they are evenly spaced.) Spread your hands apart and close to the person on each side of you. Hold the edges of the parachute with the fingers on top and the thumbs underneath. Does everyone have a good grip? . . . Now, pull the parachute toward you. Go ahead; pull as hard as you can. Good. Now, shake it as fast as you can . . . shake harder . . . faster . . . and stop. Let's call that *flutter* because that's what we made the parachute do. We need some definite signals in order for all of us to work together: we just did *flutter, stretch,* and *stop.* Let's learn a few more." (Make your own signals or use the following suggestions.)

Stretch—Pull parachute to tighten it (waist high).
Flutter—Shake parachute (waist high).
Stop—Keep hands still.
Down (*and stretch*)—Kneel and hold parachute against ground or floor; *stretch* it so that it is flat (no air underneath).
Lift—Stand, hold onto parachute, and extend arms overhead as high and as forcefully as possible (parachute billows). The lift may be started from a standing position or a *down* position.
Mushroom—Lift parachute as before, but make it rise higher by taking 3 or 4 steps toward the center. Rather than being umbrella-shaped, the parachute will more nearly resemble the shape of a mushroom.
Jell-O Mold—After making a mushroom, change one hand at a time to turn so that everyone's back is toward the center. Step backwards toward the center, quickly lie *face down,* pull the parachute over your head, and flutter kick (keep knees on the floor). The parachute will slowly fall in the center, the air from the flutter kick will cause it to rise near the outer edges (like a Jell-O mold with a hole in the center). This is a spectacular "disappearing act" and makes a good ending for a program.
Note: The key to success is to step toward the center far enough before lying *face down.*
Swing—With feet stationary and approximately shoulder-width apart, hold the parachute with both hands and swing it left and right in rhythm. When only the hands are moved, the parachute will stay parallel to the floor, and the movements can be fast. If the arms are used so that they swing *down* and left, *down* and right, a flowing movement results in a lift and fall of the parachute. Although the feet stay in place, a little knee action will help produce a wider and higher movement of the parachute.

Circle—Hold the parachute with the left hand, keep it stretched, and jog counterclockwise. Reverse the direction—hold the parachute with the right hand and jog clockwise.

Travel—Count off by two's around the parachute. While the 1's hold the parachute high, the 2's release it and weave in and out counterclockwise around the circle until they get back to place. (This is like a grand right and left in square dancing, only without joining hands.) Let the 2's hold the parachute while the 1's repeat the weaving.

Wring the Dishcloth—This results in turning the parachute inside out. Place six or eight key students together on one side. With everyone holding onto the parachute, go *down* and *stretch* and *lift*. As the parachute rises, everyone *except* the key students releases it and steps away. Maintaining their hold with one hand, the key students go under the parachute and run forward. If space permits, they enjoy a long run with the parachute floating behind them like a huge cape ("Batman!"). Give everyone a chance to be a runner.

Points to Ponder

Cut unnecessary cords from the parachute, and use them to extend or repair volleyball nets or as lines for games. Cut apart the tape loops that are usually near the outer edges so that the chute will lie flat.

Participants need to be spaced evenly around the parachute so that it is supported all around. In some classes, the larger children may need to be interspersed among the smaller ones.

Teach the children to store the parachute. One way is to roll all edges toward the center with players dropping out as it gets smaller, then fold the long roll end over end. Store in a box or bag.

PARACHUTE GAMES

The following games are given as examples only. Let the children create others.

1. *Knock It Off* (K-6). Divide the children into two teams so that each team forms one-half of the circle around the parachute. Place two distinguishable balls on the parachute—one for each team. Stretch the parachute until the leader calls, "Knock it off!" This is the signal to make the parachute *flutter* in an attempt to knock the opponents' ball off. Players may bat a ball off or back on the parachute with *one* hand, but not both. The team whose ball remains on the parachute longer scores a point.

Variation: Use only one ball and let players *flutter* the parachute in an attempt to knock the ball off over the heads of the opposing team.

Note: Try balls of different weights, and select one that is not too heavy. A volleyball, plastic ball, or one made of paper usually works well.

2. *Still Shots* (K-6).   With players around the parachute, let them count off by five's. Explain that on a signal, everyone will *lift* the parachute and step in to form a *mushroom.* As the parachute is lifted, a leader will call a number. All players with that number will release the chute and find a place underneath it so that they are not touching anyone. The outside players will let the parachute fall *easily* as they slowly count to five. During this time, each of the players underneath the chute will assume a still position that portrays any athlete *in action.* On the count of five, the parachute is lifted for all to see the "athletes." As it falls, those underneath return to the circle in their original places. Give students an opportunity to comment on what they saw before another number is called.

PARACHUTE RHYTHMS

Again, these are only examples of activities. Let the children choreograph others. The movements are given below the verses.

1. *Jingle Bells* (K-6).
"Dashing through the snow, / In a one-horse open sleigh, / O'er the fields we go, / Laughing all the way;
[*Circle counterclockwise*]
"Bells on bob-tail ring, / Making spirits bright, / What fun it is to ride and sing, / A sleighing song tonight!
[*Circle clockwise*]
"Jingle bells! jingle bells! / Jingle all the way!
[*Flutter*]
"Oh, what fun it is to ride, / In a one-horse open sleigh!
[*Lift*]
"Jingle bells! jingle bells! / Jingle all the way!
[*Flutter*]
"Oh, what fun it is to ride, / In a one-horse open sleigh!"
[*Lift*]
"A day or two ago, / I thought I'd take a ride, "And soon Miss Fannie Bright, / Was seated by my side;
[*Circle counterclockwise*]
"The horse was lean and lank, / Misfortune seemed his lot, "He got into a drifted bank, / And we, we got upsot!"
[*Circle clockwise*]
"Jingle bells! jingle bells! / Jingle all the way!
[*Flutter*]

"Oh, what fun it is to ride, / In a one-horse open sleigh!
[*Lift*]
"Jingle bells! jingle bells! / Jingle all the way!
[*Flutter*]
"Oh, what fun it is to ride, / In a one-horse open sleigh!"
[*Jell-O mold*]

2. *Jump Jim Jo* (3-6). Boys alternate with girls in a circle around the parachute.

"Jump, jump, jump, Jim Jo;
[*Shake—2 slow, 3 fast*]
"Take a little whirl and around you go.
[*Lift and turn once around*]
"Slide, slide, and point your toe;
[*Swing left, swing right, and point left foot*]
"And you take another partner and you jump, Jim Jo"
[*Lift and girls move one place counterclockwise past boys*]

Repeat all of dance. If familiar, the song may be sung; if not, it is availabe on a recording (*Folkraft* #1180).

LET'S MAKE A DANCE (K-6—without music)

Highlights—creative interpretation of words, independent thinking, working independently and with others, exploration, combining movements to create a sequence, combining sequences to make a dance; *Equipment*—optional—a hand drum or tambourine; *Area*—activity room or classroom; *Number of players*—suited best for entire class.

The following suggestions are given as types of experiences that help children feel successful, enjoy moving, and gain an appreciation for some of the skills involved in dance. The degree to which the ideas presented may be explored and developed will vary with the ages of the children, the space available, and most importantly, your interest.

It is impossible to predict the length of time to spend on a particular concept because each idea could be explored indefinitely, always refining the movement and improving the quality. However, we have grouped some experiences in order to establish a framework for a class period, as well as to provide continuity.

(1) Individually (K-6)

(a) *Travel and stop on signal.* With the children spaced with freedom to move, ask them to travel to another space (without

touching anyone) and to stop when you beat the drum once (or say, "Stop!"). Repeat this several times varying the length of time to travel. Work toward controlled movements and very strong (balanced) stops.

(b) *Different ways to travel and stop without a signal.* Ask the children to travel and stop on their own. Encourage finding a *different* way to travel after each stop, varying the distances traveled, and stopping in different body positions.

At later times, continue the concepts in the above suggestions and gradually add the following when the children are ready. Always emphasize good body control when traveling or stopping.

—Travel using different heights or levels—high, low, and those in between.
—Travel using different parts of your body to support your weight—hands, feet, hips, shoulders, front side, back side, and combinations of several parts.
—Travel at different speeds—slow, very slow, fast, very fast, and speeds in between.
—Travel in different directions—forward, backward, and sideways.
—Travel using different parts of the body to lead—hand, head, elbow, shoulder, hips, etc.
—Travel different pathways—straight, curved, zig-zagged.
—(3-6) Change from a stop, after each way of travel, to only a slight pause between movements.
—(3-6) Combine several concepts—as you travel, show changes in levels, body parts used, speeds, directions, pathways—sometimes pausing, and sometimes coming to a complete stop between movements.
—(3-6) Find a sequence of movements to repeat—work on perfection.

(c) *Shapes and forms.* Ask the children to make their bodies into different shapes (rounded, stretched, curled, long, flat, twisted, etc.). Let them explore ways to make the shapes using different levels. Use the following as guides.

—Combine a variety of shapes changing from one to another with continuous movement so that there is no stopping. One movement *flows* into the other, but is under enough control at all times that it could be stopped at any moment.
—Combine a variety of shapes, changing from one to another with a sudden thrust or explosion.

(2) With a Partner (2-6)

(a) *Turning and sharing spaces.* Let the children choose partners, and ask them to find ways to share their spaces with each other using turning movements and different speeds and levels. Find *three* ways to repeat with good body control.

(b) *Meeting, turning, and parting.* Ask partners to work together to find a way to meet each other, turn around each other, and part or separate. Give them time to work out a way that shows changes in levels and speeds. Stress good body control.

(c) *Shapes and forms.* With a partner, interact by forming shapes with the body while sharing the same space.

—Let one, partner form a shape and hold it; his partner assumes a shape in relation to it. Partners continue alternating turns.
—Partners combine a variety of shapes with slow, continuous movement until they sense a time to stop.
—Partners alternate turns at changing shapes with a sudden thrust or explosion.
—Partners change from one shape to another varying speeds by choice.

Points to Ponder

The meanings of certain words (*levels, sequence, speeds, pathways,* etc.) will need some explanation, especially for the very young children.

When working with a partner, children will need to talk. Help them establish a noise level conducive to learning and working.

When observing children, try to select only one person to watch a few seconds, then another. It is very hard to watch the group as a whole and know whether or not each child understands.

Expect *different* movements from each child. For example, one may elect to travel using his hands and feet as a bear walks, while another may travel using his hands and feet as in a cartwheel. *Both* are successful, each in his own way.

There are countless opportunities to praise because every child who tries succeeds. Encourage smooth, controlled movements. Give ample time to work out ideas.

LET'S MAKE A DANCE (3-6—with music)

Highlights—creative interpretation of music, independent thinking, exploration, sharing ideas with a small group, combining sequences of movements to make a dance; *Equipment*—any selection of recorded music (see Points to Ponder); *Area*—activity room or classroom; *Number of players*—small groups of 2-6 each.

For best results, use the experiences and suggestions in *Let's Make a Dance* (without music) before working *with* music.

The idea now becomes to create movements and sequences of movements to fit a particular recording. You may select the music yourself or discuss it with your class and try some of their choices.

Ask the children to arrange themselves in groups, with 2-6 per

group (let them choose the people and the number). Tell them that you will let the music repeat several times for about ten minutes while they work together to create movements to fit the music. The following suggestions may be helpful:

(1) *Listen* to the music and *think* of possible movements. Try them out—explore different ideas.
(2) *Share* ideas with your group. Try to find movements to repeat.
(3) *Explore* everyone's ideas.
(4) *Build sequences* of movements to repeat.
(5) *Organize* your dance: Do all move together? . . . alternately? . . . alike? . . . differently? . . . in which direction? . . . at what level? . . . at what speed? . . . How will it begin? . . . end?

Before letting them find space to work, explain that they will need to discuss ideas, but to do so quietly so that they do not disturb other groups, and to progress as far as possible, but not to worry if they have not finished in ten minutes.

While they are working, visit each group to encourage, comment, etc. Be careful *not* to tell them what to do, although thought-provoking questions would be desirable.

After approximately ten minutes (depending on the progress being made), stop the music and let the groups take turns presenting their ideas. Ask those watching to give constructive criticism (ideas for improvement of movements, timing, direction, etc., but not in reference to the skill of a particular child).

After each group has performed and constructive criticism has been offered, give them a few minutes to work on their dance. They may or may not wish to use the suggestions given.

At later times, let each group choose a recording and work independently (away from the others if possible). When each group is ready, give it a chance to perform for the others.

Points to Ponder

Many children have amazed their teachers, as well as their peers, with their creative abilities when given a chance to explore. The most meaningful experiences are those in which the children have a choice in selection of music. Examples of recordings they chose are selections from various show tunes, *The Nutcracker Suite,* folk dance music, holiday themes, and, of course, current popular tunes.

Occasionally a child prefers to work alone—let him do so if he wishes. However, if he *needs* interaction with others, but always prefers to work alone, encourage others to invite him to join a group.

Give children several opportunities to create dances. Let them work with different people, with groups of different numbers, and with different types of music. Few, if any, areas offer more opportunity for creative expression, group interaction, and feelings of success.

RHYTHMIC SPORTS (3-6)

Highlights—individual, creative expression, body control; *Equipment*—a recording of very slow tempo; *Area*—activity room or classroom; *Number of players*—unlimited.

"Have you ever seen a slow-motion, instant replay of a football or baseball play on television? . . . Remember how the players seemed to almost float in the air? Do you think you could have enough control over your bodies to move in slow motion? . . .

"Let's pretend that all of you are going to throw a baseball as it would look in slow motion. Show me how you would move. [Chances are, most of the children will move much faster than they think they are moving. Keep working with them until their movements are light, slow, and balanced.] Can you make your movements show me that you are throwing the ball so that it goes a long distance? Can you move even slower? That's the idea. Now, without telling anyone, choose any sport or activity you know, and pretend to be any player you wish in that activity. I'm going to play a record that will help you move slowly. Listen to it for just a minute, and think about how you would move to be the player or athlete you've chosen. [Play the music briefly.] Everyone ready? . . . Make sure you have enough space so that you will not interfere with anyone. Try to move so that I'll know immediately which sport you've chosen. [Put the record on and walk around the room giving help as needed.] You're a boxer; how can you move even slower? . . . Show me how you would fall if you got knocked down. Hey! What a great football player you would make; can you punt the ball, too? . . . What happens to your body *after* the ball is kicked? . . ."

As movements become more controlled, add the challenge of being able to come to a complete stop in a balanced position (like a still shot). "This time as you are moving, I am going to stop the music by quickly turning down the volume at different times. Each time the music stops, try to hold the position you're in. Of course, if you are off balance, go on into a balanced position as quickly as possible, but *freeze* so that not a muscle is moving until you hear the music again. Do you think you can do that? . . . Let's try!" Play the

record a few seconds and lower the volume abruptly. Vary the length of time that they must hold their poses or still positions. Encourage them to react quickly to the stopping and starting of the music.

Points to Ponder

Many sessions throughout the year may be profitably spent in this activity. Some additional suggestions are:

1. Give opportunities to pantomime different kinds of sports.
2. Let children have a chance to observe and help each other.
3. Let groups of two, three, or four interact as they work together.
4. Use recordings that the children think are good for slow motion.
5. Select some recordings that suggest both fast and slow movements.

STUNTS

(1) Heel Slap (K-6)

Heel Slap is an individual stunt that may be done in a limited space. This stunt and *Heel Click,* which follows, quickly refresh students in the classroom. Each participant, starting from a standing position, jumps and kicks his feet high in back as if trying to spank himself with his heels. While in the air, he slaps his heels with his hands. Optional—Start the stunt with hands already in the back.

(2) Heel Click (K-6)

In a stride position (feet apart), jump high in the air; at the peak of the jump, hit heels together, and land in place on both feet. Although *Heel Click* is a relatively simple stunt, it can bring great satisfaction to the less-skilled performer; it can also be a great challenge for the well-coordinated student because of variations:

1. Turn while clicking heels and land facing in the opposite direction.
2. Click heels together two times before landing.
3. Click heels together on the right side or on the left side. *Example:* If heel click is on the left, the performer shifts his weight to his *right* foot, and leaves the floor from that foot instead of from both feet.

(3) Push Back (K-6)

This is a modified version of a push-up, and it may be done usually without moving any furniture. Each person stands facing a desk, table, chair, or something else of about that height. He places

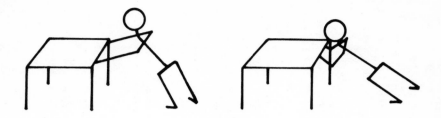

Figure 3 PUSH BACK

his hands about shoulder-width apart on the desk and walks his feet back a few feet as shown in Figure 3. (The distance will vary according to the height of the individual.) Keeping his feet together and in place, his back and knees straight, he slowly bends his elbows, lowering his body so that his chin touches the desk, then he straightens his elbows, pushing away from the desk. Repeat the action as many times as possible.

Note: Children may need to work in pairs to anchor the desks or chairs for each other. The arms should be straight before lowering the body each time.

December   LESSON PLAN GUIDE   Grades K-2

WEEK	MONDAY	TUESDAY	WEDNESDAY	THURSDAY	FRIDAY
1	Ball-handling skills Rope jumping I See	Parachute activities Parachute games	Explosion Monkey Tag Old Mother Witch	Classroom: Heel Slap Push Back Crane Dive Bicycle Race Endurance Hop	Favorite Activities
2	Parachute activities Parachute rhythms	Stations: 1. Target 2. Soccer Steal 3. Rope jumping 4. Walkie-Talkie	Let's Make a Dance (without music)	Classroom: Hot Potato Bicycle Race Mousetrap	Favorite Activities
3	Let's Make a Dance (without music)	Stations: 1. Moon Man 2. Target 3. Monkey Tag 4. Walkie-Talkie	Classroom: Stride Ball I See Sock It to Me	Classroom: Think and Do Right On/Left Off	Favorite Activities
4	Stations: 1. Stride Ball 2. Rope jumping 3. Target 4. Soccer	Classroom Stations: 1. Right On/Left Off 2. Target 3. Stride Ball 4. Walkie-Talkie	Let's Make a Dance (without music)	Classroom: Endurance Hop (K-1) Heel Click (2) Push Back Mousetrap	Favorite Activities

December   LESSON PLAN GUIDE   Grades 3-6

WEEK	MONDAY	TUESDAY	WEDNESDAY	THURSDAY	FRIDAY
1	Let's Make a Dance (without music)	Smush (3-4) Spud (3-4) Rotation Dribble (5-6)	Let's Make a Dance (without music)	Classroom: Heel Slap Heel Click Push Back Crane Dive Bicycle Race Endurance Hop	Parachute activities Parachute games
2	Let's Make a Dance (without music)	Stations: 1. Target 2. Ball handling (3) Keep Away (4-6) 3. Soccer Touch 4. Walkie-Talkie	Parachute activities Parachute Rhythms	Classroom Stations: 1. Target 2. Bowling 3. Endurance Hop 4. Walkie-Talkie	Favorite Activities
3	(Creative) Soccer Game (3) Lane Soccer (4-6)	Parachute Rhythms Rhythmic sports	Stations: 1. Target (3-4) 2. Par Three (5-6) 3. Bowling 4. Walkie-Talkie	Classroom: Sock It to Me Exchange Tag Mousetrap	Favorite Activities
4	Let's Make a Dance (with music)	Parachute Rhythms (3-4) Let's Make a Dance (with music) (5-6)	Explosion Spud Smush Bowling	Classroom: True or False Bicycle Race Exchange Tag	Let's Make a Dance (with music)

CHILDREN LEARN WHAT THEY LIVE

If a child lives with criticism, He learns to condemn.
If a child lives with hostility, He learns to fight.
If a child lives with ridicule, He learns to be shy.
If a child lives with shame, He learns to feel guilty.
If a child lives with tolerance, He learns to be patient.
If a child lives with encouragement, He learns confidence.
If a child lives with praise, He learns to appreciate.
If a child lives with fairness, He learns justice.
If a child lives with security, He learns to have faith.
If a child lives with approval, He learns to like himself.
If a child lives with acceptance and friendship, He learns
    to find love in the world.

——Dorothy Law Nolte

January

TO THE TEACHER—On Being Consistent

Around lunch time one day, two young friends sat down on the front steps to rest after vigorous play. One was overheard saying to the other, "Hey, go ask your mom if we can have some cookies. O.K.?" The second one replied, "She'd say it's too near lunch time." The first one tried several times to persuade his friend to ask, and finally said, "Well, tell her we're starving. She wouldn't want you to starve, would she?" His friend looked him straight in the eyes and, without hesitating, said, "Look, friend, my mom is the only adult I know who's consistent, and I wouldn't tempt her for anything!"

It is only a part of being human to feel better physically and emotionally some days than others. However, to let these feelings influence our actions and reactions toward others results in frustration for all concerned. Mature adults can usually cope with inconsistent reactions from others. Yet, for a child, inconsistency from an adult can produce long-lasting frustrations and feelings of insecurity.

GYMNASTIC SKILLS (K-6)

Highlights—individual challenge and success, independent thinking, body control, spatial awareness; *Equipment*—Per child—one hoop; Per 4-6 children—one tumbling mat; two plastic bottles; one 4' dowel rod; one wooden box approximately 18" x 18" x 18" (See Points to Ponder for improvising equipment); *Area*—activity room, classroom, or playground.

Gymnastics is one of the most challenging and self-satisfying activities. Many children who have never excelled in other sports have amazed themselves, their peers, and their teachers with their abilities to perform individually in gymnastics. Yet, gymnastics is often omitted in the elementary schools. In part, this is due to thinking that expensive equipment and special instructors are necessary. However, when viewed in the same light as soccer, basketball, and other sports, basic skills in gymnastics can be taught quite effectively by classroom teachers—and with little or no expense. Emphasis is placed on helping children learn to control their bodies while moving in various ways and in relation to various objects.

Every child can succeed, regardless of age, and find challenge according to his ability. Use the suggestions that follow, and add others as you see the need while observing your class.

(1) *Balance on different body parts (K-6).* With the children well spaced, ask them to see how many ways they can find to balance in place on two body parts. Keep encouraging the use of two *different* body parts. Continue working on balance—using three body parts, four, five, etc. Work toward finding the *best* balanced positions (those with wide bases and low centers of gravity).

(2) *Travel—taking weight on different body parts (K-6).* Ask the children to see how many different ways they can travel by placing their weight on different body parts. Encourage placing different body parts at different levels (high, middle, and low) while traveling. Every child—from the poorly skilled to the highly skilled—will be able to find several ways to be successful, but each will be performing at his level of ability. Always stress smooth, controlled movements.

(3) *Bend, curl, stretch, and twist (K-6).* With children well spaced, ask them to remain in place and see how many ways they can *bend* their bodies, or parts of their bodies, on each level (high, middle, and low). Ask them to hold each position a few seconds before going to the next.

When understanding is apparent, add exploring ways to *curl, stretch,* and *twist.* Give ample time to explore each on different levels, and stress holding each shape a few seconds.

(4) *Sequences (3-6).* Ask the children to work out a sequence of movements that includes bending, stretching, curling, and twisting (in whatever order they desire). Ask them to put the movements together so that one flows smoothly into the next. This will take a little time, but there should be no talking because each child should be absorbed in finding his own solution. Walk around, observe each child, and make positive comments when possible. If a child needs help, *don't tell* him what to do, but *guide* him through questions to which he responds through movement. Example: "You've got a very nice sequence, Mary. Now, how could you make each movement take you to a *different* level?" or "Great, Tim! Can you think of a way to move more smoothly from one position to the next?" Allow time for volunteers to show their sequences. If all wish to, let several demonstrate at a time.

(5) *Bottles and Canes (K-6).* For every 4 children, place two plastic bottles approximately 4' apart; place a cane (see Points to

Ponder) across the bottle tops. Ask the children to *take turns,* and see how many different ways they can find to go over the cane and land softly with good body control. After each has had several turns, ask them to explore different ways to go *under* the cane.

According to the levels and abilities of the children, the following suggestions may be added:

—When going *over* the cane, make a different shape in the air each time before landing softly on both feet. Others are: place the feet far apart; place the feet close together; place the feet high, etc., before landing softly on both feet.

—When going *over* the cane, start by facing one direction and land facing another.

—To go *over* the cane, travel from two hands to two feet. Others are: from one foot to two feet; from one foot to one foot; from two feet to two feet; from two feet to one foot.

—When going *under* the cane, lead with different parts of the body.

—To go *under* the cane, use turning, curling, and stretching movements.

(6) *Mats (K-6).*   For every 4 children, place a mat lengthwise in front of them. (See Points to Ponder for mat substitutes.) Ask them to take turns exploring different ways to travel from one end of the mat to the other, keeping their bodies under control. Allow ample time for exploration; then, and at later times, work on the following concepts:

—Find different ways to roll very slowly down the mat, very quickly, etc.
—Find different ways to use hands and feet in traveling down the mat.

(7) *Sequences on mats (3-6).*   Ask each child to work out a sequence of movements to use while traveling down the mat. Examples are: "Begin with a stretch, add a curl and a roll, and end with a stretch." "Repeat the sequence, but make one part very slow and one part very fast," "Work out a sequence of your own that shows a change in direction, a change in speed, and good body control."

(8) *Boxes (K-6).*   With 4 children per box (see Points to Ponder for substitutes), ask them to take turns finding ways to get from one side of the box to the other. Additional suggestions are:

—Jump forward off the box and land *softly* on both feet.
—Jump forward off the box, land softly on both feet, curl, and roll.
—Jump forward off the box, land softly on both feet, curl, roll, and balance.
—Jump forward off the box, stretch in the air, and land softly. (Repeat the above suggestions jumping sideways and backward.)
—Jump off the box and touch both feet with your hands before landing softly on both feet.

—Jump off the box and spread both feet far apart before landing softly on both feet.

—Jump off the box and click both heels together (as many times as possible) before landing softly on both feet.

Add others as you and your children discover them.

(9) *Hoops (K-6).* Give each child a hoop (for substitutes see Points to Ponder) and ask him to find a space not too near anyone. Allow a few minutes to see what each can do with his hoop—staying in his own personal space. Then, ask all of the children to place their hoops on the floor (check spacing) and see how many *different* ways they can get from one side to the other. Allow time to explore; then, add the following suggestions:

—Using one body part inside the hoop, go from one side to the other. Use a different body part and repeat. Do the same using two, three, and four body parts inside the hoop.

—Find a way to lift a different part of the body high each time you go from one side to the other.

Points to Ponder

Equipment for gymnastic skills can be easily and inexpensively made or improvised. For *hoops,* substitute 8' lengths of rope, yarn, or cord. For *wooden boxes,* cut and stack squares of corrugated cardboard, and tie them together; cardboard boxes filled with folded newspaper work well, but they're heavier to lift. For *mats*, folded blankets may be used, or inexpensive individual "rest mats" may be purchased at most discount stores. *Canes* may be made by using small bamboo poles, yard sticks, wooden dowel rods, or any similar item. For *bottles,* use empty gallon-size plastic bottles (milk, bleach, etc.). If additional height is desired, invert one, place it above another, and tape both open ends together.

Although having all children simultaneously working with the same kinds of equipment is preferred by some teachers, it is not always possible. An alternate suggestion is to let the class work together when doing things that do not involve equipment or small apparatus, but set up stations when apparatus is required. If stations are used, make sure the children understand the task at each; cue cards may be helpful. Also, have enough equipment at each station to eliminate much, if any, waiting in line.

Help children learn to use *all* of the available space; they will have a tendency to bunch together.

Although there should be a free and open atmosphere for learning, there should also be order and discipline. Many times these result naturally because everyone is occupied—but not always! If

discipline becomes a problem, work *with* the children to establish rules to follow. For example: only one person on a mat at a time, conversation in a low tone is allowed if one child is helping another, etc.

During a class period, work on only a few concepts. Continue these and add others at later times. Never consider them finished because each child can always find other ways to respond, or can improve those he knows.

Always stress good body control, soft landings, and good use of available space.

It is difficult to watch a whole class and see *individual* responses. Try to get in the habit of watching one student at a time, but always be aware of the whole group.

Don't expect or aim for the same response from all children. For example: Johnny may respond to *traveling on two body parts* by walking on his hands while Jimmy walks on his feet. Both have correct responses—each according to his ability. Help the children understand that each person is different and should work on his own rather than trying to imitate another.

Praise each child as often as possible!

DOUBLE TROUBLE (2-3)

Highlights—tossing a ball vertically, catching a ball during competition, alertness; *Equipment*—one ball—6"-8" in diameter—for each group; *Area*—playground, paved area, or activity room; *Number of players*—suited best for 6-12 per game.

Arrange players approximately 3' apart in a circle and let them count off in order, calling each number twice before progressing to the next number—this will result in an arrangement as shown in Figure 1. Choose one player to stand in the center and start the play by tossing the ball vertically (overhead), calling out any number other than his own, and quickly stepping out of the way. The object of the game is for both players (whose number was called) to try to catch the ball before it bounces. The one who succeeds remains in the center and quickly calls the next number. If both players catch the ball simultaneously, the caller calls another number.

If necessary, modify the game so that the ball may be caught before or after one bounce.

Points to Ponder

To help maintain a consistent circle, the caller may call, "Space yourselves!" before calling a number.

If there is not an even number of players, assign one number to three players.

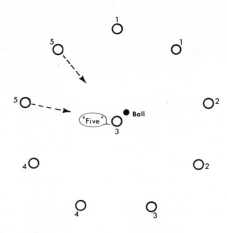

Figure 1 DOUBLE TROUBLE

Called players should return to their original places so that corresponding numbers are always side by side.

Encourage the player who catches the ball to call another number quickly so that there is *constant* action.

Paper balls may be used if the game is played without allowing a bounce.

The vertical toss is not an easy skill for young children to master. Precede the game with many opportunities for tossing the ball overhead, in front of and behind the body, and so on until the children understand how to make the ball go in any desired direction. Individual paper balls are quite practical to use for developing skills and providing maximum participation.

WHAT'S OUR BAG TODAY? (K-6)

Highlights—creative movement responses to words, guessing; *Equipment*—none; *Area*—classroom; *Number of players*—unlimited.

Before playing the game, help children to become familiar with words of opposite meanings (antonyms). Give them opportunities to express their individual interpretations of the words—each response must be through body positions or facial expressions, but it should be a silent response. Some suggested words to use are: fat-skinny; happy-sad; light-heavy; hot-cold; soft-hard; young-old; mean-nice; high-low.

Begin the game by choosing a leader and an IT. The leader chooses two words (of opposite meanings) and leads the group in a chant. IT stands away from the group with his eyes closed and his

back turned while the class chants and performs the following: "We are very, very happy [all show happiness];/ We are very, very sad [all show sadness];/ Sometimes happy [all show happiness];/ Sometimes sad [all show sadness];/ What's our bag today? [all follow the leader's decision]." IT listens throughout the chant. At the end, with his back still turned and his eyes still closed, he must quickly guess which they are portraying. If he guesses correctly, he remains IT for another turn. If his guess is incorrect, he quickly chooses a replacement and is automatically the leader for the next game.

Points to Ponder

Children may be in any formation (informally grouped or simply standing beside their desks).

Rather than letting IT become the next leader, the leader may choose a replacement.

Encourage the leader to decide quickly what he will do at the end of the chant so that there is no delay in the game.

STOP THIEF (3-6)

Highlights—throwing a ball at a moving target, leisure-time activity; *Equipment*—one ball—6"-10" in diameter, 1 pin (plastic bottle), and 2 bases; *Area*—playground or activity room; *Number of players*—two teams of 4-8 players each per game.

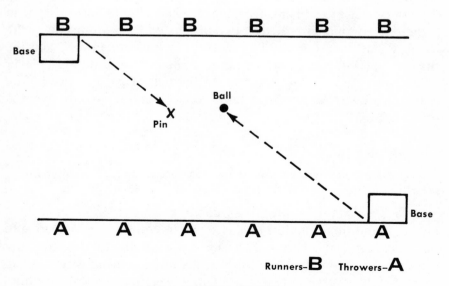

Figure 2 STOP, THIEF!

Players are positioned as shown in Figure 2. Note that the ball and the pin are set *closer* to the B team (runners) than to the A team (throwers). The game begins when the player on the base of the A team looks at his opponent (the runner at the opposite end of the B team) and says, "Stop thief!" On this signal, both players run toward the ball and pin. The B player picks up the pin and tries to return to his base before the A player can throw the ball and hit him *below the head.* Whichever player is successful scores one point for his team. After each has a turn, he goes to the opposite end of his own line. Players on each team shift one position toward their base and the game continues. When each person has run, change the roles of the teams, as well as the positions of the ball and pin.

Points to Ponder

The equipment necessary for the game may be made quite easily and inexpensively. The ball may be one of tightly packed sheets of newspaper wrapped with masking tape; the pin may be a plastic bleach or detergent bottle; and the bases may be made by folding a vegetable sack and securing the corners; lines or ropes may be substituted for bases.

Note that the pin and ball are closer to the running team to equalize the challenge. To keep the distance consistent, use a base or similar object to mark the spot.

If time is wasted in retrieving the ball after it is thrown or in setting up the pin, give the last two players on the waiting end of the runners' line this responsibility since both the "stolen pin" and the thrown ball will end up on the runners' side. (After running, a player would serve twice as retriever to set the ball or pin in place before joining his line.) Whatever method is used should serve only to speed up the game.

MOTION (3-6)

Highlights—teasing, alertness and quick reaction, party-type activity; *Equipment*—none; *Area*—classroom; *Number of players*—unlimited.

IT stands in the center of the room, and all other players form a circle around him. IT closes his eyes while you point to someone to be the leader. Ask the leader to raise his hand quickly to make sure everyone understands who will lead because his name is not called. Immediately, everyone (except IT) starts clapping a steady rhythm. When IT hears the clapping, he opens his eyes; but he must remain in

the center of the players so that he cannot face everyone at once. The leader, as inconspiciously as possible, changes the clapping to another rhythmical movement, and all other players must copy his movement as quickly as possible. IT has a total of three guesses to find the leader. The object of the game is for the group and the leader to disguise the leader. If IT finds the leader within three guesses, he chooses a replacement before the count of three, and the game continues as in the beginning. If IT fails to guess the leader, the leader chooses the new IT for the next game.

Points to Ponder

The players need not necessarily be in a circle, but they should be positioned so that IT is in the center and cannot face everyone at once, otherwise the leader would never have an opportune time to change the action. Desks need not be moved, however.

Although it is tempting to tell the children not to give the leader away by constantly looking in his direction, first try letting them play the game a couple of times and observe what happens. If it becomes apparent that they need help in disguising the leader, making the game more challenging for IT, offer some thought-provoking questions: "If Benjie is the leader, what are some ways we can cover up for him? . . . What happens if all of us look at him? . . . If we don't look at him, how will we know to change the action?" It will not take them long to realize that (1) those near the leader can take their cues from others across the room and that (2) everyone can glance at the leader occasionally, but should concentrate on other players most of the time. The leader may need some help in developing ways to be more inconspicuous when changing from one action (movement) to another. For instance, if the action is one that involves no noise (like patting his shoulders), and he wishes to change to something that makes a noise (such as snapping his fingers), he could mimic the new action, while others away from him exaggerate the sound in the new action in an effort to confuse IT.

It may also be necessary to discuss knowing when to change movements and how to change smoothly from one to another. IT may need help in the timing of his guesses. He should not guess until after a change, or until he has some reason to suspect a person, and then should make one guess at a time, rather than simply making three rapid guesses at random.

Encourage a blending of active and less active movements that

may be done *in place*; the game is not suited to movements involving traveling.

Motion makes a good break between periods of physical inactivity.

BAMBOO DANCING (4-6)

Highlights—jumping in and out of two moving poles, endurance, timing, and coordination; *Equipment*—two bamboo poles (or something similar), approximately 8' long for each set of "trappers"; a record player and a recording of "Tinikling" (*RCA Victor EPA4126*); other recordings of moderate waltz tempo may be used—"The Black Hawk Waltz" (*Imperial #X6006*), instrumental recordings of well-known tunes such as "The Sidewalks of New York," "Take Me Out to the Ball Game," and others; *Area*—activity room or classroom; *Number of players*—3-6 players per set of poles.

Bamboo Dancing is an activity that usually appeals to both boys and girls, but it is especially challenging to boys. Perhaps the best known dance of this kind is "Tinikling," a folk dance of the Philippine Islands where bamboo grows in profusion. The dance represents trappers trying to trap the long, fast-moving legs of the "Tikling" bird.

Trappers. Two people are needed for each set of poles. The poles are placed parallel to each other, approximately 16"-20" apart on the floor. A trapper sits at each end of the set; he may sit cross-legged or rest on his knees and heels (however he is comfortable). The poles are held firmly, but with the fingers slightly toward the outside so that they will not be hit when the poles are struck together to make the "trap."

The Trap: This is a steady 3/4 rhythm of moving the poles together for 1 count and back to their original positions for 2 counts. The *Cue Call* is: "In, Out, Out."

Count 1—Lift the poles and strike them together once just above the floor.
Count 2—Separate the poles and strike them once against the floor.
Count 3—Strike the poles against the floor a second time.

Repeat the movements in a steady 1, 2, 3 rhythm.

Letting the ends of the poles rest on a wooden block approximately 2" x 24" makes it possible to *slide* the poles together and produce a different sound effect.

Dancers: The number of dancers per set of poles is determined by the length of the poles. The longer poles will accommodate

two dancers, once they know the steps. The starting position is customarily with the right side toward a set of poles (trap) and facing one end of the trap. Dancers should be in bare feet, although sneakers are acceptable.

Basic Step: The dancer stands outside the set of poles (right side toward poles) with his weight on his right foot and his hands on his hips. *He faces the same direction throughout this step.* His *Cue Call* is: "Out, In, In."

Count 1—Step onto the left foot (outside the poles).
Count 2—Leap onto the right foot (inside the poles).
Count 3—Leap onto the left foot (inside the poles).

The first count for the repeat begins with a leap onto the right foot (outside the poles so that the left side is now toward the poles). Continue alternating from one side to the other in a steady rhythm. To prevent giving too much time to count 1, keep the free foot above the poles ready to go back in on count 2.

Basic Step Patterns: The suggested steps that follow are intended only as ideas of the kinds of things that can be done. Once the students become skillful (and if properly challenged), there will be no end to the interesting patterns that they can create.

—*Turn:* This is simply making a turn to face the opposite end while inside the poles on the counts of 2 and 3. The turn may be during every other *Basic Step,* during each *Basic Step,* or after any number of steps. Whenever it is done, it results in the dancer's exiting on the same side he entered. The *Cue Call* is: "Out, Turn, Turn; Out, Turn, Turn."

—*Box:* The box is a *Basic Step* ("Out, In, In") followed by one step out of the trap and two steps traveling forward beside the poles ("Out, Walk, Walk"). To re-enter the poles, the dancer turns toward his left as he leaps onto his left foot (outside the poles) to begin the next *Basic Step* followed by the walk. Continue alternating the two to make the box pattern. The *Cue Call* is: "Out, In, In; Out, Walk, Walk; Out, In, In; Out, Walk, Walk."

—*Diagonal:* This is a *Basic Step* made while traveling diagonally toward the opposite end of the poles, and followed by one step out of the poles and two steps made while turning. The next *Basic Step* takes the dancer back to his starting position to repeat the turn. The *Cue Call* is: "Out, In, In; Out, Turn, Turn; Out, In, In; Out, Turn, Turn."

—*Stride Jumps:* The dancer begins the step in stride position—straddling the poles. The first jump is outside the poles (both feet) followed by two jumps inside the poles (both feet). The *Cue Call* is: "Out, In, In." Once learned, this step is usually preceded by a *Basic Step* or some other step designed to place the dancer inside the poles before going into the *Stride Jumps.*

Figure 3

—*Travel:* To travel is to progress from one set of poles to the next. To allow this, various arrangements of the poles are possible. Some of these are: a circle formation simulating spokes in a wheel, a line formation with sets parallel to each other, or one set placed across the center of another set to allow four dancers. These three arrangements are shown in photographs in Figure 3. Whatever the arrangement, the dancer begins by dancing one *Basic Step* from one side to the other side of his set. This is followed by a *Basic Step* outside the poles (between his set and the next set). He continues in the same manner around the circle or down the line—one *Basic Step* through each set of poles and one in between each two sets of poles. If the arrangement is in circle formation, the travel is continuous until the dancer is back to his original place. If the sets are in a line formation, after the dancer crosses the last set, he then uses his next three steps to turn and re-enter the poles toward the other end (to allow room for those following him).

Points to Ponder

The rhythm is easily established by clapping hands (with or without the music) rhythmically or by stepping in place in 3/4 time. This helps insure that each beat receives the same amount of time.

The movements involved in trapping may be learned by letting everyone sit and clap hands together once and move them apart to tap on the floor (desks or knees) twice. Repeat until the movements are smooth and steady.

The basic movements involved in any of the dancers' steps may be learned simply by running slowly in place. "Stand tall, place hands on hips, and [in a steady rhythm] leap alternately from one foot to the other [as in running], allowing only the balls of the feet to contact the floor. The free foot is lifted high in back."

While learning the steps, tape lines, jump rope, lummi sticks, shoes, or similar objects placed approximately 16"-20" apart on the floor may be used to simulate the poles. If these are set up so that several lines of children can all face the same direction and all start together, it is easy to spot those who may need individual help. Once the children understand the footwork involved in a step, let them try it to the music. Children may wish to work individually or in pairs.

All of the preceding suggestions may be done *without* bamboo poles. The number of poles available, the length of the poles, and the space available will determine the organization at this point. Ideally, there should be a set of poles for every 3-6 students. However, if only one or two sets are available, groups could take turns using the poles while the others practice the steps using lines, ropes, shoes, and so forth. A set of poles could also be used as a station to which small groups rotate from stations having different kinds of activities.

Trapping is as important as dancing. Let the children practice trapping without music and without dancers. Add the dancers only *after* the trappers are successful. The trapper must concentrate on both the music and the movements of poles.

The dancer must concentrate on the movements in the dance. Once he knows the steps, the hardest part will be the first step to get started (he steps onto his left foot—outside the poles—as the poles come together). It may be wise to let the trappers start first and trap a few times before the dancer attempts an entry.

Trust is the order of the day! The dancers must have confidence in the trappers, and the trappers must have confidence in the dancers. Should the dancer hesitate to see if the poles are going to be apart, or should the trappers wait to see if the dancer's foot will be out of the way, the whole rhythm will be lost.

The skill of bamboo dancing is much like that of learning to ride a bicycle in that, after several difficult attempts, all of a sudden "you've got it," and the skill is mastered for life.

Perhaps the greatest enjoyment of all comes when a class has choreographed its own bamboo dance. It is simply a matter of changing to a different step pattern as the themes change in the music.

Many creative steps and step patterns are possible—with or without partners—once the children understand the *Basic Step* and how to trap.

GLOW-WORM—American Mixer (5-6)

Highlights—easy walking patterns to music, constantly changing partners; *Equipment*—a record player and a recording of "Glow-Worm" (*MacGregor #3105*) or any record with a definite 4/4 tempo; *Formation*—a double circle of partners holding inside hands and facing counterclockwise—around the circle—boys on the inside, girls on the outside.

Footwork

The footwork is opposite throughout—boys begin on left foot, girls on right foot. The directions given for footwork are for the boys.

Walk forward three steps (left, right, left) and stomp the right foot, but do not transfer weight to right foot. Face partner, drop hands, and walk backward three steps (right, left, right) and stomp the left foot. Walk forward moving diagonally toward the right (left, right, left) and stomp the right foot (facing a new partner). Join both hands with the new partner, and walk clockwise around (right, left, right) and stomp the left foot. Repeat from the beginning with a new partner each time. The *Cue Call* is: "Forward, 2, 3, Stomp; Away, 2, 3, Stomp; Change, 2, 3, Stomp; Swing, 2, 3, Stomp."

Points to Ponder

This dance is classified as a mixer because the steps are very simple and the change of partners is a part of the dance. Because the footwork is easy, teach the patterns of movements first (forward, away from partner, diagonally to new partner, and swing once around). Once they understand the pattern, have them practice walking three steps and stomping one time. Repeat until they get the feeling of *not* transferring the weight to the stomping foot—it is free to begin the next walk.

When the steps are smooth, combine all four parts (forward, away, change, and swing) without the music. Let them *listen* to the music while you call (or demonstrate) the four parts. Add the movements to the music as soon as possible.

Encourage each child to add his individual personality to the dance by varying the steps, snapping fingers, livening up the stomps, or by gestures when meeting new partners, and so forth.

CREATIVE EXERCISES (3-6)

Highlights—sharing ideas with a group, independent thinking, creating and fitting movement to music; *Equipment*—a record player and a recording of "Mame" or any lively 4/4 music; *Area*—activity room or classroom; *Number of players*—suited best for 6-8 per group.

There are various techniques that may be used to introduce this activity. You will develop your own according to your personality, imagination, and relationship with your class and according to their experiences and creative abilities. The following technique is intended to serve only as an example.

With the class seated comfortably, let them listen to the music and clap the rhythm softly. See if they can tell when the music changes to another part or theme, how many parts there are, and when a part is repeated. Once they understand the rhythm and changes in the music, discuss movements that would *fit* the music: "Who can show us just one thing we could do or way we could move that would fit? . . . Good, Becky—step, step, step, swing; step, step, step, swing. Do her movements fit the music? . . . Could you think of a way she could use the same movements to travel forward, around, or to the left or right? . . . How long would she repeat the movements? . . . Yes, until the music changes. How many times is it before *our* music changes? . . . Yes, four times. Who can show us another movement that would fit? . . . Hey, Charles has a good one. What does that remind you of? . . . basketball?—Bounce, bounce, bounce, shoot; bounce, bounce, bounce, shoot. And each of you will think of many others. In a few minutes, we're going to divide into small groups and let each group work out some exercises or movements that fit our music. Although each group will be trying to solve the same problem, do you think each group will solve it with the same movements? . . . Probably not, because there are many different ways to successfully solve a problem." It may be necessary to explain that they may use movements that they already know, or they may be original. The important thing to remember is that the movements must fit the music, and the changes should be made smoothly. Explain that when they get in their groups, you will play the record several times while they work together on solving their problem. Clear up any questions, and assign them in groups of 6-8 to a specific area to work. Visit the different groups to encourage further exploration, but be careful *not* to tell them what to do.

After several minutes, signal them to stop and sit. Give each group a chance to show its movements while the others watch.

Encourage sharing ideas that would make the movements fit the music better.

After each group has demonstrated its exercises or movements, let the whole class select one movement from each group to repeat a certain number of times (according to the music). This should give four or five different activities to combine into an exercise routine to the music.

Points to Ponder

Make the exercises more meaningful by involving the children in selecting the music they would like to use. This can be from the school collection, or individuals may bring their own records.

Any one of several methods may be used for getting into groups—counting off, assigning groups, groups by choice, and so forth.

There was deliberate omission of a definite formation. Encourage various formations—circles, diagonal lines, crosses, semicircles, "V" shapes.

The process may extend over as long a period of time as there is interest in polishing, smoothing out, and refining the movements. Later, the routine may be used as a warm-up activity preceding other activities.

SING A SONG OF SIXPENCE—English Singing Game (K-2)

Highlights—performing predetermined or interpretive movements to music, dramatizing words in a song; *Equipment*—optional—a record player and a recording of "Sing a Song of Sixpence" (*Folkraft #1180*); *Area*—activity room or classroom; *Formation*—single circle with hands joined facing center.

Song and Actions

"Sing a song of sixpence pocket full of rye, [*All walk clockwise around circle*] Four and twenty blackbirds baked in a pie, [*Walk toward center and stoop*] When the pie was opened, the birds began to sing, [*Jump and open arms wide*] Wasn't that a dainty dish to set before a king? [*Walk back to place and bow*] The king was in the counting house counting out his money, [*Pretend to count money*] The queen was in the parlor eating bread and honey, [*Pretend to eat*] The maid was in the garden hanging out the clothes, [*Pretend to pin clothes on line*] Along came a blackbird and snipped off her nose." [*Pretend to fly around and snip off a nose*] Repeat all as desired.

Points to Ponder

Let the children learn the song before introducing the actions. Although specific movements were suggested to dramatize the words of the song, it would be much more meaningful and challenging to the children if they created their own: "Now that we know the song, how would you like to act it out? What could we do to the first part of the song? [They may decide to all do the same thing together or for each to do something different.] How can we pretend we're being baked in a pie? How can we show that the pie was opened?"

Although a record was suggested, it is not essential since the tune is familiar to most people.

VIRGINIA REEL—American Folk Dance (4-6)

Highlights—moving in line formation to music, square-dance type skills; *Equipment*—a record player and any lively 4/4 music ("Virginia Reel," *RCA Victor #41-6180* or "Virginia Reel," *Folkraft #1161*); *Area*—activity room or classroom; *Formation*—sets of six to eight couples each. Boys stand side by side, facing their partners. The couple (in each set) nearest the music is the head couple; the couple at the opposite end (of each set) is the foot couple.

Cue Calls and Actions

Part One

"*Forward and Bow*"—All walk toward partner and nod head. Walk backward to place.

"*Right Hands*"—Join right hands with partner, walk once around clockwise and back to place.

"*Left Hands*"—Repeat with left hands (walking counterclockwise).

"*Both Hands*"—Repeat with both hands (walking clockwise).

"*Do-Si-Do Right*"—Fold arms "Indian style," walk around partner passing right shoulders then left shoulders. Walk backward to place. (Face same direction throughout.)

"*Do-Si-Do Left*"—Repeat, passing left shoulders first.

Part Two

"*Head Couple All the Way Down and Half Way Back*"—The head couple in each set joins both hands and slides down the center to the foot of the set and half way back; others clap.

"*Reel*"—The head couple joins right hands and passes right shoulders so that the boy is facing the girl at the head of the set, and his partner is facing the boy at the foot of the set. The head couple separates, and (with left hands) each swings the person he (she) is facing and returns to the center of set to swing each other with the right hand. The reel continues (alternating left hand to line and

right hand to partner) to each person in the line. When the reel is complete, the head couple joins both hands and slides back to the head of the set. Then, each turns *away* from each other and leads his line (girls follow head girl, boys follow head boy—walking behind the original line) to the foot of the set. At the foot, the head couple joins both hands high to form an arch. The other couples meet, pass under the arch, and move back to place; the "old" head couple remains at the foot of the set. Other couples will have progressed one space toward the head of the set.

Repeat from beginning with a new head couple each time.

Points to Ponder

As far as possible, have the same number of couples in each set. If a set has less than the others, it simply means that it will finish a few seconds earlier and wait until all sets are ready to repeat *Part One.*

Each *Cue Call* in *Part One* takes 8 counts of the music. (For instance, on "Forward and Bow," there are 4 counts for partners to meet and bow, and there are 4 counts to walk back to place.)

Encourage short steps and moving *with* the music rather than simply counting steps.

Although walking was suggested, skipping may be used to liven it up.

Correlating the *Virginia Reel* with social studies adds interest, enthusiasm, and motivation.

When dancing in the classroom, moving the furniture toward the center of the room leaves space to form sets along the sides and ends of the room.

Children and adults enjoy this activity; however, it can be monotonous to watch as a spectator. Therefore, if it is performed in a program, consider ending it after only three or four couples have been the head couple.

LIMBAR (3-6)

Highlights—individual challenge, festive-type activity; *Equipment*—one bamboo pole per 4-6 children (see Points to Ponder); Optional—a recording of calypso-type music; *Area*—activity room or classroom; *Number of players*—suited best for 4-6 per group.

Most children have seen the limbo performed on television. They love the challenge of seeing how close to the floor they can lower the pole and still be successful in getting under it. Explain that

the dancer faces a pole held horizontally, and keeping his weight on his feet, must go under the pole without touching it. Get someone to help you hold the pole about shoulder high while a few volunteers demonstrate. If the dancer is successful, the pole is lowered a few inches for his next turn; if unsuccessful, the pole remains at the same height for his next turn. An easy and practical system for heights is to use *shoulder, waist, top of legs, knees,* and *calf of leg.* Each person is responsible for his height each turn. Let the children choose groups of 4-6, get a pole, and find a good space in which to work. Ask them to work out taking equal turns holding the poles. Music may or may not be provided.

Points to Ponder

Poles may be from 3'-5' long. Substitutes are: yard sticks, rope (yarn or cord), or wooden dowel rods.

Usually, children are not used to bending backward. Therefore, spend only a few minutes at a time on the activity, and ask them to take turns rather than continuing until they miss.

No one is eliminated. Each continues at the last height he was unsuccessful.

At first, children will try various ways to get under the pole. Eventually, they will discover that they must lean backward and spread their feet apart; the front part of the body faces the pole while going under.

January   LESSON PLAN GUIDE   Grades K-2

WEEK	MONDAY	TUESDAY	WEDNESDAY	THURSDAY	FRIDAY
1	Gymnastic skills	Explosion Old Mother Witch Touché Turtle	Gymnastic skills	Classroom: What's Our Bag Today? Heel Slap Push Back Mousetrap	Favorite Activities
2	I See Gymnastic skills (K) Jack Be Nimble (1-2) Monkey Tag	Gymnastic skills	Ball-handling skills (K-1) Double Trouble (2) Rope jumping	Sing a Song of Sixpense Gymnastic skills (K-1) Jump Jim Jo (2)	Favorite Activities
3	Let's Make a Dance (without music)	Stations: 1. Ball-handling skills 2. Rope jumping 3. Soccer Touch 4. Walkie-Talkie	Think and Do What's Our Bag Today?	Gymnastic skills	Favorite Activities
4	Gymnastic skills	Parachute games	Ball-handling skills	Mousetrap Sing a Song of Sixpense	Favorite Activities

January   LESSON PLAN GUIDE   Grades 3-6

WEEK	MONDAY	TUESDAY	WEDNESDAY	THURSDAY	FRIDAY
1	Gymnastic skills	Double Trouble (3) Smush (4) Stop Thief (3-4) Indian Ball (5-6)	Gymnastic skills	Classroom: Motion What's Our Bag Today? Hot Potato	Favorite Activities
2	Gymnastic skills	Target One Against Three Spud	Gymnastic skills	Creative exercises	Favorite Activities
3	Double Trouble (3) Stop Thief (3) Keep Away (4) Rotation Dribble (5-6)	Creative exercises True or False	Gymnastic skills (3-4) Glow-Worm (5-6)	Ball-handling skills (3) Bamboo Dancing (4-6) Limbar	Favorite Activities
4	Creative exercises (3) Bamboo Dancing (4-6)	Gymnastic skills Limbar	Parachute rhythms	Parachute games (3) Virginia Reel (4-6)	Favorite Activities

CURIOSITY

Tell me, tell me everything!
What makes it Winter
And then Spring?
Which are the children
Butterflies?
Why do people keep
Winking their eyes?
Where do birds sleep?
Do bees like to sting?
Tell me, tell me please, everything!

Tell me, tell me, I want to know!
What makes leaves grow
In the shapes they grow?
Why do goldfish
Keep chewing? and rabbits
Warble their noses?
Just from habits?
Where does the wind
When it goes away go?
Tell me! or don't even grown-ups know?

Harry Behn

February

TO THE TEACHER—On Free Play

It is generally accepted that most children like to play and will do so on their own. There are those who contend that free play is the only physical education that elementary children need. There are also those who feel that children need to be always involved in an organized, structured program of activities.

During free play, children are free to do (within reason) whatever they desire. Usually they will organize themselves either in a large group or in several small groups. This experience is invaluable, they make and/or change rules as needed, solve their own problems, choose the people with whom they wish to play, and are totally free of any adult standards or values being imposed upon them.

In a structured program, children are exposed to a variety of activities and skills. These experiences offer each child an opportunity to be successful in many different activities to which he might not ever have been exposed. Being organized so that every child is included prevents the few highly skilled boys and girls from taking over and excluding the less skilled and more inhibited children who desperately need to be involved.

There are many advantages and disadvantages found in each situation. We feel that children like and need guidance, organization, and structure as well as opportunities for free play. Plan free play (*Walkie-Talkie*) stations in which there is a choice of equipment, and involve the children as much as possible in planning their physical education.

MIDNIGHT (K-3)

Highlights—running/chasing/tagging, teasing and chanting; *Equipment*—none; *Area*—playground; *Number of players*—unlimited.

"Once there was an old fox who lived in the woods not far from a place where there were lots of chickens. Do you know what a fox would do if he caught a chicken? . . . That's right, he would have a real feast, wouldn't he? Well, these chickens were very brave and were always teasing this old fox. He would try very hard to catch

them, but he was afraid to chase them until midnight when all of the people were asleep. The chickens knew this and would follow him around saying: 'What time is it, Mr. Fox?' The fox would turn around, and all of the chickens would freeze in their tracks while he looked at his watch and told them what time it was. If he said, 'One o'clock' [or some other time], the chickens would follow chanting: 'What time is it, Mr. Fox?' until he faced them again. But what do you think the chickens would do if the fox said: 'Midnight!'? . . . That's right—run back to the chicken coop as fast as their little legs would carry them. We could choose a fox and play that game. Would you like that?"

Discuss the area to be used for the chicken coop where the chickens can run to be safe from the fox. Choose a fox and begin the game. Help the children learn to venture close enough to the fox to challenge him, but stay far enough away to have a chance to escape. After the fox chases them home, help him quickly choose a new fox (from the children he did *not* tag) to continue the game.

Points to Ponder

Children may need to be reminded that catching or tagging a player involves only a *tap*.

Encourage the children to look for empty spaces in order to avoid running into each other.

The area designated as the chicken coop may be an imaginary line between two plastic bottles, anywhere beyond a rope or line on the ground, or past a shadow produced by a tree, building, and so on. Whatever the area, encourage running *past* the line to leave space for others who follow.

FIRE CHIEF (1-2)

Highlights—running parallel to others, racing against others; *Equipment*—none; *Area*—playground; *Number of players*—unlimited.

The players are arranged as shown in Figure 1, and the running distance is approximately 40'-60'. Players count off by 4's, with each number representing a fire truck. One player is the Fire Chief who, keeping his place in line, calls loudly, "Calling all fire trucks number 2!" (He may call any number other than his own.) All number 2 trucks run to the opposite line and back to place. The Fire Chief judges which truck returns first, and the winning driver becomes the Chief for the next time. Trucks must stay in lanes as automobiles do

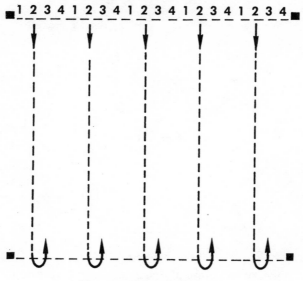

"Calling all firetrucks Number 2!"

Figure 1 FIRE CHIEF

in heavy traffic. If any truck fails to go all the way to the opposite line before returning, he is disqualified (cannot be the winner).

Points to Ponder

Before playing the game, it might help to use a chalkboard to illustrate the fact that the shortest distance between two points is a straight line.

After the children are in position to play, give each number a "walk through" to make sure they know where to run and how to stay in lanes.

The game may be made more challenging by the Chief's calling two or three numbers at once—"Calling all fire trucks numbers 2 and 3!" If he wishes to call all trucks, he yells, "Four alarm!"

A modification of the game would be to vary the action to include skipping or galloping.

SCOOP BALL (K-6)

Highlights—using a scoop as an extension of the hand, hand-eye coordination, individual challenge; *Equipment*—one scoop and ball—described in Points to Ponder; *Area*—activity room, playground, paved area, or classroom; *Number of players*—unlimited.

Children of all ages (and even adults) enjoy activities that

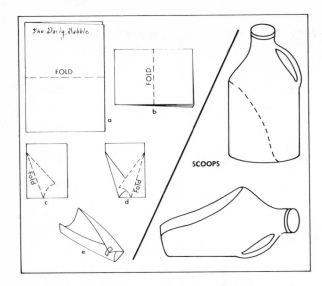

Figure 2 SCOOP BALL

involve a piece of equipment used as an extension of the hand to receive or catch another object. There are numerous types of scoops that can be purchased; however, an inexpensive one can be easily made from a piece of cardboard (or similar material) or several sheets of newspaper folded and rolled in the shape of an "open cone" as shown to the left in Figure 2. More durable and still inexpensive ones may be easily made by cutting the bottom out of a plastic bottle—it may be cut straight across or at a slant as shown to the right in Figure 2.

Before using the scoops, give the children many ball-handling opportunities—individually and with partners—using large balls (paper balls, volley or playground balls, or the inexpensive vinyl balls). Later, let them have some time to manipulate and experiment with smaller objects such as discarded tennis balls, small paper balls packed firmly, beanbags, or small rubber balls. When they show some degree of control, introduce activities involving the scoop and the small ball.

The suggested methods and activities that follow are intended to serve only as ideas and/or types of things that have been created by other classes. The possibilities for expansion are as numerous as the number of individuals involved.

The degree to which children will be able to advance in the progression given will be determined by their stages of development as well as their abilities. Challenge them as far as seems appropriate for your particular situation.

—Do your own thing (K-6).   Give each child a scoop and a ball and ask him to stay within a given area to find out how many different ways he can use them. Walk around helping individuals as needed: "You really have mastered that, Ruth; now can you think of another way to use the scoop?" or, "Good try, Pat, what could you do to make the ball bounce just a little higher;" or, "Very nice, Tracy; could you use the scoop this time to throw the ball against the wall?"

—All together now (K-6).   Ask the class to follow your directions so that all are attempting the same skills. Some suggestions are:

—toss the ball just overhead and catch it in your scoop.
—toss it, a little higher and catch it in your scoop.
—toss it, so that you have to *stretch* to catch it.
—toss it and catch it just *before* it touches the floor.
—place the ball in the scoop, toss it, and catch it in the scoop.
—roll the ball against the wall and catch it in the scoop.
—bounce the ball on the floor and catch it in the scoop.
—bounce the ball against the wall and catch it in the scoop.
—(add others).

—Double up (3-6).   Ask each person to quickly get a partner and find a good space not close to another couple. Let *one* from each couple get two scoops and one ball to share with his partner. Ask couples to work on some specific tasks or skills such as:

—roll the ball to each other and catch it in your scoop.
—toss the ball to each other and catch it in your scoop.
—start close together, and each time the ball is caught in the scoop, move a little
  farther apart; for each "miss," move closer together.
—using only the scoop to throw and to catch the ball, find the distance farthest
  apart at which you and your partner are successful most of the time.
—toss the ball so that your partner has to *stretch* (jump) high to catch; *stretch* to
  either side to catch it; reach or move forward to catch it.
—keep moving (back and forth, around) all the time you are passing and
  receiving the ball.
—with the ball in the scoop, toss it to your partner from overhead, from either
  side, from behind you, from a low position.
—(add others).

Get together (3-6).   Ask the children to get in groups of their choice—the groups may be three, four, or five in number. Tell them that the faster they can do this and sit quietly, the sooner they

will get to play. When all are ready, give them some specific directions to follow in creating or designing a game such as:

—"When I say, 'Go!,' each group will find a space not too close to another group.
—When you are ready, choose one person to get a scoop for *each* person in your group and *one* ball for the group to share.
—You will have five minutes to work as a group and create a game using the ball and scoops.
—Do you know what you're going to do when I say, 'Go?' Any questions? Go!"

Walk around and make sure that the groups understand the task. Where necessary, offer thought-provoking questions: "Hey, you have a great thing going; now what could you add to make the game move a little faster? Is there a way to get each person in the activity most of the time?" After ample time, call the groups together and tell them all of the positive things you noticed. Ask some questions to which their responses are to be made when they spread out into their areas to work: "Think about these things as you work next time: (1) Are the rules adequate? (2) Can you really play the game well? If not, what can you do to make the game more successful? (3) Is everyone involved? (4) Are you really controlling the scoop?" Work as long as seems feasible. Perhaps at some later period they could have more opportunities to *perfect* the game, give it a name, and choose a leader to explain it to the class. Each group may also wish to play some of the games designed by other groups.

Tie-it-in (5-6).   After children have had the above kinds of experiences over a period of time (several class periods), other areas in the upper grades may be tied in or correlated quite easily. Thus, experiences are possible in situations that make learning more relevant and in which motivation is already present. Many sessions throughout the year may be planned by expanding the ideas offered below:

Language Arts: Write descriptions of the games created; read the games to the class; reconstruct sentences, correct spelling, and so forth, as offered by the class, and then compile the written work into booklet form.

Math: Work out scoring; draw the shapes and sizes (to scale) of the courts or areas used in the games.

Art: Portray on paper the games and actions; design a cover sheet for the booklet.

Points to Ponder

We have given many more suggestions for working with scoops than are intended for any one month. Spend ample time experimen-

ting with the individual ideas, and intersperse other types of activities throughout the year.

Scoops may be easily accumulated by asking (in advance) those who can do so to bring an empty plastic milk or bleach container. Be sure to show them a sample for size and ask them to rinse the container before bringing it. Usually one with a handle is a good size.

Although beanbags and paper balls may be used for many of the activities suggested, accumulate some small balls that bounce to use for those requiring the object to roll or rebound.

Walk among the individuals to offer positive remarks, but step back sometimes to watch the whole group and to follow the actions of one person.

Be sensitive to whether or not the children are doing *what you asked*. The task may need repeating several times.

Always have the equipment ready and easily accessible— perhaps a box, vegetable sack, or laundry bag could be used to store the equipment.

Challenge the children often by asking them to hold the scoop sometimes in one hand and sometimes in the *other* hand as they work.

It is quite distracting to talk when children are constantly "playing" with the scoop and/or ball. Yet, the temptation is almost too great (even for adults). Some teachers have eliminated this problem by having the children place the ball in the scoop and place both of them on the floor. If juggling beanbags become a problem, just have each child place his beanbag on his head while you are talking.

YOU NAME IT (3-6)

Highlights—tagging/dodging, working with another person; *Equipment*—a rope 8'-10' long per two players; *Area*—playground or activity room; *Number of players*—unlimited, but arranged in pairs.

With the children standing or seated so that all can see and hear, quickly select two players for demonstration. Ask one to stand with his back to the rope; ask the other to face him, but stand out of reach as shown. Explain that the one at the line is the *tagger* and his partner is the *dodger*. When the dodger says, "Go!," he tries to cross the line without being tagged. The tagger may move only *from side to side* (he may not move forward or backward) in the game, as shown in Figure 3. The dodger may move in any direction he chooses to outwit the tagger and to cross the line. Whenever one player is

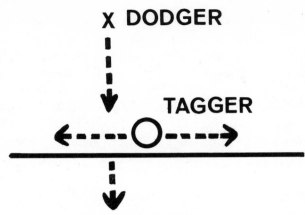

Figure 3 YOU NAME IT

successful, the two reverse roles and the game continues. If there are no questions, let the two demonstrate the game. Without much discussion, ask everyone to select a partner, get a rope, and begin play. The game is quite active; therefore, after only a few minutes ask the children to sit quietly while they think about some things:

—Is your game going well? How could you improve it?
—Does the dodger have a fair chance? Is your area wide enough?
—Is the tagger moving only from side to side? How can you outwit him?
—When you need to rest, sit with your partner and discuss a name for the game.

Points to Ponder

Substitutes for ropes are: drawn lines or two plastic bottles set 8'-10' apart.

Let the class observe a few selected partners and discuss some things they noticed that might be helpful to everyone.

Because it can be organized quickly and requires little preparation, use this game often during the year either at the end of a less-active period or as a station to which small groups rotate.

If the number of players is uneven, use one group of three who simply take turns within that group.

NERVOUS WRECK (1-6)

Highlights—alertness and control, teasing a player, party-type game; *Equipment*—one ball—6"-10" in diameter (preferably one made of paper or yarn) for each group; *Area*—classroom; *Number of players*—approximately 6-8 per group.

Nervous Wreck is a game that is challenging to adults as well as to children. It is often enjoyed as a party game.

IT holds the ball and stands in the center of a circle of 6-8 players who have their hands behind their backs. The object of the game is for each circle player to catch the ball *if* IT tosses it to him, but not to move either hand so that IT can see it in the event that IT pretends to toss the ball but does not release it. When a player *errors* (misses a tossed ball or moves his hand(s) from behind him when IT pretends to toss the ball to him but does not release it), he must turn his back to the group until another player errors, whereupon he may turn back. There is never more than one person's back turned at a time.

Points to Ponder

Give different people a chance to be IT; encourage them to make accurate tosses. Balls thrown out of reach do not count.

Players should be approximately 6'-10' away from IT, depending on the abilities of the group—adjust the distance as necessary.

Consider the lack of physical activity in the game, and use it as a station, or a "quickie" between long periods of sitting.

CLUB GUARD (5-6)

Highlights—throwing at a guarded stationary target, moving quickly to guard an object, teamwork; *Equipment*—one ball—6"-10" in diameter—and a plastic bottle or club per group; *Area*—playground, paved area, or activity room; *Number of players*—4-6 players per game.

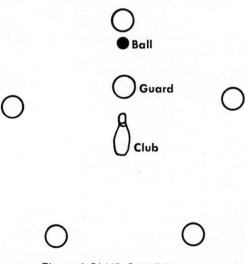

Figure 4 CLUB GUARD

Before playing a game requiring as much skill in handling a ball as *Club Guard,* parts of several class periods should be spent in letting children work in 2's, 3's, and 4's. During this time they need to concentrate on passing the ball to each other as quickly and as accurately as possible.

The game begins with players arranged as shown in Figure 4. The Guard gives the signal to start the play by tossing the ball to any circle player. The object of the game is for a circle player to throw the ball at the club and knock it down. If he is successful, he becomes the Guard, and the game continues as in the beginning. The responsibility of the Guard is to move around the club in such a way as to prevent its being knocked down by the ball *or* by himself. If the Guard should knock it down, he quickly chooses a replacement and the game continues.

Points to Ponder

It is quite tempting, as a player, to hold the ball in an attempt to "throw the Guard off guard" or to throw the ball at the club even when it is apparent that the Guard is positioned to prevent a hit. Players will need *much* help in teamwork—quickly passing the ball among each other until the Guard is caught "off guard" for an "open shot." Grasping this concept of teamwork is difficult and will not happen overnight.

Players will need help in maintaining their distances from the club. The distance should be one that allows fast and accurate passes, as well as a fair chance for the Guard. Some classes have added a helpful rule—the Guard checks the players for distance before he tosses the ball to begin the play.

Any ball of appropriate size may be used; paper balls work well.

BRANDING CATTLE (K-4)

Highlights—dramatizing the branding of cattle, responding to music or a drum beat; *Equipment*—a recording of "Branding Cattle" *(Phoebe James #AED8)* or a drum or tambourine; *Area*—activity room.

Without a recording of "Branding Cattle" (K-4). Before giving any directions for the game, let the children become familiar with the sounds of the tambourine. Let them practice the responses together.

Figure 5 BRANDING CATTLE

Gallop—Beat a steady 2/4 rhythm, as shown in Figure 5, using the tambourine or a drum. Let the children practice galloping freely around the available space being careful not to touch anyone or anything.

Lasso—Beat the tambourine or drum loudly and slowly *three* times for each child to pretend to swing a lasso around his head thrice in time with the tambourine. Then, add a loud, quick beat to "throw" the lasso and rope a calf.

The struggle—Shake the tambourine (beat the drum) slowly for the calf to struggle to get loose.

The fall—Strike the tambourine (drum) loudly once for the calf to fall.

Tie the critter—Beat a walking rhythm for each child to pull his rope tight, walk up to his calf, and tie its two front legs (arms) and two hind legs (legs) together.

Get the iron—Beat a walking rhythm to get the "branding iron" (a few steps away) from a make-believe fire and take it back to the calf.

Brand the critter—Shake the tambourine (drum) vigorously to quickly press the "branding iron" against the rear quarter of the calf.

When they understand the responses to the sounds of the tambourine or drum, let each child choose a partner of his choice. Ask the partners to decide who will be the cowboy and who will be the calf first. (Explain that they will take turns playing each part.) Remind them to use all of the available space and to be careful not to interfere with other cowboys or calves. Let the calves be creative in their responses to having a hot iron pressed against their hides.

With a recording of "Branding Cattle" (3-4). A set of directions is given with the record. However, the following variation is suggested because it permits more activity for each child. Let each child select a partner of his choice and take turns at being the cowboy or the calf as described previously, the only difference being that they now respond to the music.

Points to Ponder

Listening skills are an important part of this activity. Make sure that the children really know what each sound of the record or tambourine (drum) means. Let them respond creatively to the gallop,

lasso, and so forth; but be sure they understand the types of movements called for by each sound. The very young children may need to practice responding to each sound several times before attempting to put them into a sequence. And, if a group works better with *all* members being cowboys with make-believe calves (rather than with partners), this is fine.

Encourage using *all* of the available space and not touching anyone. If there is consistent running into each other, don't hesitate to stop the activity to discuss how to avoid collisions. If the problem does not correct itself within a reasonable time, discontinue the activity and work on finding empty spaces in which to gallop, and so on; otherwise, the objectives of the lesson will be lost and only confusion will result.

Before introducing the activity, make it more meaningful by discussing cowboys, cattle ranchers, cattle, the reason for branding them, what it means, and whether or not it hurts.

FROM A TO Z (K-6)

Highlights—visualizing letters of the alphabet, moving efficiently in relation to others; *Equipment*—none; *Area*—activity room; *Number of players*—unlimited.

From A to Z may be played several different ways depending upon the abilities of the children involved. Some of these are described below.

Individually (K-6). With the children spaced so that they have room to work, ask them to see if they can make their bodies into the shape of the letter O (or any appropriate letter). Let them choose whether they will stand or lie on the floor, but give them the direction from which the letter should be read. Sometimes you may specify whether they should stand or lie down. Give individual help where needed.

In partners (K-6). Do the same thing with one partner forming the letter called while the other one stands and assists him in making it more perfect. Alternate turns.

In teams (4-6). Each child now becomes *part* of a letter that will be formed by the whole team. When the letter is called, they may stoop or lie on the floor, but the whole team should do the same. The first team to finish by having completed a letter wins. Make sure that everyone knows which direction the letter should face. If space allows, have each team's letter face the same direction. It may be necessary to assign a leader for each team.

Points to Ponder

With the younger children, make the letter on a chalkboard or show them one on an alphabet card before asking them to make its shape.

Capital letters should be used, and the letters called should be appropriately difficult for the children involved.

Give them opportunities to see the letters formed by others in the class.

MENDED HEARTS (K-6)

Highlights—cooperation toward a common goal, fitting pieces of a puzzle together; *Equipment*—several valentines (construction paper) each a different color and each cut into identical jigsaw puzzle pieces; *Area*—classroom; *Number of players*—suited best for 4-6 per team.

Divide the class into equal teams of 4-6 players and assign each team a different color. If there are five teams—the red, blue, yellow, green, and purple teams—then five paper valentines (one of each color) are needed. Make a pattern as shown in Figure 6 for the valentines or cut them all at the same time. Do the same when cutting them into jigsaw puzzle pieces so that the skill in assembling them will be equalized.

Have a leader from each team decide on a place in the room where his team will assemble its "heart." Shuffle all pieces and place them anywhere in the room. When a starting signal is given, all players help gather the pieces of their color and take them to the designated spot where they quickly "mend their heart." The first team to do so exclaims, "Mended heart!"

Points to Ponder

Involve extra or handicapped players by having them place the pieces in preparation for the game.

The grade level and the abilities of the group are the determining factors in cutting the valentines into pieces. Generally, younger children can easily assemble 3-5 pieces, whereas most older students can work with as many as 6-10 parts. Making a distinction between the front and the back of the valentine is helpful.

The competitive element is not essential to the enjoyment and benefits of the game; using *groups*, rather than *teams*, with no stress on speed or on a *winner*, is fun, too.

Figure 6 MENDED HEARTS

SEVEN JUMPS (K-6)

Highlights—creative responses to music, moving freely without touching others; *Equipment*—one record player and a recording of "Seven Jumps" (*RCA Victor #41-6172*); *Area*—classroom or activity room; *Number of players*—unlimited.

Traditionally, *Seven Jumps* is performed in a circle with everyone doing the same thing at the same time. There are two parts for which directions accompany the recording.

The modification that follows offers more opportunity for independent thinking and variety of response.

Part One: For 16 measures, each child uses any movements he wishes that go with the music.

Part Two: There are two sustained notes. On the first one, each child assumes a balanced position (pose) and holds it. When the second note is heard, he changes to a different position and holds it until the music changes to repeat Part One.

Part One will always sound the same, although the movement responses may be different. Part Two will add one sustained note each time for a total of eight on the last repeat. For each sustained note, the movement response should be different.

Points to Ponder

Let the children listen to the music long enough to get the ideas described above. Then, let them space themselves with room to move.

The most natural response for Part One is skipping. Encourage a variety of responses such as: skipping-traveling freely into open spaces; and skipping-traveling forward and back, side to side, around in a circle. Children will think of many other movements. For Part Two, stress different levels (high, low, and in between), different shapes (stretch, twist, curl, etc.), and holding each position (pose) very still.

INDIAN DANCE (3-4)—(Prayer for Rain)

Highlights—"Indian-like" movements, moving to music or a drum beat; *Equipment*—a record player and recording of the "Indian Dance" (*Folkraft #1192*). A hand drum may be used as an accompaniment to the record, or as a substitute for it, by beating a steady 4/4 rhythm, accenting the first beat each time; *Area*—activity room or classroom; *Formation*—"Indians" seated cross-legged in a single circle and facing the center with arms folded shoulder high in front of chests.

Cue Calls and Actions

Part One

"*Down, 2, 3, 4; Up, 2, 3, 4*"—Bend forward from waist and back up to position.

"*Down, 2, 3, 4; Up, 2, 3, 4*"—Repeat above.

"*Open, 2, 3, 4; Close, 2, 3, 4*"—Open arms wide to look at the sky; refold arms and look straight ahead.

"*Open, 2, 3, 4; Close, 2, 3, 4*"—Repeat the opening and folding of arms.

"[Look] *Right, 2, 3, 4;* [Look] *Front, 2, 3, 4*"—With right hand placed above the eyes, look around to the right and back to the front.

"[Look] *Left, 2, 3, 4;* [Look] *Front, 2, 3, 4*"—Change hands and repeat toward the left and back to the front.

"[Listen] *Right, 2, 3, 4*"—Cup right hand behind right ear and listen.

"[Listen] *Left, 2, 3, 4*"—Cup left hand behind left ear and listen.

"*Tap* [and] *Tap* [and] *Tap* [and] *Tap*"—Fold arms and alternate tapping elbows with opposite fists (right fist taps left elbow, and so forth).

Part Two

Repeat the calls in Part One, omitting the taps—Repeat the actions in Part One; but, instead of tapping the elbows, rise to a stooping position, facing counterclockwise around the circle. This leads into Part Three.

Part Three

"*Right* [and] *Left* [and] *Rain, Rain, Rain*"—Slap the floor with the right hand, then with the left hand. Cup both hands in front of the mouth, look up at the sky, and say, "Rain, rain, rain!"

"Right [and] *Left* [and] *Rain, Rain, Rain"*—Repeat above, but rise to the feet while calling for rain.

"Toe [and] *Heel* [and] *Toe* [and] *Heel* [and] *Toe* [and] *Heel* [and] *Toe* [and] *Stoop"*—Turn in place, *or* progress counterclockwise around the circle with three toe-heel steps, and stoop in place.

"Right [and] *Left* [and] *Rain, Rain, Rain"*—Repeat slapping floor and calling for rain.

"Right [and] *Left* [and] *Rain, Rain, Rain"*—Repeat slapping floor and calling for rain.

"Toe [and] Heel [and] Toe [and] Heel [and] Toe [and] Heel [and] Yell"—Repeat the toe-heel steps and jump high with a quick "Indian yell" or war whoop at the end.

A heel-toe step is done by stepping on the ball of the foot—*Toe* [and]—then lowering the heel to the floor—*Heel* [and]—and taking the weight on the heel. Alternate feet while moving counterclockwise.

Points to Ponder

Let the children first listen to the music (or the beat of the drum). Then teach the movements before putting them with the music. The directions given are only one version of the dance, there are many others. Perhaps the very best version for your students would be the one they choreograph themselves. They could listen to the music or the rhythm of the drum and then work in small groups. Each group could create movements for one part or for the whole thing.

If a hand drum is not available, one can be made easily by using an empty cylindrical oatmeal container.

Figure 7

The dance may be dressed up even more by putting a make-believe fire in the center of the circle. Some classes use sticks placed over red tissue paper with a flashlight shining underneath it.

The toe-heel step may be made more characteristic or "Indian-like" by adding the bending motions and hand actions shown in the two photographs in Figure 7.

Children usually enjoy this type of activity. It becomes even more relevant if it is tied in with classroom studies.

A true story: A group of third graders in North Carolina substituted "snow" for "rain" in this dance one Wednesday. It snowed so much that night that all the schools were closed Thursday and Friday.

February   LESSON PLAN GUIDE   Grades K-2

WEEK	MONDAY	TUESDAY	WEDNESDAY	THURSDAY	FRIDAY
1	Scoop Ball	Stations: 1. Scoop Ball 2. (Long) rope jumping 3. Target 4. Walkie-Talkie	Classroom: Seven Jumps Sing a Song of Sixpense Sevens and Threes	Classroom: Mended Hearts What's Our Bag Today?	Favorite Activities or Parachute Games
2	Branding Cattle From A-Z	Midnight Back Away Monkey	Stations: 1. Bowling 2. (Short) rope jumping 3. Scoop Ball 4. Walkie-Talkie	Classroom: Hot Potato (K) Endurance Hop (K) Nervous Wreck (1-2) Sock It to Me	Midnight Moon Man (K) Fire Chief (1-2) I See
3	Stations: 1. Bowling 2. Scoop Ball 3. Monkey Tag 4. Walkie-Talkie	Touché Turtle (K) Fire Chief (1-2) Old Mother Witch Jumping Brooks	Classroom: Seven Jumps Let's Make a Dance (without music)	Classroom Stations: 1. Target 2. Stride Ball 3. Lummi Sticks 4. Walkie-Talkie	Favorite Activities
4	Bowling Touché Turtle Explosion	Stations: 1. Soccer Touch 2. Midnight 3. Back Away 4. Walkie-Talkie	I See Jumping Brooks Monkey Tag V-r-r-room	Classroom: Sock It to Me What's Our Bag Today? Bicycle Race Mousetrap	Favorite Activities

February   LESSON PLAN GUIDE   Grades 3-6

WEEK	MONDAY	TUESDAY	WEDNESDAY	THURSDAY	FRIDAY
1	Scoop Ball	Stations: 1. Scoop Ball 2. (Short) rope jumping 3. Right On/Left Off 4. Walkie-Talkie	Classroom: Let's Make a Dance (3) (without music) Seven Jumps Bamboo Dancing (4-6)	Classroom: Bicycle Race Hot Potato Sock It to Me	You Name It True or False Midnight (3) Touchdown (4) Club Guard (5-6)
2	From A-Z Branding Cattle (3-4) Rhythmic Sports (5-6)	Classroom: Nervous Wreck Exchange Tag Mousetrap	Indian Dance (3-4) Seven Jumps Bamboo Dancing (5-6)	Classroom: Mended Hearts True or False Bowling	Stations: 1. You Name It 2. Spud 3. Midnight (3) Scoop Ball (4-6) 4. Walkie-Talkie
3	Classroom: Let's Make a Dance (without music)	Stations: 1. (Long) rope jumping 2. Scoop Ball 3. You Name It 4. Walkie-Talkie	Bridge Bowling Spud	Classroom Stations: 1. Nervous Wreck 2. Lummi Sticks 3. Target 4. Walkie-Talkie	Favorite Activities or Parachute (3) Caputre the Flag (4) Indian Ball (5-6)
4	Stations: 1. Target 2. Back Away 3. Stop Thief (3-4) Club Guard (5-6) 4. Walkie-Talkie	Classroom: Let's Make a Dance (with music)	From A-Z One Against Three Smush	Favorite Activities or Parachute	Indian Dance (3-4) Branding Cattle (3-4) Glow-Worm (5-6) Virginia Reel (5-6)

A CURRICULUM FABLE

Once upon a time, the animals had a school. The curriculum consisted of running, climbing, flying, and swimming, and all of the animals took all of the subjects.

The Duck was good in swimming—better, in fact, than his instructor—and he made passing grades in flying; but he was practically hopeless in running. Because he was low in this subject, he was made to stay in after school and drop his swimming class to practice running. He kept this up until he was only average in swimming, but average was acceptable, so nobody worried about that except the Duck.

The Eagle was considered a problem pupil and was disciplined severely. He had beaten all of the others to the top of the tree in the climbing class, but he had used his own way of getting there.

The Rabbit started at the top of the class in running, but he had a nervous breakdown and had to drop out of school because of so much make-up work in swimming.

The Squirrel led the climbing class; but his flying teacher made him start his flying lessons from the ground instead of the top of the tree. He developed a charley horse from overexertion on his take-off and began getting C's in climbing and B's in running.

The practical Prairie Dogs apprenticed their offspring to a Badger when the school authorities refused to add digging to the curriculum.

At the end of the year an abnormal Eel who could swim well and run, climb, and fly a little was made Valedictorian.

——Anonymous

TO THE TEACHER—On Responsibility

One of the claims made by most educators is that they teach children to accept responsibility. Most teachers set this as one of their objectives and plan many classroom discussions around accepting responsibility for such things as: one's own decisions and actions, one's personal belongings, planning and organizing activities, cleanliness and safety of self and surroundings, and helping others. The possibilities for discussion are limitless. However, assuming that children will learn responsibility by means of lectures or discussion is like assuming that they will learn how to read by hearing about reading. Experiences in reading are provided throughout a child's school life, and he is given more difficult tasks as he is ready for them. More and more teachers are realizing that in order for the best learning to occur, the application of the principle of learning by doing must be consistent in all areas. Fortunate indeed are the children whose teachers plan living experiences and guidance for them in learning to accept responsibility.

CREATIVE GAMES (3-6)

Highlights—creative and independent thinking, cooperative group planning; *Equipment*—one ball (any kind) and one plastic bottle; *Area*—activity room, playground, paved area, or classroom; *Number of players*—suited best for 4-6 per group.

With the class seated comfortably, your introduction to the activity will be determined by your personality, imagination, and relationship with your class as well as the children's previous experiences, backgrounds, and abilities. The ideas that follow are intended to serve only as examples.

"Have you ever wondered how a particular game got started? Who made it up? Why certain rules were made? Have you ever tried to make up a game? I'll bet you could create some games that are more fun than any we know! In a few minutes we will divide into several groups and each group will have the same problem to solve—to create a game! Do you think that each group will solve the

problem just alike? . . . Probably not, because we are all different and each of us is full of ideas to share. Although we have the same problem, there are many different ways to successfully solve it."

It may be necessary to define and stress the word "create" to insure their understanding that the game from each group must be original insofar as they know. The problem should be stated very clearly to them, that is, to create a game in the space and time they will be given. They must use the equipment they will have, provide activity for each person in their group, and allow each member to suggest ideas. In addition, they must give their game a name and elect one person as their leader who will later explain their game to the class.

Have them count off by fours (fives or sixes, depending on amount of space, equipment, and size of class). Explain that when they get to the area to which you will assign them, each group is to choose one person who will get one ball and one plastic bottle. Explain also that as a group is ready, they may begin discussing, trying out ideas, making rules, and so forth. Tell them that they will have approximately fifteen minutes before you will signal them to stop and sit wherever they are. Before assigning areas for the different groups, answer any questions for clarification purposes. Assign them definite areas of the playground or activity room to begin solving their problem. Visit the different groups as a "spectator," to clear up questions, or to encourage further exploration. Be careful *not to tell them what to do.*

When approximately fifteen minutes have passed (or whenever they appear ready) signal them to stop and sit. Ask each group leader (in turn, or as they volunteer) to give the name and explanation of his group's game and organize his group to demonstrate the game just long enough to show how it works. During this time, ask the other groups to watch to see if the demonstrating group solved the problem. Encourage them to think of things they think would make the game being demonstrated safer, more challenging, active, or interesting. The possibilities for creative thinking, sharing of ideas, decision making, respecting the rights and feelings of others are unlimited.

Note to the teacher—Don't panic! There is a lot involved in this process. It cannot be accomplished in one class period; nor should it be. When you finish reading these suggestions, you will readily see how the process could extend over a long period of time. You will think of numerous ways in which to correlate language arts, arithme-

tic, social studies, and art other than those offered later in Points to Ponder.

Points to Ponder

Consider equipment—each group may be given the same equipment, different equipment, or no equipment at all. Ideas of what to use could easily come from the children (old tires, brooms, jar lids, ropes, bamboo poles, Indian clubs, beanbags, paper balls, hoops, etc.).

Only one method of getting into groups was given. Ultimately, strive to reach the point at which children could be asked to get into groups of 4-6 on their own, find an area in the available space, and begin their project.

According to the interest, motivation, abilities, and maturity of the children, the process may continue daily or periodically for refinement and exploration.

Correlation with other studies stimulates interest, makes learning more relevant, and gives more opportunities for each person to discover or contribute his individual talents. Some suggestions from which you may build are offered below:

—Tie in your class discussions of the democratic process. "How did you select a leader? Did one person dictate what you would play? How were decisions made? Why were certain rules made? How were problems solved? Do you see any connection between the rules of a game being followed by each player and the laws of our land being obeyed by each member of society? Do you think a small number of people is more effective than a large number? Why? How did you feel in your group? Were your ideas considered? How do you think others in your group felt? . . . involved? left out?"

—Tie in language arts by having each group get together and write up its game including the name, equipment needed, illustrations or diagrams, number of players, and directions for playing. One person in each group could be responsible for editing and refining the writing. A collection of games during the year may be made into a booklet. If a particular child is talented in this area, he could be the editor.

—Tie in art by letting children design the cover and illustrate the book. Those talented in this area could volunteer to to the art work.

Each child needs to feel that he contributed something. With the variety of talents involved in this activity, there should be at least one (and hopefully many) opportunities for each child to experience the feeling of success and belonging. Every child has one or more talents; an alert teacher will help him to discover them.

After the initial sharing of each group's game, the class should feel free to offer suggestions for improvement, make comments about things they really liked, discuss whether or not the group solved the given problem, and so forth.

Groups may elect to learn the games that the other groups created. By letting each member of a given group aid one of the other groups in doing this, you are giving priceless opportunities for developing leadership in each child.

The exploration and refinement of games may be continued as long as there is high interest. Be sensitive to this, and try to cut it short or expand it as necessary so that it ends on a pleasant and successful note.

RACE BALL (1-6)

Highlights—throwing a ball quickly and accurately, running to a designated spot, cooperating as a team member; *Equipment*—one ball—approximately 6"-10" in diameter—and one marker (pin, plastic bottle, etc.) per team; *Area*—playground or activity room; *Number of players*—suited best for two or more teams of 4-8 players per team.

Race Ball is a type of relay game insofar as the first team to finish wins; however, several members from *each* team are active at the same time.

Holding a ball, a Leader from each team faces his players as shown in Figure 1. On signal, the Leader tosses the ball to the player on either end of his team. The player receiving the ball tosses it back to the Leader and immediately turns, runs around a marker 40'-60' behind the Leader, returns to his place in line, and stoops. Simultaneously, the Leader continues (in order) to toss the ball to each member of his team who immediately runs around the marker, back to place, and stoops. When the last player returns the ball, the Leader places the ball on the ground (floor) and makes the same run. The team to finish first with all players stooping wins. To repeat the game, ask each Leader to quickly choose a new Leader for his team.

Points to Ponder

Before playing the game, give the children many opportunities to handle a ball—individually and with a partner. They should feel comfortable with a ball before confronting the competitive element in this game.

Different types of balls and skills may be used depending on the abilities of the children, for example: toss and catch any size ball;

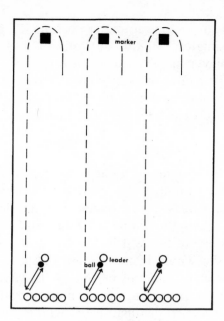

Figure 1 RACE BALL

bounce-pass and catch any size ball; toss, strike or tap (as in volley ball), and catch a light weight ball; pass and trap (as in soccer) a soccer or utility ball.

Stooping to end the play is added only as a means of making it easier to distinguish the winning team.

Make sure that each team has the same number of players. If one or two teams have one less player, equalize the challenge by having the first runner on each team run first *and* last.

Place the markers and let the teams walk through the activity once for complete understanding. Check to see that all players are equidistant from the Leaders and the markers before giving the signal to begin.

JUMP ROPE RELAY (3-6)

Highlights—jumping rope in a competitive situation, cooperating as a member of a team; *Equipment*—a jump rope (approximately 8' long), a marker (plastic bottle), and a starting line for each team; *Area*—playground or activity room; *Number of players*—suited best for two or more teams of 3-5 players per team.

Prior to playing the game, make sure that all of the players can jump an individual rope while running and that they have performed simple running relays.

With each team in relay formation behind its starting line, place a marker approximately 40'-60' in front of each team. On your signal, the first player in each team jumps the rope continuously as he runs *around* his team's marker, back to place, hands the rope to the next person in line, and goes to the end of his line. Each player repeats the action until all have run. The first team to finish wins.

Points to Ponder

Teams should be equal in number to equalize the competition. If there is an uneven number, let the first person on each team that has one less player run last before his team is considered finished.

The players waiting to jump should remain *behind* their starting lines. If a player inches forward in front of the line to get an early start, disqualify the whole team. Discuss this rule before the relay begins, and enforce it from the beginning. Discuss why the rule is important—as in official track meets, swim meets, and so forth.

To make it easier to distinguish the winning team, add the rule that the players must stoop after they have finished.

Ropes may be easily made by cutting regular plow line into lengths (approximately 8'). Wrap masking tape around the area to be cut, and cut through the tape to keep the rope ends from unraveling. Ropes may also be made of plastic clothesline, although they will be a little lighter in weight.

SWING ALONG (K-6)

Highlights—judging the speed of a moving object, jumping over a moving object; *Equipment*—a jump rope (approximately 8' long) for each child; *Area*—activity room, paved area, or playground; *Number of players*—unlimited.

There are several names given to this activity, but the one recently given by a group of children is *Swing Along.*

Space the children a few feet apart and give each child a jump rope. Ask them to double the rope and hold the two ends in one hand. Use as many of the following suggestions as seem feasible for your particular class.

Individually: "Can you swing your rope on the floor in a circular motion in *front of you* and jump it every time it comes around? Can you keep all of the rope close to the floor? Try it a few times. Can you keep swinging and jumping as you travel around the room? Look for empty spaces so that you don't interfere with others." Let them continue trying these kinds of things as you give individual help where needed.

In twos: "Find a partner near you and put one rope away. Let me know when you are ready by being very quiet—in a space large enough in which to work. Each of you will have a chance to swing the rope for your partner; it doesn't matter which you do first—you decide. Hold one end of the doubled rope and make the rope travel on the floor in a circular motion *around you* so that your partner can jump it. Can you use your other hand and swing the rope so that it travels in the opposite direction? Try passing it from one hand to the other as it swings around you so that you face the same direction as the rope swings." Give them ample time to be successful, and give individual help where needed. Let partners alternate swinging and jumping the rope.

In fours: "You and your partner join another set of partners and put away one rope. When you are ready, choose one person to hold the end of the doubled rope and swing it around as before while the other three jump it. Try traveling counterclockwise around the center person as the rope is traveling clockwise (and vice versa). Can you stand beyond the length of the rope and take turns running in, jumping the rope, and running back to place before the rope comes around again? [Move around the area to offer suggestions.] Do you think you could jump when the rope is a little closer to you next time? Do you think you jumped too soon or too late? How do you know *when* to jump? Can you think of other ways to use your feet to get over the rope?"

All together: "Everyone except Martha please put away your ropes and form a large circle around Martha. Move back far enough for Martha to hold the end of a *fully extended* rope and swing it around and around close to the floor without touching you. Practice a few times, Martha," (To prevent the center person from getting too dizzy or too tired, ask him to kneel and pass the rope from one hand to the other as it goes around.) From this point, players may run in, jump, and run out on their own or run in according to the calls of a leader. Some favorites are: (1) when the month of one's birthday is called, (2) when a color one is wearing is called, (3) when the color of one's eyes is called, (4) when the first letter of one's name is called, (5) when one's number is called (having counted off by fours). Sometimes two or more months, numbers, and so on may be called together, sometimes everybody may be called at once.

Points to Ponder

In swinging the rope, the hands should be kept low; let the children discover this for themselves as much as possible.

Give them time individually to practice swinging the rope so that it travels completely *around* them before they join a partner.

The main purpose in suggesting that the rope be doubled when jumping individually, in twos, or in fours is to conserve space.

Most children will be able to kneel and switch hands in order to make the rope travel *on the floor*; however, some of the younger ones may need to turn around with the rope. In such cases, ask them to occasionally reverse the direction in which they swing the rope to prevent dizziness.

If space or the number of available ropes do not permit the activity as written, use it as a station to which small groups rotate from other games requiring small numbers of players.

A tennis shoe or deck tennis ring tied to the end of the rope when it is fully extended gives it the weight necessary for swinging.

BIRD IN THE NEST (3-4)

Highlights—moving quickly with another person, competing as a member of a team; *Equipment*—two plastic bottles (bases, markers, etc.) for each team; *Area*—playground, or activity room; *Number of players*—two or more teams of 4-8 players per team.

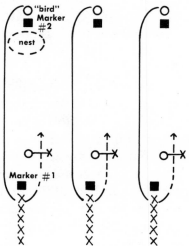

Figure 2 BIRD IN THE NEST

"Have you ever watched closely how a bird makes a nest? How does that little bird ever get all of the pieces put together? . . . That's right, she carries *one piece* at a time and places it exactly where she wants it. She does a good job of making it round, doesn't she? The

game we are playing today is called *Bird in the Nest* because we'll look like a bird making a nest and hopping into it."

As others watch, place one team in relay formation at one marker with one of its players—the "bird"—standing approximately 40'-60' in front of and facing his team as shown in Figure 2. Let them walk through the action once: The "bird" runs across to his team, *around* Marker #1, takes the first player in line, and—with hands joined—they run back to Marker #2. The "bird" leaves the player stooping in front of Marker #2, runs *around* it, and runs back to repeat the action bringing the second player in line to join the first player. As each player is brought over, the "bird" places him with the others to form a circle (nest). When the last player is brought over, the nest should be complete. The "bird" runs around the Marker #2, down to Marker #1, around it, and back, hopping into the nest to end the game. Explain that several teams will be doing the same thing side by side. The winner is the first team to have its bird in its nest, but all rules must be followed. If there are no questions, space the teams far enough apart and give the starting signal.

Points to Ponder

Plastic bottles or some other kind of markers for the "bird" to *go around* will eliminate the temptation not to run all the way. Otherwise, children get so excited that they sometimes unwittingly "fudge" a little. A team should be disqualified if its "bird" fails to run around either marker.

Teams should be equal in number. If there is one less player on a team, ask the first player taken to the nest to return to his team (while the "bird" is taking other players). Thus, he will be first and last, this will equalize the competition.

At the end of each race, ask the "bird" to quickly choose a replacement to begin a new race.

ACCENTS AND PATTERNS (5-6)

Highlights—creating movements in relation to a rhythmical pattern, moving and working harmoniously with a small group; *Equipment*—chalk and chalkboard, record player, and a recording in 4/4 time. (*Note:* If a record player is not available, substitute a tambourine or drum to beat the rhythmic patterns); *Area*-activity room; *Number of players*—suited best for 3-8 per group.

The most common time signatures are 2/4, 3/4, and 4/4. Currently popular is the 2/4 beat; this may be used in place of the

Figure 3

4/4 rhythm. Explain to the children that in 4/4 rhythm there are four beats (quarter notes) to a measure, and the first beat of each measure is accented. Demonstrate this on the board (as illustrated in Figure 3), showing the accented first beats. These four measures make a rhythmic phrase in which a pattern is established. Have the children clap the rhythm, emphasizing the first beats with louder claps. Ask them how they could emphasize the first beats if they were *moving* to the rhythmic phrase. They will discover that a strong movement (large, heavy, or loud, such as a leap, swing, jump, or stomp) or a change in direction or position (a turn or a movement from high to low) could emphasize the accented beats. In this particular rhythmic pattern, the strong movement would be followed by three less emphatic ones (such as three running steps) or by a follow-through of the strong movement (*Swing*, 2, 3, 4).

Discuss the word "pattern" to help children learn that a pattern of movement is the same set of movements repeated. Example: *Leap,* 2, 3, 4, *Turn,* 2, 3, 4–*Leap,* 2, 3, 4, *Turn,* 2, 3, 4.

Compare a music composition to an English composition in which music phrases are *sentences* and music parts ("when the music changes . . .") are *paragraphs.* Illustrate the other three rhythmic patterns on the board (as shown in Figure 3-B through 3-D) and the children clap each pattern.

Divide the class into four groups so that there will be four "paragraphs" to fit the music, and assign a pattern (diagram) to each;

play the record and ask each group, in turn, to clap its specified pattern to the music. Play the record again, and have each group create a set of movements to the rhythmic pattern; allow time for individual experimentation and for group choice of movements. Move around from group to group to give suggestions or help as needed. Let each group perform for the others; then put the "four paragraphs" together to the music. This experience in fitting movement to music affords students an insight into how dances and routines are created (choreography).

Points to Ponder

The formation in which a group works often determines the choice of movements. Ask the children to think of different ways in which to begin—a circle, a line, parallel lines, a square, or a free formation. They have a choice, also, of starting positions—kneeling, standing, sitting, or a combination of these.

Using a record to which the children can relate increases their interest and involvement. If any of the illustrated rhythmic patterns are not suitable for a particular recording, change the accents accordingly.

In helping children grasp the concept of moving to a pattern, give as few demonstrations and suggestions as possible. (Children tend to work from the presented ideas rather than creating their own.) Their movements will be less inhibited and the results will be amazingly original.

PARTNER TAG (1-6)

Highlights—tagging, chasing, and dodging with a partner, regard for the safety of self and others; *Equipment*—markers or ropes to define boundary lines and an object (marker, lummi stick, rolled newspaper) that can be carried by two players; *Area*—playground or activity room; *Number of players*—unlimited.

To prepare for safe play, ask all children to walk anywhere within bounds without touching anyone; follow this by having them *run* without touching. Let children choose partners (an extra player could join two others) and walk together holding hands without touching others; follow this by having them *run* together successfully. Designate one pair as IT, and give them an object to carry between them. The two who are IT count aloud to five and then attempt to tag another couple without releasing the object. When they are successful, they give the object to the couple tagged. The

count to five is repeated and the game continues. Players may not release hands.

Points to Ponder

To tag safely, children should tap rather than hit or push.

Partner Tag is an active game for all players and is, therefore, a good activity for cool and windy weather.

If releasing the object or hands becomes a problem, have the players decide on a solution. (Eliminating problem players for a short time is usually all that is needed to correct the problem.)

Boundary lines should be far enough apart to allow freedom of movement and safe play, but confined enough for successful play.

VICTORY LANE (1-6)

Highlights—running in a straight path parallel to others, alert response to visual signals, racing against others; *Equipment*—parallel lines (ropes, markers): For Grades 1-2—20 yards apart, For Grades 3-4—30 yards apart, For Grades 5-6—40 yards apart; *Area*—playground; *Number of players*—unlimited.

Starting Signals

On Your Mark—Official's arm outstretched and parallel to the ground
Get Set—Arm stretched overhead
Go!—Arm moved forcefully downward

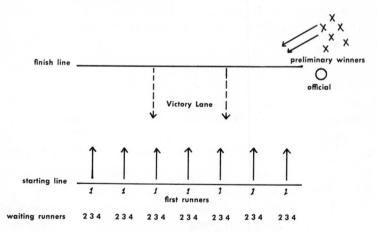

Figure 4 VICTORY LANE

Responses to Signals

On Your Mark—Runners place both hands on the ground behind the starting line and kneel on one knee.

Get Set—Lift the knee off the ground and lean forward; keep eyes *on the official.*

Go!—Push off by digging into the ground with the front foot; keep low to the ground for the first few steps, then rise gradually as the speed increases.

Have players stand behind the starting line and count off by fours. Show them how to give and respond to the starting signals. Select a child (or use a handicapped one) to be the *official*. His responsibilities are to stand at the finish line, give the hand signals (no audible signals are given), and proclaim the first two winners in each race. All #1 players compete first; have the others take several steps backward to await their turns as shown in Figure 4. Watch for starting line violations, and also remind runners to keep their eyes on the official (they often watch the runner beside them and get a late start). The official gives the signals and then watches so that he can announce the first- and second-place winners. These two stay with him at the finish line, and the others return to place as the players of the second heat prepare to compete. When all four *heats* (races) have been run, there will be a final race among the winners down *Victory Lane* (from finish line back to the starting line).

Points to Ponder

Children instinctively slow up as they approach a finish line. Help them understand the advantages of running at full speed as they cross it.

The fourth-heat players need to recuperate before dashing down Victory Lane. Utilize this time by reviewing the starting signals with the class and letting all of them, led by one official, give the starting signals.

FIELD DODGEBALL (5-6)

Highlights—accuracy in hitting a moving target, wise decision-making, anticipating the moves of others; *Equipment*—one ball—approximately 6"-8" in diameter—and one marker; *Area*—playground; *Number of players*—approximately 12-18 players per game.

Following the diagram in Figure 5, team A (the throwing team) is spaced within the designated area and must stay beyond the restraining line except when retrieving a throw-away ball. Team B (the running team) forms two lines as shown. On a starting signal, the first player in *each* of team B's two lines runs through the playing area, around the marker, and back to tag the next player in *his* line

who runs immediately upon being tagged. (There will always be two runners.) Each run from the line scores one point. Simultaneously, team A picks up the ball, which is on the ground, and tries to prevent team B from scoring by hitting a B runner anywhere below the head. When a runner is hit, he raises one hand to indicate that he is out and also to signal the next player in his line to run.

A runner may pause, stop, change directions, hide behind an opponent, or run anywhere within the boundary lines in an attempt to dodge the ball. If he runs out-of-bounds, he is automatically out, and therefore, raises his hand, and the next runner in his line starts.

A player on the throwing team may pass the ball to a teammate who is in a better position to hit the runner, or he may throw at the runner himself. He may *not* hold the ball more than three seconds or take more than one step with the ball in his hands.

When three outs occur, teams change places, and the game continues as in softball. The team with the higher score at the end of a previously determined number of innings, or period of time, is the winner. Make sure that the losing team had as many " times at bat" as the winning team.

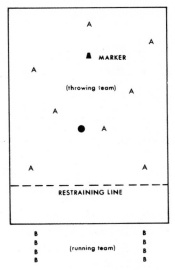

Figure 5 FIELD DODGEBALL

Points to Ponder

This is a fast-moving game with teamwork and *quick thinking* being the keys to successful play. When introducing it, a diagram is of tremendous value in giving an overall understanding of the game.

You may wish to discuss only the basic rules at first so that little time is spent before getting into action. Although fewer players than are usually in one class make for a better game, it is sometimes wise to let the whole class play in one game when learning it. Later, there can be two separate games if space permits, or part of the class could be engaged in activities requiring less space.

Make the rules as simple as possible and use the children's suggestions in making rules as the necessity arises. Below are some examples of things that might need discussing:

—Who will give the starting signal? Only one signal is needed because once the game begins, the play continues until there are three outs.

—How will we know when three seconds have passed? This need not be a *strict* rule and perhaps could be solved by having the members of the running team slowly count to 3 when they feel someone is abusing the rule. The thrower must throw by the count of three or the running team is automatically given a run.

—Why do you think you may take only one step when the ball is in your hands?

—The runner does not have to travel any particular path to get around the marker.

—Would you throw the ball at a runner when one of your team members was not in a position to get the ball in case you missed? If you saw a teammate doing this anyhow, where would you try to position yourself to be of most help?

—Would you throw the ball at the runner when you could pass it to someone in a better position to make an out? Why?

—What, besides raising his hand, could a runner who is out do to help you know he is out? (He could *walk* out-of-bounds to go back to the end of his line.)

—When you are a runner, *where* would you try to run? . . . Of course, as far away from the ball as possible. Would you have a better chance to score if you and the other runner were close together? far apart? near the middle? near the boundary lines?

Although definite boundary lines are helpful, imaginary lines between four plastic bottles or other visible markers work well. Ropes, bases, or plastic bottles may be used to indicate the restraining line and the marker behind which the runners must go. Paper balls may be used if packed tightly so that they can be thrown easily. Scoring may or may not be used.

Change and/or add rules as necessary.

OBSTACLE COURSE (K-6)

Highlights—competing against self, mastering specific obstacles, personal achieve-

ment; *Equipment*—anything that children can go around, in, out, under, over, through, or can throw, roll, jump, climb, walk, or can use as a target; *Area*—playground or activity room.

Planning an obstacle course and making the rules can be an interesting, challenging, and creative experience for all grades. It can involve an entire class period or only a few minutes before or after other activities. This is left to the discretion of the teacher and interest of the children.

Each class can originate its own, but just for example, the course might be similar to the diagram shown in Figure 6.

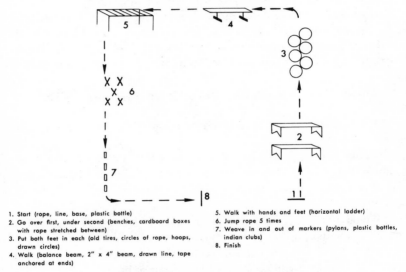

1. Start (rope, line, base, plastic bottle)
2. Go over first, under second (benches, cardboard boxes with rope stretched between)
3. Put both feet in each (old tires, circles of rope, hoops, drawn circles)
4. Walk (balance beam, 2" x 4" beam, drawn line, tape anchored at ends)
5. Walk with hands and feet (horizontal ladder)
6. Jump rope 5 times
7. Weave in and out of markers (pylons, plastic bottles, indian clubs)
8. Finish

Figure 6 OBSTACLE COURSE

Points to Ponder

Make use of anything that is already available such as trees, basketball goals, horizontal ladders, poles, hanging bars, balance beams, benches, jungle jims, climbing ropes, etc. Other inexpensive items, such as plastic bottles, jump rope, old tires, cardboard boxes, etc., can be easily obtained.

When setting up the course, leave running distance between each two activities, and alternate those requiring leg and arm strength.

The course can be circular, straight, zig-zag, rectangular, or any other arrangement. The important thing is that the children know the order of activities and the rules that apply to each.

Running, skipping, walking backward, hopping, galloping, and other movements may be incorporated to add variety.

Once learned, the course may be used as an active way to begin or end a class period.

Nearly all children like to compete against time, that is, to see if they can improve the length of time it takes them to finish a certain thing. If a stopwatch or a watch with a second hand is available, try adding this competitive element at any grade level. Thus, each child tries to improve his own score from day to day rather than competing against someone else. If watches are not available, you can get the same effect by counting. Let the children work in small groups; while one child is running, the others in the group count softly together: "One-and-two-and . . . ."

YOGI BEAR (1-2)

Highlights—throwing and catching a ball, running/chasing/dodging; *Equipment*—any size ball or object that can easily be thrown and caught; *Area*—playground, activity room, or paved area; *Number of players*—suited best for 6-8 players per game.

Yogi Bear is another name for the game of *Center Base*. The forest rangers (players) are in a circle having a picnic. Yogi Bear (IT) steals the picnic basket (ball) from the center, tosses it to one of the rangers, and runs out of the circle. The ranger who caught it places the picnic basket back in the center and tries to tag Yogi Bear before Yogi can get back in the circle and touch the basket. If Yogi is tagged, the ranger becomes the new Yogi Bear. If Yogi is not tagged, he has another turn—and so the game continues.

Note: Players may leave or enter the circle at any point in their chase. They may not run far away from the circle. The ranger chasing Yogi is not allowed to stay inside and guard the basket; he must go outside, but he may do so from any place in the circle.

Points to Ponder

Many different objects may be used instead of balls. Some of these are beanbags, erasers, plastic blocks, paper or yarn balls. If a ball is used on a hard surface, place it in a deck tennis ring, hoop, or circle of rope to keep it from rolling away during play.

The game may be taught with the entire class in one large circle or by using one group to demonstrate as others watch. This is a

matter of choice; the important thing is that once it is learned, play should continue in small groups so that each child can be involved.

MAN FROM MARS (K-2)

Highlights—distinguishing colors, running/chasing/tagging; *Equipment*—none; *Area*—playground; *Number of players*—suited best for entire class.

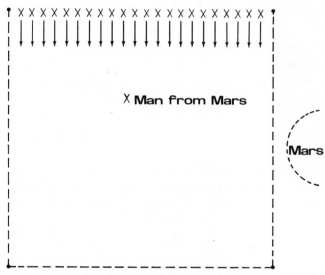

Figure 7 MAN FROM MARS

Man From Mars was originally designed to help children distinguish colors and their various shades.

Following the diagram in Figure 7, the Man from Mars begins the game by saying, "I'm the Man from Mars! I'll chase you to the stars—because you have on *red*!" (Blue, green, or any other color may be called.) All of the players wearing the color called must run to the opposite end of the designated area as the Man from Mars tries to tag as many as possible, sending them to Mars. Then, the Man from Mars repeats his rhyme, calling another color. When all children have run, the Man from Mars chooses a replacement from those *not tagged*; those tagged re-enter the game and play resumes from the opposite side of the area with the new Man from Mars.

Note: Those running out-of-bounds to avoid being tagged are automatically considered tagged.

Points to Ponder

Before playing the game, some discussion about the colors of clothes the children are wearing would be helpful. Sometimes it is

also helpful to decide on four or five predominant colors worn by the class and ask each child to "be that color" to which his clothes are closest. Some classes have found it fun to make arm bands, using four or five different colors of scrap material or crepe paper, to wear during the game.

Encourage safe play and honesty in admitting when tagged.

Marked boundary lines are not necessary. Using imaginary lines from markers or plastic bottles set approximately 60' apart on the playing area will be adequate and will require very little preparation.

COFFEE GRINDER (K-6—Individual Stunt)

Place the right hand on the floor, stiffen the right arm, and lock the elbow while extending the body out until it is straight with the right side toward the floor. The body is balanced and supported by the right arm and sides of the feet.

As soon as each child feels balanced, let him "walk" his feet forward so that he circles the supporting hand, which pivots on the floor. Increasing the speed and placing the free hand on the hip may be added as individuals are ready. Let them experiment using the left hand and circling in the opposite direction.

CHINESE GET-UP (3-6—Couple Stunt)

Have two children who are of comparable size sit on the floor, back to back, and lock elbows with each other. Each bends his knees and places his feet together, flat on the floor, and as close to his hips as is comfortable.

Each pushes against the floor with his feet and at the same time *against* his partner's back with his back in an effort to rise together smoothly. Once they rise, ask them to re-seat themselves without unlocking elbows or having to move the feet from their original positions.

If they fail to get up, it is probably due to knees or feet being separated or to pulling away from the partner rather than pushing back.

After the demonstration, let them find partners according to size. If there is an extra player, let him join a couple and share turns.

Success cues: Matched partner; sit tall; knees together; *push!*

Points to Ponder

Chinese Get-Up is the type of activity that may be approached through the problem-solving technique, which places the responsibility for learning more directly on the children.

Example: "When I say, 'Go!' I'd like each of you to find a partner and sit back to back, lock elbows with your partner and rise together to a standing position without releasing elbows. Think about what you're to do, the kind of partner you think you'll need—the two of you may talk quietly together as you're working. Are there any questions? . . . Ready? Go!"

Walk around to the pairs and assist when necessary without *telling* them what to do: "What do you think is your problem?" (If their sizes are not matched well enough, allow them to find another partner in a pair with the same problem.)

Many children may find other ways to solve the problem of rising together, while many others may simply go ahead and do the *Chinese Get-Up.* As long as they solve the given problem, they are successful. Let them discuss (or show) things they tried and explain what they had to change (and why) to make it work.

March   LESSON PLAN GUIDE   Grades K-2

WEEK	MONDAY	TUESDAY	WEDNESDAY	THURSDAY	FRIDAY
1	Jumping Brooks Swing Along I See	Stations: 1. Swing Along 2. Monkey Tag 3. (Short) rope jumping 4. Walkie-Talkie	Explosion Jumping Brooks (K) Yogi Bear (1-2) Midnight	Classroom: Endurance Hop Coffee Grinder Heel Slap What's Our Bag Today?	Ball-handling skills Bowling Moon Man (K) Partner Tag (1-2)
2	Obstacle Course Man From Mars Yogi Bear (1-2) Back Away (K)	Stations: 1. Scoops 2. V-r-room 3. (Long) rope jumping 4. Walkie-Talkie	Back Away Swing Along Midnight (K) Victory Lane (1-2)	Classroom: What's Our Bag Today? Hot Potato Mousetrap	Stride Ball (K) Race Ball (1-2) Man from Mars Jumping Brooks
3	Obstacle Course Monkey Tag (K) V-r-r-room Victory Lane (1-2)	Stations: 1. Swing Along (K) Yogi Bear (1-2) 2. Target 3. Monkey Tag 4. V-r-r-room	Bowling Race Ball (1-2) Midnight Touché Turtle (K)	Classroom Stations: 1. Walkie-Talkie 2. Lummi Sticks 3. Heel Slap 4. Stride Ball	Favorite Activities or Parachute
4	Explosion Old Mother Witch (K) Man from Mars Partner Tag (1-2)	Stations: 1. Bowling (K) Yogi Bear (1-2) 2. Midnight 3. Swing Along 4. Walkie-Talkie	Favorite Activities	Classroom: Sock It to Me Stride Ball Bicycle Race	Obstacle Course Man from Mars Monkey Tag (K) Fire Chief (1-2) I See

March   LESSON PLAN GUIDE   Grades 3-6

WEEK	MONDAY	TUESDAY	WEDNESDAY	THURSDAY	FRIDAY
1	Obstacle Course Partner Tag Victory Lane Jumping Brooks	Stations: 1. One Against Three 2. You Name It 3. Scoop Ball 4. (Short) rope jumping	Creative Games		Classroom: Sock It to Me Exchange Tag Bowling
2	Swing Along Jumping Brooks Jump Rope Relay	Touchdown Partner Tag (3-4) Bird in the Nest (5-6) Field Dodgeball (5-6)	Stations: 1. Swing Along 2. Scoop Ball 3. Jumping Brooks 4. Walkie-Talkie	Classroom: Chinese Get Up Coffee Grinder Bicycle Race Mousetrap	Bowling Smush Spud Explosion
3	Partner Tag Bird in the Nest (3-4) Touchdown (5-6) You Name It	Classroom: Let's Make a Dance (with music)(3-4) Accents and Patterns (5-6)	Stations: 1. (Long) rope jumping 2. Swing Along 3. Scoop Ball 4. Spud (3-4) Club Guard (5-6)	Classroom Stations: 1. Nervous Wreck 2. Chinese Get Up 3. Crane Dive 4. Push Back	Obstacle Course One Against Three Give Me Ten Race Ball
4	Stations: 1. Target 2. (Long) rope jumping 3. Jumping Brooks 4. Swing Along	Partner Tag Jump Rope Relay Victory Lane	Obstacle Course Race Ball (3) Capture the Flag (4) Field Dodgeball (5-6) True or False	Classroom: Hot Potato Bowling Mousetrap	Favorite Activities or Parachute

TAKE TIME

Take time to think . . .
>It is the source of power.

Take time to read . . .
>It is the fountain of wisdom.

Take time to pray . . .
>It is the greatest power on earth.

Take time to love and be loved . . .
>It is a God-given privilege.

Take time to be friendly . . .
>It is the road to happiness.

Take time to laugh . . .
>It is the music of the soul.

Take time to give . .
>It is too short a day to be selfish.

Take time to work . . .
>It is the price of success.

Take time to play . . .
>It is the secret of perpetual youth.

Author Unknown

April

TO THE TEACHER—On Attitude

An attitude is a contagious thing! Very few of us possess such resistance and stamina that our attitude is not in some way improved or impaired by every individual with whom we come into contact. This influence is felt constantly in our everyday lives, and, in turn, affects all those with whom we work. Children, being in their formative years, are armed with little or no resistance, and are therefore easily influenced by parents, teachers, and other adults, as well as by their peers.

Although many other factors must be taken into consideration, the attitude of the teacher toward any subject or activity at school greatly influences that of the child. Because most children enjoy "playing" usually very little is required to motivate them in physical education. The points of concern, however, are the kinds of experiences to which they are exposed and whether or not physical education is treated as any other area of learning. If the choice of activities is *always* theirs in physical education, more often than not the boys will choose some national sport such as football, baseball, or basketball—in their quite normal desire to emulate their television, high school, or college heroes—and only those who are already more highly skilled will be chosen for a team.

How rewarding it must be to have a group of children who enjoy any activity you introduce! In most cases, this is possible because your attitude is contagious!

BALLOON BALL (K-6)

Highlights—kinesthetic awareness, striking a moving object so that it rises; *Equipment*—one balloon per child; *Area*—classroom or activity room; *Number of players*—unlimited.

Playing with an inflated balloon is one of a child's favorite activities. It can be made simple enough for the very young child or complex enough to offer a challenge even to adults.

Give each child an inflated balloon (not quite to full capacity)

"Can you strike or tap the balloon so that it rises straight overhead?"

Figure 1

and tied at the opening to prevent leakage. For a brief time, let the children experiment to discover the different kinds of things they can make their balloons do without causing them to burst or to interfere with anyone. From this point, the extent to which some of the following challenges can be met satisfactorily will depend on the ages and skill levels of the children. Although grade levels are given, progress according to the children's abilities.

Keep it up (K-6). Ask the children to find a space not too close to anyone and to keep their balloons in the air. Ask them to respond through movement to your questions. Some suggestions are:

—"Can you strike or tap the balloon so that it rises straight overhead? (See Figure 1)
—Can you use a *different* body part to strike the balloon?
—How many *different* body parts can you use? [hands, feet, knees, elbows, head, shoulders, back, etc.]
—Is your balloon rising straight overhead? [You shouldn't need to chase it.]
—Watch the balloon as you strike it; where must you hit it to make it go straight up?
—Use only *one* hand to keep your balloon up.
—Do the same using *only* the other hand.
—Use one hand—then the other.
—How *high* can your hand be *when* it strikes the balloon?
—How *low* can you let the balloon fall before you strike it?
—Strike the balloon so that you must move to a different space to strike it again.
—Watch for other people and their balloons—look for empty spaces."

Sitting, kneeling, lying (4-6). With the children spaced com-

fortably, ask them to keep their balloons in the air while keeping their bodies in various positions. Some suggestions are:

—"Keep the balloon in the air, but support your weight on something *other* than your feet.
—Can you find a different position? . . . How many positions can you find?
—Can you strike the balloon so that it floats back to you so that you do not have to move?"

Points to Ponder

Balloons are quite inexpensive; in fact, they are often given away as advertisement by various companies. Also, each child may be able to bring one or two on the days this activity is planned. Although round shapes work best, other shapes provide interesting challenges. If they are not inflated too near to capacity, usually they will not burst easily.

For the very young child, this activity offers invaluable experiences in hand-eye coordination and body control. The light and gentle movements of the balloon give him adequate time to focus on the part of the balloon he wishes to strike. The floating action also allows children time to position themselves where they need to be in order to strike the balloon so that it travels in the desired direction. This awareness will aid them later in learning to handle an object that is heavier and traveling at a faster speed.

When children are working on any of the skills suggested (or any that you and they may have added), give them enough time to accomplish the task. Some children will be much more skillful than others, but everyone should be able to feel successful according to individual abilities.

A balloon for each child gives the teacher and students opportunities to communicate and work together to learn skills. However, if enough balloons are not available, the activity works well as a station where 4-6 children work on the given skills while the rest of the class works in small groups using other kinds of equipment. After a period of time, all groups would rotate to a different activity.

STRIKE IT (K-6)

Highlights—striking a moving object, spatial awareness; *Equipment*—one ball per person (see Points to Ponder); *Area*—a smooth surface—preferably an activity room; *Number of players*—unlimited.

Explain to the group that when you finish talking, each of them will be given a ball. They will also have a few minutes to discover

how many different kinds of things they can do with the ball, but it must always be under control. (A brief discussion of the meaning of the word "control" may be necessary.)

Observe the kinds of things they do with the balls as an indication of their individual abilities and needs.

Basics for Grades K-6

Try to establish an atmosphere in which everyone listens to directions, understands that the key word is *control* (and not force), and tries to master the skills given. Let them know the signal you will use for them to stop, hold their balls *still,* and listen to the next directions. Some skills to work toward are listed below. Add others that you and the children develop.

—"In your own space, try tossing the ball up so that it bounces right in front of you.
—Keep working on it until you have good control.
—Instead of catching it this time, see if you can tap [strike] it so that it rises and bounces again.
—If you lose control, catch it and start over.
—Try to keep the ball in your own space.
—What part of the ball must you strike to make it go straight up?
—How many times can you strike it before you have to catch the ball?
—This time, try tapping or striking the ball so that you must move to another space to strike it after each bounce.
—Look for the empty spaces.
—Keep the ball near enough to be under control at all times.
—Find a partner, put one ball away, and stand a few feet apart.
—Strike the ball and make it bounce in front of your partner so that he can strike it and make it bounce in front of you.
—How long can you keep the ball going without losing control?"

Additions for Grades 3-6

—"Strike the ball so that your partner has to move [to either side, forward, backward] to strike it after the bounce.
—Keep working on this with both of you moving continuously.
—Make sure you control the ball at all times.
—Each of you get a ball and find a space away from others.
—Can you keep your ball in the air by striking it and *not letting it bounce?*
—Try to stay within your space—if you lose control, just catch the ball and start over.
—Most of you are using your fingers and fists—what other body parts can you use to strike the ball? That's good; I see some using heads, arms, elbows, shoulders, knees, and feet.

—Where must you contact the ball to make it go straight up?

—Now, use only three body parts to strike the ball *try not to let the ball bounce.*

—Using only your hands, try to strike the ball 7 times or more before losing control or letting the ball bounce.

—Keep working on it—think about what you're doing, where you must contact the ball to make it rise.

—Quickly, get a partner and put one ball away.

—See how long you and your partner can keep the ball in the air *without catching* it or letting it *bounce.*

—Find another set of partners and put one ball away.

—How long can the four of you keep the ball in the air?

—Make sure you strike *underneath* the ball so that it rises."

Points to Ponder

The type of ball recommended is a lightweight, 8"-9" vinyl or plastic ball. These kinds of balls are very inexpensive (less than seventy-five cents), easy to control, and excellent for the young child because, in most cases, he is not afraid of them. Once a child understands the movements involved in ball handling, he will usually be able to transfer this learning to handling balls of various weights and sizes. If, however, it is impossible to obtain a ball for each child, some possible alternatives are: (1) use the number of balls available and let the activity be a station to which children rotate from other activities, and (2) if there is a ball for every two or three children, let them take turns observing each other.

In all of the suggested activities, enough time should be given for children to understand the concepts involved. The whole idea is for a child to learn where his body (or its parts) should be positioned in order to strike a ball and cause it to go in any desired direction. Far more material has been presented than should be introduced in any one lesson, and many class periods could be devoted to improving the skills involved. Before working with a partner, children should first be able to control the ball by themselves.

It is quite normal, at first, for children to be excited over everyone's having a ball. Give them a few minutes in the beginning of each lesson to use the balls freely as long as they use good judgment. The excitement soon wears off, and they usually will concentrate on the skills within a short time. Help the children understand that there is a time to *listen* and a time to *move*, and that they should respond to your questions and directions by thinking and moving rather than verbalizing. They need to know that when you ask them to stop, all balls are to be held *still* so that everyone can hear the next directions.

(A good signal is to simply say, "Stop!"; however, one that is most effective and quite pleasant is a tambourine—two light taps mean *start* and one tap *stop*.)

By carefully observing the whole class and individual children, you will be able to sense the need for further directions as well as for individual help. If, for example, some children find difficulty in striking the ball and causing it to rise straight overhead, let the class observe someone who does it well: "What did Curtis do that made the ball rise straight overhead? Where were his hands when they struck the ball?" (Let them discuss what Curtis did and then let everyone try again.)

Encourage not interfering with others, looking for empty spaces, helping one's partner(s), and *always* keeping the ball *under control*.

WALL BALL (3-6)

Highlights—judging speed and direction of a rebounding ball, moving in relation to a moving ball, controlling a ball while striking it; *Equipment*—one ball—approximately 8"-10" in diameter—per person, and a wall; *Area*—activity room; *Number of players*—the number of players is determined by the available wall space.

Wall Ball is another favorite activity of children (adults enjoy it, too) and may be played individually or with a partner.

Before introducing a game-type situation, give each child a ball and ask him to experiment with striking the ball so that it rebounds from the wall. The ball may bounce once, twice, or not at all before he strikes it again. (If there is a lack of equipment or wall space, see Points to Ponder.) Allow sufficient time for the students to adjust to various situations. Encourage them to try to strike the ball after each bounce, after no bounce, from a low position, from a high position, etc.

Players may be challenged to create their own games, including the rules, or they may play any of the following.

Solo. This is a game in which each player competes alone. He stands behind a line approximately 5' from the wall and puts the ball into play with an underhand volleyball serve. The ball must hit the wall, rebound behind the line, and bounce only once before he strikes it again. His score is the number of times he is successful before missing. Winners may be determined by either of two methods: (1) the player who is successful (consecutive hits) the

longest period of time, or (2) the one with the largest number of consecutive hits (points) at the end of a specified length of time. All players should begin at the same time when in competition.

Note: Balls hitting on the line are considered good. Tape or white shoe polish may be used for the line, and the distance may be changed if necessary.

One Against One. In this game, eliminate the 5' line used in the game of *Solo* because part of the skill and strategy is in sometimes making the ball rebound close to the wall. The two players competing against each other toss a coin (or call a number, etc.) to decide who will serve first, thereafter, they alternate the serve. Players take turns striking the ball after one bounce until one of them misses thus allowing his opponent to score a point. The first player to score five points wins the game, and a new game is begun with the *loser* serving first.

Note: Each player should call the score before he serves (giving his own score first). If necessary, the width of the playing area may be limited to approximately 10'.

Two Plus Two. In this game, two players play together as a team against two players who play beside them, but with a different ball. On signal, one player from each team serves its ball. After each rebound from the wall, partners alternate striking the ball until one team misses, thus giving the opponents a point. The team reaching five points first wins a game. Any number of games may be played.

Doubles. Doubles involves two sets of partners (four people) and one ball. Play is the same as described in *One Against One,* except that there are two players on each team. The two partners must not only alternate turns playing the ball with the other team, but must also alternate play between themselves. For example, if player #1 from team A serves the ball and player #1 from team B plays it, player #2 from team A must play it next, then #2 from team B, and so on. (As long as the ball remains in play, a player will play it every fourth time.)

Note: This game is quite challenging and probably should not be attempted until players are more highly skilled in striking skills. It may be made even more challenging by using a smaller ball.

Points to Ponder

If a gymnasium or multipurpose room and a ball per person are available, usually everyone in a class has enough wall space to

experiment with striking skills. The balls need not be as expensive as volleyballs or even playground balls. In fact, the inexpensive vinyl balls are much more easily controlled. They may be purchased at most discount stores for as little as fifty cents each. If wall space or the availability of balls presents a problem, any of the suggested activities may be set up as a station to which players rotate from other types of games.

Once children have a ball in their hands, it is difficult to give many directions. Tell them some of the first things they are to work on *before* giving them the balls.

Perhaps, before trying any game situations, players should spend parts of several class periods simply learning the skills—the different parts of the hands that can strike the ball, the amount of force necessary to make the ball rebound a short or long distance, where the body must be for best control, the adjustments and compensations necessary for various plays, and so forth.

Because the activity requires constant movement, players will not be able to play for long periods of time. Be sensitive to their need to rest or change to a less vigorous activity.

VOLLEY TENNIS (5-6)

Highlights—judging the speed and direction of a bouncing ball, teamwork, striking a ball during competition; *Equipment*—one ball—approximately 8"-10" in diameter, lines or markers to outline a court approximately 25' x 50', and a net 3' high; *Area*—paved area or activity room; *Number of players*—suited best for 12-16 per game (6-8 per team).

Volley Tennis is so named because it combines the ball-handling skills of tennis (volleying the ball or striking it after one bounce) with the playing procedures of volleyball (positions, scoring, and rotation of players).

The game is an excellent lead-up to tennis because it involves the important concept of correctly positioning oneself for the greatest advantage in striking a ball, whether it be before or after the ball bounces. This concept is often foreign to most children because they will invariably get too close to a bouncing ball to strike it successfully.

Precede the game with experiences in striking a ball before or after it bounces. (Use *Strike It* and *Wall Ball* previously described.) Children also need to understand and experiment with the skills involved in the serve before attempting to play the game.

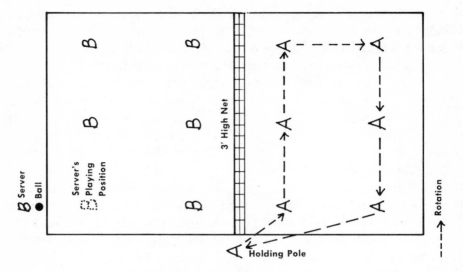

Figure 2 VOLLEY TENNIS

Players are positioned on the court as shown in Figure 2. Server B stands *behind* the end line. He drops the ball to the floor, and on the rebound, strikes it underhanded with any part of his hand or fist. The ball must travel over the net and into any part of the opponents' court; line balls are good. On the serve, the ball may not bounce before it crosses the net. The server has only one serve; if he misses, the serve goes to the opponents.

The receiving player *lets the ball bounce* and then either strikes it so that it goes back across the net or taps it to one of his teammates. Thereafter, the ball may be volleyed (struck before it bounces), or it may be tapped or struck after it bounces. The ball may be played any number of times on one side of the net before it is returned over the net. It is considered a *miss* if:

—the ball bounces twice before it is played.
—a player is hit by the ball (he should manage to get out of its path).
—the ball hits the floor, wall, or any obstacle out-of-bounds.
—any player touches the net while the ball is in play.
—a player *pushes* rather than strikes or taps the ball.
—the ball bounces over the net without being hit (the ball cannot bounce and then go over the net).
—a player reaches across the net to play the ball.

Scoring, rotation of players, court positions, and other game procedures are the same as for volleyball and other net games.

Rules in a Nutshell

1. Only the serving team can score; the receiving team wins the serve instead of a point.
2. The players on the *receiving* team rotate when they win the serve. (Both teams do not rotate at the same time.)
3. The same player continues to serve as long as his team scores; he has only one attempt each time he serves.
4. Players rotate clockwise as shown in the diagram. This is called *circle rotation.*
5. A game is completed at 11, 15, or 21 points. A team must have two points more than its opponent in order to win. (If the score is 11 points to 10 points, the game is incomplete; 12 points to 10 points will complete the game.)
6. The server calls his own score first, then opponents' score, and then says, "Ready?"
7. When a ball is served, it must *clear* the net; otherwise, it is a miss. During play, however, a ball that touches the net as it goes across is considered good, and the ball remains in play.

Points to Ponder

If net posts or standards are not available, use bamboo poles or broomsticks to hold the net (or rope); have one player from each team hold a pole and then rotate into the game as shown.

Each player is responsible for the area in front and on either side of him. He does not back up to play a ball.

Although the ball may be played with any part of the hand or fist, it is generally under better control if the hand or the heel of the hand is used.

RESCUE RELAY (3-6)

Highlights—running while holding hands with a partner, changing directions quickly; *Equipment*—two starting marks (lines, bases, or plastic bottles) for each team; *Area*—playground or activity room; *Number of players*—two or more teams of 6-8 players each.

Rescue Relay is a running event in which a leader (1) stands in front of, and 20' to 60' away from his team (2, 3, 4, 5, 6), which is in relay formation with one player behind the other. When the relay is concluded, all players on a team will be behind the starting position of the player 1.

When a starting signal is given, player 1 runs to his team, takes the hand of player 2, and "rescues" him (brings him back to the starting mark without releasing his hand). Player 1 stays at the starting mark; player 2 returns to rescue player 3 by taking his hand

and bringing him back. Player 2 stays and player 3 continues the relay in like manner. When all runners have been rescued and are standing in order behind player 1, they stoop to indicate completion of the relay. The first team to do so is the winner.

Points to Ponder

Disqualifying a team for releasing hands helps them to understand the importance and the fairness of game rules. Explain that crossing the line too soon also gives an unfair advantage to a team.

Before playing the game, have pairs of players run anywhere within an area without releasing hands. This gives them a pregame activity and an opportunity to run with a partner.

Teams should be equal in number. Use extra or handicapped players to give signals, watch for fair play, or to judge.

THROW AND GO (K-6)

Highlights—forcefully throwing a ball for distance, running competitively; *Equipment*—a distinguishable ball and a starting mark for each team; *Area*—playground or activity room; *Number of players*—three or more teams of 3-6 players each.

Teams may be in file formation—one behind the other—or they be informally grouped, standing or sitting, while they await a turn. Teams need not be equal in number. It is actually better if they are not equal in number so that the same players will not always compete against each other.

The first player on each team holds a ball and stands on his mark. When a starting signal is given, he throws the ball so that it goes straight ahead and as far as possible. He then runs quickly to retrieve *any ball other than his own* and brings it back to his starting mark. The first runner to do so scores a point for his team.

Points to Ponder

With the advent of vinyl balls, there is usually no problem in securing a variety of distinguishable balls of like weight and size. Colored tape or regular masking tape can also be used to make interesting marks on balls that are otherwise alike.

Any skill that forcefully sends a ball can be used and developed through the game. Primary students would probably toss or throw the ball; other students might pitch, roll, kick, or throw the ball in a specific way. A softball throw could be used, but because of the

distance involved, teams should have a maximum of two or three players each.

Often, primary students are concerned because the last person back sometimes has to return with his own ball. This is an opportunity for discussion and thinking: "What other ball could he bring back? . . . That's right, there was no other choice for him. Does it really matter in this game if the *last* person does have his own ball?"

Because teams need not be equal, there will be no extra players. Handicapped or nonplaying students can give signals and judge winners.

Players on each team keep score for themselves.

SPACESHIP (1-3)

Highlights—listening for a signal while running, stopping quickly and finding an empty space; *Equipment*—none; *Area*—playground or activity room; *Number of players*—suited best for 10-20 per game.

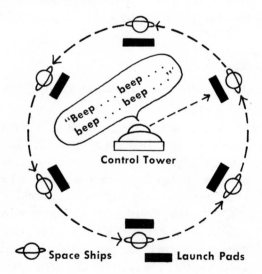

Figure 3 SPACESHIP

Players stand one behind the other in pairs to form a circle with a center player as the control tower as shown in Figure 3. The front players are launch pads; those in the back are spaceships.

The control tower cups his hands around his mouth and turns slowly as he calls aloud, "Beep-beep-beep-beep-beep-beep----." This signals all spaceships to run counterclockwise around the circle of

launch pads *who do not run.* The spaceships continue to run until the control tower is suddenly silent. The instant the tower becomes silent, he runs to stand *in front* of a launch pad, and all spaceships quickly do the same. There will be one spaceship left without a launch pad—he becomes the control tower for the next game. (Each time the game is repeated, the players have changed roles.)

Points to Ponder

If a spaceship slows down intentionally in attempting to find a launch pad, he has discovered a way to become the control tower. This privilege at times outweighs the prestige of finding a place to land. Without embarrassing anyone, help the children understand that the game will be more fun if everyone makes a real effort to find a landing place as quickly as possible.

Encourage and remind children to look for empty spaces and to run, pass, or stop without touching others.

Before playing the game, have all spaceships run while the launch pads remain in place so there will be no confusion as to who runs.

HEN AND CHICKS (K-3)

Highlights—listening to detect the direction of a sound, teasing; *Equipment*—none; *Area*—classroom; *Number of players*—unlimited.

"Once there was a mother hen who had five little baby chicks. Those little chicks were always playing tricks on their mother. They would hide from her sometimes, and she would just call and call, trying to get them to answer her. Do you know how a hen calls her chicks? . . . That's right, she says, 'Cluck, cluck, cluck,' and all of her chicks answer, 'Peep, peep, peep' but because they're hiding among all the other chicks in the barnyard, the hen has to listen very carefully and walk all among the chicks to try to find hers. So the mother hen made a rule. Every time the hen said, 'Cluck, cluck, cluck,' all of *her* chicks had to answer with three peeps—and *no other chicks were allowed to answer."*

Explain that one person will be the hen and that there will be five chicks scattered among the remainder of the class. All players will remain seated and will have their hands cupped around their mouths. Explain, also, that those who are *not* chicks are very important to the game—they have their hands cupped because they are helping the chicks play their trick. Every time the hen calls her

chicks (three clucks), all five chicks—and *only* those five—must answer (three peeps). As the hen finds a chick, that chick removes his cupped hands from his mouth and watches the game. He does not answer the hen anymore. The hen must find all chicks within a given time, or the game will start over with a new hen and a new set of chicks. When everyone understands, choose a hen and have her close her eyes or leave the room while five chicks are *quietly* selected.

Points to Ponder

Very young children may tend to answer the hen whether they are chicks or not. Keep working until *only* the chosen five answer. Help the others feel their importance to the game in their role as decoys.

Encourage the hen to move among the players, call often, and *listen* to the responses, rather than simply trying to guess who the five chicks are the minute the game starts.

Limit the game to a reasonable length of time so that it does not drag. Also, give everyone a chance to be the hen or a chick.

COTTONTAIL HOP (K-6)

Highlights—chasing, tagging, and dodging, moving in relation to others; *Equipment*—none; *Area*—playground or activity room; *Number of players*—unlimited.

Choose five "Peter Cottontails," and ask all other players to space themselves within the given area. (If outdoors, limit the area to make for a better game.)

On a signal, the "Peter Cottontails" try to tag (touch) as many players as they can. In order to be *safe*, a player must put both hands up beside his ears to represent rabbit ears and place both feet together, although he may hop or stand still.

Encourage players to be daring and to remain within the boundary area. A player running out-of-bounds is automatically out. All tagged players are out and must stand or sit away from the group until a new game begins. Play until only five players remain. If the game is repeated, let each of the untagged players be the new "Peter Cottontails" for the new game.

Points to Ponder

Explain the game in its entirety while the children are standing or seated so that all can hear.

If possible, use something to distinguish the "Peter Cottontails." The little ones might enjoy wearing a head band with "rabbit ears." The older ones could tie a kerchief or scarf around them.

Eliminated players do not remain out for a long period of time, and they usually enjoy watching the others play.

An appropriate starting signal is for the "Peter Cottontails" to get together and sing (or say) the first part of the familiar song: "Here comes Peter Cottontail . . . "

Because the game is quite active and because it does eliminate some players rather quickly, it makes a good activity to end the class period. Those eliminated simply prepare to go back to the classroom.

FOUR SQUARE (K-6)

Highlights—leisure-time activity, controlling a ball; *Equipment*—one ball—approximately 8"-10" in diameter—that bounces well; *Area*—activity room, paved area, classroom, or playground; *Number of players*—suited best for 4-8 per game.

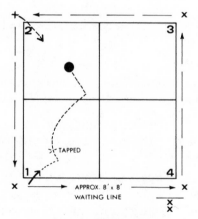

Figure 4 FOUR SQUARE

The basic game of *Four Square* is described below. Following it are several variations. Use those that best fit the abilities of your children.

Four Square (basic game)

Use 6 players to demonstrate the game. Assign a square to each of 4 players, and have the remaining 2 players stand behind the waiting line, as shown in Figure 4.

The player in the #1 square is the server and always starts the

game by saying, "Ready?"—to which the other players respond, "Serve!" He drops the ball into his own square and after the first bounce, taps (strikes) it into one of the other three squares. The skill in the game is to tap the ball every time it bounces in your square and cause it to fall into another player's square. Play continues until someone misses. A miss is when a player taps the ball before it bounces or fails to tap it into another square. When a player misses, he goes to the end of the waiting line. Other players rotate one position toward square #1 (depending on which player misses), and the first waiting player enters the game at square #4. The object of the game is to become the server and to hold that position as long as possible.

Note: Balls that bounce on outside lines are *good;* balls that bounce on inside lines are *not* good. See if your class can determine why this is a rule.

(1) Variation—Four Square Catch

Generally, the hand-eye coordination and agility of the six- and seven-year-old are not developed fully enough to successfully play the game as written above. However, if you substitute "toss and catch" as the only skills involved, the game becomes one that offers both fun and challenge. The game remains the same except that each person *catches* the ball after the first bounce in his square, then *tosses* it into another's square. That person does the same.

(2) Variation—Four Square Tap

Progress from the variation suggested for first grade as you feel your class is ready. Instead of tossing the ball into another's square, catch it as before, then bounce it into your *own* square, and tap it into another's square. Each person *catches, bounces,* and *taps.*

(3) Variation— Doubles

This is the same as the basic game of *Four Square* except that there are 2 players (partners) at each square who alternate turns at playing the ball when it bounces in their square. Failure to do so is a miss. Both partners remain together; that is, they rotate together and are eliminated together.

(4) Variation—Around the World

Before saying "ready," the server calls "around the world" and

serves to the player on his right. Each player in turn must tap the ball to the square on his right. This continues until there is a miss. (The server may serve to his left and each would in turn tap the ball to his left.)

(5) Variation—War

The server calls "war" before saying "ready," then he serves the ball to any of the other players. The one to whom he served must return the ball to the server's square. The two of them continue playing the ball back and forth until one misses or until the server calls "cease fire." If the latter occurs, play resumes among any of the four players.

(6) Variation—Battle

The server calls "battle" before saying "ready," then he serves and plays the ball to anyone, but the other players must always play the ball back to the server. This continues until someone misses or until the server calls "cease fire." When the latter occurs, play resumes among any of the four players.

(7) Variation—Spell It

The server calls "spell _____" (an unfamiliar word) before saying "ready." As he starts the play, he gives the first letter in the word to be spelled. Each time a player plays the ball he must give the next letter. This continues until the word is spelled or a player misses at which time a new game is started. If a player gives an incorrect letter it is considered a miss.

(8) Variation—Alphabet

Before saying "ready," the server calls "alphabet." Each person playing the ball gives the next letter in the alphabet.

(9) Variation—Number Ball

Same as *Alphabet,* except that consecutive numbers are called.

(10) Variation—Paddle Ball

Paddle Ball is played like *Four Square* except that paddles (approximately the size of Ping Pong paddles) and a small ball are used (tennis balls work well).

Points to Ponder

Before playing the game, give the children an opportunity to practice the skills involved so that they will be learning only one new thing at a time. This may be done with 2-6 people in a circle (using the skills appropriate for their level—catch and bounce; catch, bounce, and tap; or only a tap). Have them try to keep the ball in the circle.

Consider the available area for play. If it is a hard surface, masking tape or chalk may be used to mark the court. If the surface is grass or level ground, rope or cloth tape work well (cut them into desired lengths, preferably six 8' pieces. The court should be prepared prior to playing. In the upper grades, the children could easily do this for you. Once they learn to improvise, they will discover several places to play the game even during leisure hours. Many walkways, sidewalks, tile floors, breezeways, etc. have natural squares built in.

Since each player is responsible for a ball landing inside his square, discuss with the class *where* they feel the player should position himself to be prepared: "The ball may land in a top corner or near the bottom of your square. Can you move forward quicker than you can move backward? Try it and see. *How* do you think you would stand to be best prepared? . . . knees and waist bent slightly? weight near your toes? or would you stand flat-footed and up straight?—*you* decide!" It should not take them long to realize that they can move more easily *forward* into their squares to receive a ball, and that a "ready" position is one with the body bent slightly and the weight forward.

When first learning the game, the younger children may need to use *both* hands and tap the underside of the ball (underhand tap). However, when they become more skillful they should be encouraged to use any method they prefer. This creates an entirely different game—one involving more speed, timing, agility, strategy, and skill in controlling the ball.

If the number of available balls requires more than 8 players per game, *Four Square* would be best used as one of three or four stations to which groups rotate after several minutes.

KING SQUARE (5-6)

King Square is the same as *Four Square* except that the area of play (court) is four times larger (approximately 16' x 16'). Some

challenging variations are for the server to call a specific body part that must be used instead of hands (foot, elbow, knee, fist).

Points to Ponder

Any of the variations of *Four Square* may be used in *King Square*. In addition, the skills will be quite different due to the enlarged area. Also, if precut material is used to form the court, cut them into 16' lengths.

April

LESSON PLAN GUIDE

Grades K-2

WEEK	MONDAY	TUESDAY	WEDNESDAY	THURSDAY	FRIDAY
1	Striking skills Balloon Ball	Explosion Touché Turtle Monkey Tag	Striking skills Strike It Cottontail Hop	Classroom: Hen and Chicks Bicycle Race Mousetrap	Stations: 1. Balloon Ball 2. Strike It 3. Scoops 4. Target
2	Ball-handling skills Four Square	Back Away Throw and Go Cottontail Hop	Stations: 1. Back Away 2. Throw and Go 3. (Long) rope jumping 4. Walkie-Talkie	Classroom: Sock It to Me Hen and Chicks Endurance Hop	Strike It Four Square
3	Stations: 1. Strike It (K) Four Square (1-2) 2. Jumping Brooks 3. (Short) rope jumping 4. Swing Along	Explosion Moon Man (K) Spaceship (1-2) Cottontail Hop	Bowling Target Right On/Left Off	Classroom Stations: 1. Balloon Ball 2. Hot Potato 3. Four Square 4. Walkie-Talkie	I See Scoops (K) Partner Tag (1-2) Spaceship (1-2) Throw and Go
4	Stride Ball Throw and Go (Long) rope jumping	Stations: 1. Strike It 2. Four Square 3. Right On/Left Off 4. Walkie-Talkie	Favorite Activities or Parachute	Classroom: What's Our Bag Today? Lummi Sticks	Favorite Activities or Balloon Ball (K) Four Square (1-2)

April

LESSON PLAN GUIDE

Grades 3-6

WEEK	MONDAY	TUESDAY	WEDNESDAY	THURSDAY	FRIDAY
1	Striking skills Balloon Ball Sock It to Me (balloons)	Striking skills Strike It	Cottontail Hop Four Square	Classroom: Bowling (K) Hen and Chicks (3) Bicycle Race Mousetrap	Stations: 1. Strike It 2. Four Square 3. Scoops 4. Walkie-Talkie
2	Obstacle Course Strike It Wall Ball	Rescue Relay Four Square Cottontail Hop	Strike It (Creative) striking game (3) Wall Ball	Classroom: Hen and Chicks (3) Motion (4-6) Nervous Wreck Exchange Tag	Favorite Activities
3	Spaceship (3) Give Me Ten Throw and Go Cottontail Hop	Favorite Activities	Rescue Relay Spaceship (3) Touchdown (3) Capture the Flag (4) King Square (5-6)	Classroom Stations: 1. Four Square 2. Strike It 3. Scoops 4. Nervous Wreck	Four Square (3-4) Volley Tennis (5-6)
4	Partner Tag Four Square (3-4) King Square (5-6)	Rescue Relay (3-4) Throw and Go (3-4) Touchdown (3-4) Volley Tennis (5-6)	Double Trouble (3) Spaceship (3) Volley Tennis (5-6) Throw and Go Wall Ball (4)	Classroom: Sock It to Me Exchange Tag True or False	Stations: 1. Four Square (3-4) King Square (5-6) 2. Bowling 3. Throw and Go 4. Walkie-Talkie

BEING HUMAN

Did you ever wonder . . . how two could see the same? . . . yet, the tale one told . . . seemed like a different game . . . and how what you told him . . . was not what he told Sue . . . each word was changed somehow . . . except for one or two . . .

It's not that he would mean . . . to jeopardize his friend . . . by painting over scenes . . . with colors sure to win . . . nor would he mean to hurt . . . one of the rest of us . . . it's that bit of being human . . . that's in the best of us . . .

Rosalie Bryant

May

TO THE TEACHER—On Feelings and Emotions

One of the most neglected needs of children is that of being able to express their feelings and emotions. A child is told not to cry, not to be afraid, not to hate anyone, yet he may have feelings of sadness, fear, or hate. We need to open the way for children to express their feelings, and to know that their friends and their teachers have the same feelings. There are countless opportunities to center discussions around feelings arising from anger, love, hate, fear, bravery, death, joy, winning, losing, and other emotions. If the discussion is about death, be sensitive to the child who may have recently lost a family member or pet.

Perhaps if we spent more time helping children accept their feelings and emotions and learn to channel them into acceptable behavior, we could do much to eliminate many potential emotional problems.

DRAG RACE (K-6)

Highlights—running parallel to others, responding to a visual signal, racing against others; *Equipment*—none except markers to indicate the starting and finishing lines, approximately 40' apart; *Area*—playground; *Number of players*—unlimited.

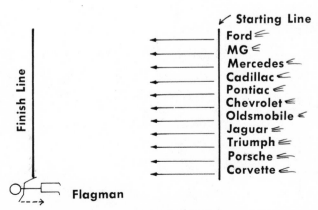

Figure 1 DRAG RACE

Players are positioned as shown in Figure 1. Each of them *silently* decides on the kind of automobile he wishes to "drive" in the drag race. The flagman stands at one end of the finish line. When he raises his arm sideways to shoulder level, all cars (players) "start their engines." When he quickly lowers his arm, all cars speed as fast as they can in an effort to be the first to cross the finish line. Each must stay in his own lane. The flagman announces the winner who announces the kind of car he drove and becomes the new flagman. Players arrange themselves for a new race as quickly as possible. They have the choice of keeping their same "cars" or driving different ones.

Points to Ponder

Let all players practice responding to the signals of the flagman before going into competition.

Nearly all children (regardless of age) tend to run *to* the finish line and stop, rather than running *across* the finish line before reducing their speed. Keep working on their understanding of when to slow down.

Each time a winner is declared, let him begin the game in the opposite direction in order to save time.

Remember that half the fun of the game is the revving noise that "drag racers" make when warming up their engines.

BULL IN PEN (2-6)

Highlights—running, chasing, and tagging, regarding the safety of self and others; *Equipment*—none; *Area*—playground; *Number of players*—unlimited.

Bull in Pen is played according to many different sets of rules. Those described here are felt to eliminate the safety hazards found in many versions of the game.

Play begins with a player (the "Bull") in the center of a circle of players whose hands are joined (the "Pen"). He tries to break through or duck under the joined hands of any two players. When the Bull is successful, all players (except the two between whom he escaped) chase him in an effort to *overtake* him before he can circle around the area and return home. Players may not wait at home or cut across to head off the Bull in an attempt to tag him. The first player to overtake and tag the Bull becomes IT for the next game. Should the Bull reach home (where the two players are waiting) without being tagged, he chooses his successor.

Points to Ponder

If the Bull is having difficulty getting out of his Pen, encourage players to surprise him by making his escape easier (by lifting their arms).

Having two players remain in the area eliminates their having an unfair advantage in tagging the Bull as he escapes, and also gives the Bull a home base for his return.

Emphasize that after the Bull is tagged, the chase ends—sometimes the players continue tagging.

Also emphasize that the Bull must be overtaken and not headed off or cut off by the tagger.

Remember that the game is very active, and children will not be able to play it for a long period of time.

COUPLE TAG (3-6)

Highlights—alertness in responding to the movements of others, chasing, tagging, dodging; *Equipment*—none; *Area*—playground, activity room, or paved area; *Number of players*—approximately 8-12 per game.

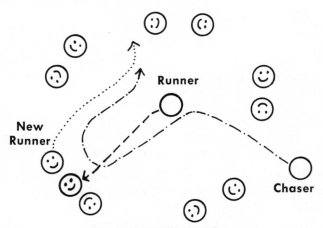

Figure 2 COUPLE TAG

Partners stand facing each other so that all except two players form a circle. One of the two extra players is the Chaser; the other is the Runner. The object of the game is for the Runner *not* to be tagged by the Chaser. To be safe, the Runner may stop *between* any set of *partners* and *face* one of them. The one to whom he turns his back will immediately become the Runner; the one he *faces* becomes his new partner as shown in Figure 2. If the Chaser tags the Runner before the Runner can find a safe place, the two reverse roles (the

Runner becomes the Chaser). The Runner and Chaser may go through the center of the circle or anywhere in the area, but they may not leave the area or cut between two partners. Partners should keep their feet facing each other and a little distance between pairs of partners so that those running can distinguish each pair. To begin play, the Chaser and the Runner should be on opposite sides of the circle.

Points to Ponder

The demands for alertness in this game are constant. To make sure that players understand *when* they are to run, have a walk-through after they are in position: "Pretend that Pat is chasing Tillie. The only way that Tillie can be safe is to stand between two partners and *face one* of them. [Demonstrate] Who would become the runner? Suppose Tillie faced the other person? Suppose she faced one person, then changed her mind, and faced the other? . . . That's right, both players would probably run, and our game would be ruined."

In the excitement of the game, children sometimes forget to face their partners. Help them understand that they can keep their toes pointing toward their partners and still turn their heads to see the game.

Encourage the runners to get a "home" as *quickly* as possible so that there is an almost constant changing of runners. If a runner does not make an effort to get a "home," if he runs away from the group, the group may count aloud to three. By the count of three, the runner must either be in a safe place or choose a replacement. Encourage giving everyone serveral turns.

If one person remains the chaser long enough to become too tired, let him exchange places with someone who is not running.

The number of players makes a difference in the success of the game. It is better to have two or three games simultaneously than to play with an entire class in one game.

LINE UP (K-2)

Highlights—skills in running and throwing during competition, softball-related knowledge; *Equipment*—one softball and 2 bases; *Area*—playground; *Number of players*—suited best for 2 teams of 6-9 players each per game.

Line Up is a very active game involving only a few skills in teaching some basic concepts leading up to softball.

Place 2 bases approximately 40' apart—one in the field and one for home plate. Explain that the game begins with one team in the field as "fielders" and the other at home as "runners." The first runner stands beside home plate and throws the ball as far as possible into the field (it must go in front of an imaginary line on each side of home base to be a *fair* ball; behind the imaginary line is *foul*). If the ball lands in the fair area, he runs and touches the other base (with his foot) and then runs back to touch home base. Foul balls do not count. Let one runner throw the ball and run the bases while the others watch.

Explain to the fielders that they will line up as quickly as possible behind the player on their team who fields the thrown ball. Have 6-8 players try this with a ball that you throw. Discuss things that would help them get in line more quickly. Explain that if the fielders can line up behind the player who fields the ball before the runner gets back to home base, he is *out*. Otherwise, he is *safe* and scores one *run* for his team. After 3 outs, the teams change places and the game continues until there are 3 more outs completing the first inning. Runs are accumulated from one inning to the next. The team with more runs at the end of a designated number of innings or length of time wins. Be sure that the innings are even so that each team has the same number of times to score.

Points to Ponder

Depending on the skill levels of individual classes, it may be wise to separate boys and girls for more challenging games.

Since it is typical of a young child to want to be the star—with little thought given to the good of the team—there will be many opportunities to help them work together. Sometimes the fielders spend so much of their time fighting over the ball that the runner scores a run before possession of the ball is gained. In the excitement, the fielder getting the ball often runs with it, thus making it hard for the other fielders to line up behind him. With your help, they will soon learn to work together.

The distance between bases will vary with individual classes.

If it is too difficult to score runs, move the base in the field closer to home. If it is too difficult to make outs, move it farther from home. Keep the same distance for both teams.

If space permits, the entire class may play two separate games or half of the class may be involved in games requiring less space.

THROW IT AND RUN (3-6)

Highlights—softball-type game, throwing and catching skills; *Equipment*—one softball and 4 bases; *Area*—playground; *Number of players*—suited best for 10 players (too few is better than too many).

Throw It and Run was designed as a practical way to teach the basic rules of softball without requiring batting. Often the younger children, especially third and fourth graders, want to play softball, but most of their time is spent waiting for a good pitch or striking out.

The game begins with the pitcher pitching the ball to the "batter" who *catches* it, *throws* it anywhere into fair territory, and runs, as in softball. From here on, the rules are the same as in softball. (See *Softball*.)

Points to Ponder

The distance between bases may need to be adjusted to the skills of the players. Use whatever distance the majority of them can accurately throw the ball. If this is done, let them know from the beginning that the distance will be increased as their skills improve.

Bases may be obtained easily and inexpensively. Some classes use carpet samples; squares cut from discarded carpet or throw rugs; legs of discarded jeans filled with sawdust, beans or very small pebbles stitched in a bag; or vegetable sacks folded into squares and stitched. You and your class will think of other ways to make them, but whatever you use, please avoid using sticks, stones, boards, or worn spots on the ground for bases.

This game is not very physically active at best; yet, it may be necessary to teach an entire class at first. As soon as possible, organize so that there are fewer in each game, thus allowing more involvement of each player.

If there are fewer than 10 players on a team, eliminate positions in the following order: right shortstop, catcher (the pitcher can run in and play the catcher's position), center field (this position can be covered by the other two fielders), and left fielder (the left shortstop can cover left field).

BEAT THE THROW (4-6)

Highlights—accuracy in catching and throwing a ball during competition, running bases in order; *Equipment*—one softball (or paper ball) and 4 bases per game; *Area*—playground; *Number of players*—suited best for two teams of 5-8 players each per game.

Beat the Throw is one of the best games to help children learn if their throwing and catching skills are adequate for softball. Most children overestimate their ball-playing skills. Often, if the distance between bases in softball is left to the decision of the children, it is too great. Therefore, teachers have used *Beat the Throw* as a prerequisite for softball: "When you can show me that most of your team can play this game with no errors, then we'll learn the game of softball. We will make the distance between bases the same as the number of feet that your team can accurately throw the ball."

Four bases are placed as in softball. The team at bat has one runner standing beside home base and the remainder of the team standing (or sitting) at least 15' away from the playing area. The fielding team has a pitcher, a catcher, and a player at each of the other three bases. (If there are more than five players, see Points to Ponder.)

When the pitcher throws (underhand pitch) the ball to the catcher, the runner begins running the bases, touching each in order. The catcher throws the ball to the first baseman who must touch first base with his foot before throwing the ball to the second baseman. Each baseman catches the ball, touches his base, and throws to the next baseman until the ball reaches the catcher who touches home base. If this happens before the runner reaches home, he is out. Otherwise, he scores one run for his team, and the game continues with the next runner. After three outs, the teams change places.

Note: Help children understand that a thrown ball travels faster than a person can run; therefore, runs are scored only on the fielding team's errors.

Points to Ponder

If there are more than five players on a team, use two basemen for a base. Let them alternate playing the base and backing up each other.

Make sure that runners understand that they must *touch* each base. Running near it is not sufficient.

A ball made of paper works well. Many children are afraid to try to catch a regular softball thrown from a distance. A ball made of paper can help eliminate this fear.

Before playing the game, let the children have several opportunities to run the bases. Let them get a partner and throw and catch the ball, gradually increasing the distance between them.

Bases may be made by cutting throw rugs into square pieces, folding vegetable sacks and securing the loose ends, or using carpet samples.

The team at bat should stay well out of the playing area. This rule should be strictly enforced for safety reasons as well as for not interfering with the play at home plate. If crowding around home plate occurs, calling an out on the batting team usually eliminates the problem.

TUNNEL BALL (3-6)

Highlights—forcefully kicking a stationary ball, accurately rolling a ball, cooperating as a team member; *Equipment*—a ball that may be kicked (soccer or utility ball), 2 bases and a restraining line; *Area*—playground; *Number of players*—two teams of 6-8 players each per game.

In the game of *Tunnel Ball,* the kicking team lines up behind a restraining line that is 10'-15' away from home base. First base is placed 30'-50' from home plate, the distance being based on the average skill of the players.

The fielding team spaces itself so that a large area of the field is covered. The distance between home plate and the fielders is also judged according to the skills of the players.

The ball is placed on home plate. The first kicker, who stands *no more than 8'* behind home plate, runs and kicks the ball forcefully toward the fielding team. He then runs and tags first base and returns to tag home.

The fielder who retrieves the ball holds it and *stays where he is,* but turns his back to the majority of the fielders. All fielders run and line up behind him, standing close together with feet in a wide stride position (feet apart). The retriever, with no help from the other fielders, bends over and attempts to roll the ball betweeen his legs and the "tunnel of legs" behind him before the runner returns home. The ball must pass completely through the tunnel. If this is accomplished before the runner tags home plate, he is out. If the runner reaches home first, a run is scored. After three outs, the teams change places.

Points to Ponder

Limit teams to the suggested number (6-8 per team). Too many players hinder the success of the tunnel. It is better to have more games played simultaneously than to place too many players in a single game.

KICKBALL (3-6)

Highlights—forcefully kicking a moving ball, running bases, teamwork; *Equipment*—a ball that may be kicked (utility ball, soccer ball, paper ball), 5 bases (one for the pitcher's mound), and a rope or line (to indicate the kicking team's "dugout"); *Area*—playground; *Number of players*—two teams of 7-10 players each.

The required skills in *Kickball* are similar to those in softball. The organization and game rules are the same. (Refer to the softball section).

The difference is that a large and inflated ball is rolled to the batter, and is kicked rather than batted.

Kickball is *not* recommended for grades 1 and 2.

Skills

Kick. The ball should be kicked just as it crosses home plate. A player who runs halfway toward the pitcher to kick the ball is endangering the fielding team, and is also gaining an advantage in his run to first base. A player who kicks the ball to the side of or behind home plate will likely kick a foul ball, perhaps many. The skill of kicking the ball at the proper place is not a difficult one, merely one that should be learned.

If the catcher is in the correct position, (6'-8' behind home plate), there will be no problem of a long run by the kicker.

Should the kicker elect not to kick a rolled ball, he should let it pass to the catcher—who returns it to the pitcher.

Pitch. The ball should be rolled to the batter. The movements involved in rolling the ball are the same as those in the softball pitch, except that the ball is released close to the ground (so that it rolls and does not bounce.)

SOFTBALL (4-6)

Highlights—batting, throwing, catching, and pitching a softball, teamwork, leisure-time activity; *Equipment*—a bat, a softball, 5 bases (one for the pitcher's mound), and a rope or line (to indicate the batting team's "dugout"); *Area*—playground; *Number of players*—two teams of a maximum of 10 players each.

The Game

Softball begins with one team at bat and the other team in the field, as shown in Figure 3. Batters take turns at home plate attempting to hit the ball pitched by the opposing pitcher. After the ball is hit, the batter becomes the runner and attempts to touch each

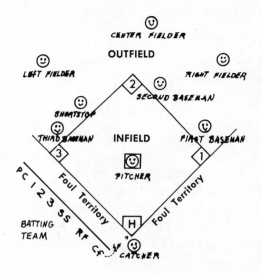

Figure 3 SOFTBALL—FIELD AND POSITIONS

base, in order, and return home to score a run for his team. He may stop on any base and continue running when the next batter hits the ball. A team remains at bat until three outs are called at which time the two teams exchange places until the other team also makes three outs, completing one inning. The game continues for nine innings with each team accumulating scores. The team with the higher score at the end of nine innings is the winner.

The rules listed below are suggested for grades 4-6:

1. A strike is:
   —a ball struck at and missed.
   —a tip ball unless it is on the third strike.
   —a foul ball unless it is on the third strike.
2. The batter is out:
   —after three strikes.
   —for batting out-of-order.
   —for interfering with play at home base.
   —for slinging the bat (releasing it) during the swing (safety rule).
   —if he tips the ball on the third strike and the ball is caught before hitting the ground.
   —if he fouls the ball on any strike and the ball is caught before hitting the ground.
3. The runner is out if:
   —he hits a fly ball that is caught.
   —the ball is held on first base before he reaches first base.
   —he is touched while off base with the ball held by any opposing player.
   —he runs more than three feet from the base line to avoid being tagged.

—he is hit while off base by a batted ball before it is touched by the fielding team.

—he fails to touch a base and does not go back to the base missed in reverse order before the ball is held on the base missed.

—he is standing off base before the ball leaves the hands of the pitcher.

Organization

Limit play to spring season. In the past, many physical education programs consisted of four main areas—softball, kickball, dodgeball, and rope jumping. All of these activities are good, but children who have been given the opportunities to learn a wide variety of activities and skills have discovered many more favorite games and sports. Their preferences are no longer confined to the above-mentioned games. To play one game the entire year denies them the time—and their right—to know and enjoy other equally enjoyable activities. It is recommended, therefore, that softball be limited to the spring season.

Separate boys and girls. In general, boys are often stronger, more skillful, and more experienced in softball than girls. There will be more opportunity for skill development and increased pleasure in playing if there are two games—one for the boys, another for the girls. Of course, highly skilled girls may join the team of their choice. If there are not enough players to have two games, see the suggestions given below.

Have a maximum of 10 players per team. If there are fourteen players on each team in a softball game, thirteen players are awaiting a turn to bat, and only three or four players are active. There is little opportunity to develop skills, learn position play, or understand the mechanics of the game.

If there are as many as fourteen boys and fourteen girls in the class, that is enough for two games of seven players per team (pitcher, catcher, three basemen, two fielders—eliminating the center fielder and the shortstop).

If the class is unbalanced (such as 19 boys and 12 girls), vary the organization. At times, let the boys have a game while the girls play some other activity. At other times, organize the class into three teams of boys *and* girls: one team is at bat, one is in the field, and the third is the skill team (working on throwing, pitching, catching, or batting). Rotate the fielding team to bat, the batters to the skill team, and the skill team to the field.

If there are eight players on a team, eliminate the center field

position. If there are ten players, add a right shortstop between first and second base.

Change positions every game. Deciding on positions before going to the playground is a time-saving move. It also gives all children equal opportunities to develop skills; otherwise, those who play the "best" generally monopolize the key positions, which are the most active.

A suggested solution is to make a softball wheel as shown in Figure 4. For each game, the inner wheel is rotated one position. Place as many positions on the outer wheel as there are team members on the inner wheel. Use heavy paper or cardboard to make the wheels.

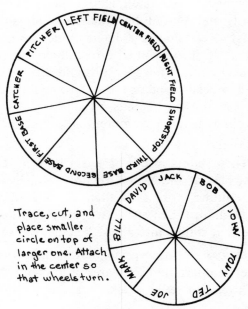

Trace, cut, and place smaller circle on top of larger one. Attach in the center so that wheels turn.

Figure 4 SOFTBALL WHEEL

Arrange distance between bases according to the skill of the players. A softball diamond is 60' square. Many sixth graders can play a successful game on a field of this size. Players should be able to accurately and consistently throw a ball from one base to another and to catch one thrown the same distance; if they cannot, the field is too large.

The distance between the bases should be as far as the majority of players can throw a ball (from 30' to 60').

Show respect for the official. Although an umpire is not

essential, it is profitable to have one. Only one person can make a decision, and this as *he* sees it. Discuss such things as fair play, unbiased decisions, good sportsmanship, rules on overthrown and foul balls, the forced play rule, responsibilities, and, *in particular,* a positive attitude toward the official. With an umpire, there is less argument, strikes and balls can be called, and the game takes form. Once a child has had the responsibility of officiating, he is less likely to question decisions.

Safety

The slinger. "Swing it, but don't sling it." Releasing the bat before the swing is completed is the most dangerous of all the softball hazards and should be considered an automatic out (for safety reasons). Releasing one hand while swinging may lead to slinging the bat, so it may be wise to call this an out, too. The bat should not travel after its release—it should drop to the ground. Send violators to a special "practice box" to work on swinging, then dropping the bat until a habit is established. Another method for solving the problem is to have a potential "slinger" carry the bat with him to first base.

The slider. Sliding into a base can be fun. It is also a strategic and important part of the game—for professionals or league players. Safe sliding requires more skill than considered necessary for an elementary-age child; it can also cause many injuries. Therefore, it is recommended that sliding into a base be an automatic out.

The brick base. Appropriate bases made from rugs cut into squares, carpet samples, mats, squares of linoleum, and such are easy to acquire. The use of rocks, sticks, boards, or bricks for bases only creates hazards.

The blocked base. "If the baseman is in the base line, the runner has the right of way"—this is the regulation rule. However, for educators at the elementary level the safety of the child takes precedence over winning the game. Prepare children for knowledge-able base play by having the basemen touch the corner of the base closest to the ball while awaiting the catch, leaving room for the runner to tag the base safely. The basemen do not play on the base except when anticipating a throw. Their playing positions are shown in Figure 3 showing field and positions.

The blocked path of the runner. The same reasoning applies

to a player who is standing on the line between the bases (which is the runner's path). The basemen and the shortstop(s) play either in front of or behind this path, as shown in the diagram.

The finger jammer. Injuries to the fingers occur usually because of an awkward, unskilled catch. "Make a pocket for the ball, and 'give' when you catch it." (Refer to the *Skills* section below.)

The batters battered. Many accidents occur because the batting team lines up as close to home plate as possible. They are not only in a precarious location, but they also interfere with the game. Place a rope (line, marker) at least 15' away from home plate and have the batters stay behind it.

Skills

Batting. It is not unusual for a beginner to face the pitcher and push the bat forward, moving it in a vertical direction. He has very little chance of making contact with the ball, which is traveling on a horizontal plane. Have him first get the feel of letting a bat *swing*—waist high and parallel to the ground. When he can do this with ease, he will instinctively begin changing weight with his swing, rocking onto the back foot with the backswing, and onto the lead foot on the foreswing. Add this accomplishment to a good batting stance, and a dramatic hit ensues—surprising him more than anyone else. The batter's feet face home plate in stride positon (feet apart), his side and eyes face the pitcher, and his shoulders rotate toward the catcher. His elbows are high and away from the body, his knees are bent, and the bat is held straight, slightly tilted up and back over the right shoulder—not resting on it. (For a right-handed batter, the bat is gripped with the right hand above the left.) The distance between the batter and home plate is such that the swing—at full extension—is over home plate.

Pitching. The pitcher is required to deliver the ball with an underhand motion. The ball is held in *both* hands while facing the plate, knees are bent, and eyes remain on the target. The elements involved are a backswing, a step and a vigorous stretch forward, and an extension of the throwing hand toward the target as the ball is released waist-high.

Throwing. Common errors in inadequate throws are: facing the target, stepping off the wrong foot for a forceful throw, and not using full extension of the throwing arm. The *side* should be turned

toward the target. As the weight shifts to the back foot, the ball is "cocked" (carried away from the target). As the weight shifts to the lead foot, the body rotates toward the target, and the throwing arm is thrust vigorously and at full extension toward the target. The ball will travel in the direction of its release.

Catching. The hands are cupped to make a softball-size pocket with the fingers of one hand angled toward the other. If the ball is caught high (above the waist), the fingers are above wrist level; if it is caught low (below the waist), the fingers are below wrist level. Accidents occur when the hands are apart with fingers spread and pointing toward the ball. As the ball is received, the hands move in the same direction as the ball ("give" . . ."go with the ball").

Base running. A runner may not leave the base until the ball leaves the pitcher's hand. He must touch *every* base! If he fails to do so, he must reverse his run, also touching each base, and beat the ball back to the base he missed. A good base-running skill drill (and a good pregame activity) is to have the entire class run the bases several times. They travel in single file approximately 3' apart around the diamond, concentrating on touching every base; they do not pass other runners.

If a runner advances on a foul ball, he may *not* be put out on his return to base. He may leave the base *after* a fly ball is caught. But if he leaves the base *before* it is caught, he may be put out on his return to that base.

Runners may not move more than 3' from the base line *to avoid being tagged.* However, they sometimes go beyond this range in rounding the corners on a fast run; this is permissible.

Knowledge

Fair and foul balls. A ball that first *hits* in foul territory is a foul ball regardless of where it rolls. Other than this, a good overall rule is: Where the ball *rolls* in the infield and where it *hits* in the outfield determine whether it is fair or foul.

Illustrations shown in Figure 5 are:

1—The ball hits foul in the infield and rolls fair (foul ball)
2—The ball hits foul in the outfield and rolls fair (foul ball)
3—The ball hits and stays foul (foul ball)
4—The ball hits and stays fair in the infield (fair ball)
5—The ball hits and stays fair in the outfield (fair ball)

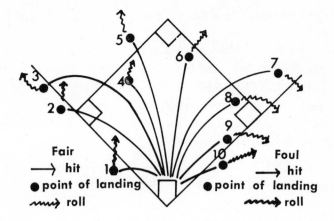

Figure 5 SOFTBALL—FAIR AND FOUL BALLS

6—The ball hits fair in the infield and rolls fair in the outfield (fair ball)

7—The ball hits fair in the outfield and rolls foul (fair ball)

8—The ball hits fair in the infield and rolls foul in the outfield (fair ball—it was fair when it rolled into the outfield)

9—The ball hits fair in the infield and rolls foul without being touched (foul ball)

10—The ball hits and stays foul (foul ball)

Foul tip. A foul tip is a batted ball that goes directly behind the batter, but does not rise above his head. It is a strike unless the batter already has two strikes (same as a foul ball). However, if after 2 strikes a foul tip is *caught,* the batter is out.

Forced play. In a forced play, the runner *must* advance to the next base: Example (1) A runner is on first base, and the batter gets a hit; the runner is *forced* to run to second base. In this case, the second baseman need only to hold the ball and tag the base with his foot to make the out. Example (2) A runner is on second base, there is no one on first base, and the batter gets a hit; the runner is *not* forced to run to third base. If he decides to run, he must be *tagged* out, since this is not a forced play.

On a forced play, tag the base (or the runner). If the play is not forced, tag the runner.

Overthrown balls. An overthrown ball is one thrown beyond the reach of a baseman. At first and third bases, an overthrown ball usually goes out-of-bounds. If it does, a runner may gain one

base on the overthrow *in addition* to the base he was entitled to as the result of a hit.

When the ball is overthrown at second base, it remains in the playing field where there are players to recover it. In this case, when it is in fair territory, runners may advance as many bases as they can.

Fly ball. A batted ball that is caught before it touches the ground, whether in fair or foul territory, is an out. A runner may advance only *after* the fly is caught.

Tie play. If a runner and the ball arrive at a base simultaneously, the runner is safe. "The tie goes to the runner."

Interference with play by batting team. Action often takes place in foul territory close to home plate, such as a wild throw to the catcher, a foul fly ball, or a foul tip. The catcher requires room to perform successfully in these plays; if batters are in the way, he is handicapped. If they interfere with his movements or with the ball, the batter is out.

Runner hit by a batted ball. A runner, off base, who is hit by a batted ball that has not been touched by the fielding team, is out.

Stealing bases. In regulation softball rules, base stealing is allowed, but the runner is required to stay on base until the ball leaves the pitcher's hand. For elementary play—except for highly skilled teams—base stealing only runs up the score and delays the game. (The catcher misses a ball. The runner on first goes to second. The catcher throws to the second baseman who misses the ball. The runner goes to third. There is a wild throw to the third baseman. The runner goes home. A score has been made on three errors.) Because elementary players have not mastered the skills required for base stealing—and preventing base stealing—it should not be allowed.

Innings. Six outs (three for each team) make one inning; three outs are only half of an inning. The game in elementary schools is usually played according to time rather than innings. The score is that of the last *full* inning.

Batting order. The outfield positions are inactive in comparison to the infield positions. Consequently, there is some compensation in putting outfielders first in the batting order. The following batting order is suggested: left fielder, center fielder, right fielder, shortstop(s), third baseman, second baseman, first baseman, catcher, and pitcher.

Misconceptions. It is suggested that the game of softball be

played no earlier than the fourth grade because the skills and reasoning powers of younger children are usually not suited to the game. When children at the primary-age level attempt to play, the game has to be modified. Such modification usually results in the learning of a few skills and a large number of misconceptions. Examples of these misconceptions—along with the correct rule—include:

1. Misconception—Four fouls make an out.
   Correct rule—There is no limit to the number of fouls.
2. Misconception—A runner hit by a thrown ball is out.
   Correct rule—A runner hit by a thrown ball is *not* out.
3. Misconception—If a runner travels halfway to a base, he must continue toward it.
   Correct rule—A runner may travel all the way to a base and return to the preceding base—if it is not occupied.
4. Misconception—Two runners on a base is an automatic out.
   Correct rule—The base belongs to the one who was there first, except on a forced play. An out can be made by tagging either runner when he is off base.
5. Misconception—A batted ball caught after one bounce is an out.
   Correct rule—A batted ball caught *before* it touches the ground is an out.
6. Misconception—A runner does not have to actually touch the base—just go across it.
   Correct rule—Runners must touch each base.

BROOM HOCKEY (4-6)

Highlights—controlling an object used as an extension of the hand, teamwork; *Equipment*—six brooms, four plastic bottles (goals), a chalkboard eraser (puck), and tape (face-off spots); *Area*—Activity room or paved area; *Number of players*—suited best for 12-35 per game.

In the game of *Broom Hockey*, the players score points by using brooms to sweep a puck (chalkboard eraser) through the opponents' goal.

Teams and brooms are arranged as shown in Figure 6. When a starting signal is given, the first three players from each team run *between* their own goal posts and into the playing area. On each team, player 1 takes the broom at the half line on the right side of the court; player 2 takes the midcourt broom; player 3 takes the third broom and becomes the goalkeeper. Players 1 and 2 may play anywhere on the court, but player 3 remains to defend the goal. Play begins immediately with the first player to reach the puck starting the attack. Broom heads must remain *in contact* or *close to* the floor.

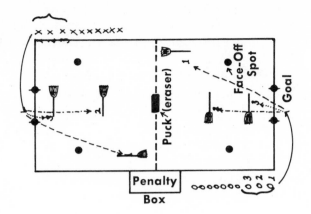

Figure 6 BROOM HOCKEY

The puck may be tapped, pushed, jabbed, or hit, but may not be covered with the broom and dragged along the floor. The penalty for violations is temporary elimination, in which the penalized player takes his broom and goes to the penalty box for a period of 20 seconds. Following the violation, the game resumes with a face-off at one of the two face-off spots on the penalized team's half of the court. In the face-off, the official drops the puck between two opposing players who have their brooms touching the floor and their backs toward their own goals.

Points to Ponder

If the number of team players is a multiple of three, have players rotate places so that they will not play the same position twice in succession.

Goal posts are approximately 8' apart. A goal does not count if the post is knocked down during play. As a safety precaution, it may be necessary to have the goalkeeper *remain on his feet,* blocking shots with his broom only.

You or a student may officiate the game; a whistle is helpful in controlling play. If the violation of lifting the broom high (high-sticking) is called as frequently as it occurs while learning the game, players will learn quickly to keep the brooms low, which is necessary for a safe game.

If there is a handicapped or a temporarily inactive player, ask him to time any players in the penalty box; otherwise, have penalized players time themselves, either by a wall clock or by

counting *slowly* to 20. Keep penalized players and their brooms safely away from the action.

If the puck travels across the sidelines or behind the goal, play continues. A goal, of course, must be scored through the front of the goal. Inactive players on the sidelines should move away from a puck that goes out of bounds so that active players may play it.

For a game on a paved area, use either a small milk carton reinforced with tape, or a small, flat tin can for a puck.

The playing area is approximately 30' x 60'.

May

LESSON PLAN GUIDE

Grades K-2

WEEK	MONDAY	TUESDAY	WEDNESDAY	THURSDAY	FRIDAY
1	Base Run (see softball skills) Line Up Cottontail Hop	Strike It Four Square	Base Run Line Up Man from Mars (K) Partner Tag (1-2)	Classroom: Heel Slap Seven Jumps Sevens and Threes	Stations: 1. Strike It 2. (Long) rope jumping 3. Scoops 4. Swing Along
2	I See Monkey Tag Touché Turtle	Target Bowling Midnight (K) Jack Be Nimble (1-2)	Base Run Line Up Old Mother Witch	Stations: 1. (Short) rope jumping 2. Four Square 3. Lummi Sticks 4. Walkie-Talkie	Favorite Activities
3	Drag Race Jumping Brooks Moon Man Cottontail Hop	Base Run Line Up V-r-r-room	Old Mother Witch Ball-handling skills Drag Race	Classroom Stations: 1. Bottles and Canes (gymnastic skills) 2. Coffee Grinder 3. Walkie-Talkie 4. Push Back	Explosion Midnight (K-1) Bull in Pen (2) Throw and Go
4	Drag Race Bull in Pen (2) Swing Along Man from Mars	Sevens and Threes From A to Z Sing a Song of Sixpence	Throw and Go Line Up (K-1) Double Trouble (2) Bull in Pen (2)	Classroom: Endurance Hop Hot Potato Mousetrap	Stations: 1. (Long) rope jumping 2. Monkey Tag 3. Stride Ball (K) Yogi Bear (1-2) 4. Walkie-Talkie

May LESSON PLAN GUIDE Grades 3-6

WEEK	MONDAY	TUESDAY	WEDNESDAY	THURSDAY	FRIDAY
1	Base Run (see softball skills) Ball Skills: (Softball) pitching catching throwing	Base Run Ball Skills: (Softball) pitching catching throwing Beat the Throw	Base Run Beat the Throw	Drag Race Couple Tag Bull in Pen	Favorite Activities
2	Ball Skills: kicking (3) fielding batting (4-6) Tunnel Ball (3) Beat the Throw (4-6)	Base Run Tunnel Ball	Bridge (3-4) Bowling (3-4) Indian Ball (5-6)	Classroom: Nervous Wreck Lummi Sticks	Base Run Tunnel Ball
3	Rules and Knowledge (Kickball, Softball) Throw It and Run	Skill Stations: 1. Pitching 2. Throwing and Catching 3. Kicking (3) Batting (4-6) 4. Base Run (timed)	Base Run Kickball (3) Softball (4-6)	Couple Tag Bull in Pen (3-4) Four Square (3-4) Indian Ball (5-6)	Favorite Activities
4	Base Run Kickball (3) Softball (4-6)	Base Run Tunnel Ball (3) Broom Hockey (4-6)	Obstacle Course Tunnel Ball (3) or Kickball (3) Broom Hockey (4-6)	Base Run Kickball (3) Tunnel Ball (4-6)	Base Run Thorw It and Run (3) Softball (4-6)

FATHER TO SON

This is your first game, son.
I hope you win.
I hope you win for your sake not mine.
Because winning's nice.
It's a good feeling.
Like the whole world is yours.
But it passes, this feeling.
And what lasts is what you've learned.

And what you learn about is life.
That's what sports is all about.
Life.
The whole thing is played out in an afternoon.
The happiness of life.
The miseries.
The joys.
The heartbreaks.

There's no telling what'll turn up.
There's no telling whether they'll toss you out in the first
       five minutes or whether you'll stay for the long haul.

There's no telling how you'll do.
You might be a hero or you might be absolutely nothing.
Too much depends on chance.
On how the ball bounces.

I'm not talking about the game, son.
I'm talking about life.
But it's life that the game is all about.
Just as I said.

Because every game is life.
And life is a game.
A serious one.
Dead serious.

But that's what you do with serious things.
You do your best.
You take what comes.
You take what comes and you run with it.

Winning is fun.
Sure.
But winning is not the point.

Wanting to win is the point.
Not giving up is the point.
Never being satisfied with what you've done is the point.
Never letting up is the point.
Never letting anyone down is the point.

Play to win.
Sure.
But lose like a champion.
Because it's not winning that counts.
What counts is trying.

Author Unknown

June

It is well accepted that most children enter school with a natural curiosity to learn. Yet, it has been said that before their school days end, we cause many of them not only to lose most of that curiosity, but also to feel that they are failures and thus become potential dropouts during their first years of school.

As the school year ends and we are evaluating our teaching, perhaps above all else we should look at *each* child and ask ourselves: "Is he anxious to continue learning?" and "Have I geared my teaching so that he has a sense of achievement as well as a feeling of challenge?"

To be completely effective, these goals should be established at the beginning of the school year and consistently worked toward every day. If your goals encompass these objectives, fortunate, indeed, is every child in your class.

PEACE TAG (K-3)

Highlights—changing directions quickly in relation to others, running/chasing/tagging; *Equipment*—none; *Area*—playground or activity room; *Number of players*—4-6 players per game.

Peace Tag was originated by some third graders when they were asked to create a game. They were asked to make any rules that they felt were necessary, give the game a name, and explain it to the class. One group created *Peace Tag,* which was immediately declared a favorite!

The game begins with one player, IT, facing 3-5 other players who are scattered within an area approximately 25' x 50'. When IT says, "War!" all other players run in an effort to keep IT from tagging them. The only way a player can be safe is to stoop, give the peace sign, and say, "Peace." If, however, a player is tagged, he becomes IT, and the game continues—no one is eliminated. Those not tagged are the winners.

226

Points to Ponder

If trying to be tagged (in order to be IT) becomes a problem, let the children discuss what is happening. Usually the discussion is all that is necessary to solve the problem. However, if more action is required, the rule could be made to the effect that each tagged player remains out of the game until all but one player is tagged. The remaining player becomes IT for the new game. No player will be eliminated for too long a period of time if the groups are kept small.

A whole class could play the game together if there is an IT for every 3-5 students. If this is done, the game could be used as a way to eliminate players at the end of a class period. Those eliminated simply prepare to go back to the classroom.

DONKEY DODGE (5-6)

Highlights—teamwork, anticipating the moves of another, passing a ball quickly; *Equipment*—one ball—8"-10" in diameter—per game; *Area*—playground, paved area, or activity room; *Number of players*—best suited for 6-8 players per game.

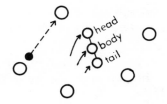

Figure 1 DONKEY DODGE

Donkey Dodge is a type of dodgeball game that requires much skill in passing and receiving a ball. It also places much responsibility on the player for quickly deciding whether to attempt to hit the target or to pass to a teammate who may be in a better position.

Players are arranged in a circle with the three center players representing the Head, the Body, and the Tail of a donkey as shown in Figure 1. They must remain hooked together by holding onto the waist of the person in front. The object of the game is for the circle players to try to hit the Tail of the "donkey" anywhere *below* that player's head. The Head and Body of the "donkey" try to protect the Tail by turning to face the ball, thus keeping between him and the ball. Circle players pass the ball to each other as quickly as possible in an effort to catch the Tail unprotected. The player who

hits the Tail becomes the Head, the Head becomes the Body, the Body becomes the new Tail, and the old Tail fills the vacancy left in the circle.

Points to Ponder

This game is quite a challenge for even the most highly skilled players. The ball must be passed quickly and accurately to another player several times before the "donkey" will be caught off guard. Nearly all players will need help, at first, in throwing the ball as soon as they receive it. Encourage them not to hesitate with the ball in their hands since that only gives the "donkey" time to rest. Setting up the play for another teammate to hit the Tail is part of good teamwork.

Playing with more than the recommended number of players does *not* make for successful play. If necessary, organize more games rather than placing more players in one game.

Since it is not necessary for the ball to bounce, one made of paper works quite well.

Encourage the players not to throw at the Tail unless his *back* is toward them. Often they will try to throw the ball so that it goes over the heads of the first two parts of the "donkey" and lands on his Tail.

The Head player may use his hands to *deflect* any balls that may be thrown at him, but he may *not* use his hands to otherwise strike the ball.

HOPSCOTCH (K-6)

Highlights—hopping, jumping, turning, leisure-time activity; *Equipment*—tape or chalk to draw hopscotch patterns, or bases to use as blocks in forming patterns. Optional—a small, flat object (thrower) that can be tossed (stone, beanbag, coin); *Area*—activity room, classroom, paved area, or playground; *Number of players*—suited best for 2-6 per game.

Observe a child while he hops (one foot) and then jumps (two feet). The well-coordinated child moves smoothly as he adjusts his body balance from one point to two. Because *Hopscotch* involves harmonious action of various body parts, it offers an opportunity to develop coordination.

The following rules are general ones and may be modified for convenience:

—one block indicates a hop (one foot); two blocks indicate a jump (two feet);

three blocks indicate triple jumps (jump into center block, jump again—placing left foot in left block and right foot in right block—then jump back into center block).

—touching a line is a miss.

—when hopping, touching the free foot to the ground is a miss.

—when jumping, both feet should land simultaneously.

—when a player reaches the last blocks in a pattern, he jumps and turns so that he faces the starting position; he then continues the actions and exits through block 1.

—touching the ground with the hand(s) is a miss.

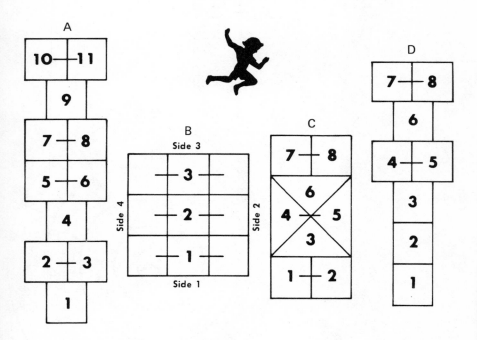

Figure 2 HOPSCOTCH

Figure 2, cont.

Points to Ponder

Traditional hopscotch patterns are shown in Figure 2A and 2D; suggestions for other patterns are shown in 2B, 2C, 2E, 2F, and 2G. Encourage the children to make original ones.

In Figure 2B, the player jumps into block 1, executes a triple jump, and then jumps out. Then he jumps into block 2, does a triple jump, repeats block 1, and then jumps out. He then takes a long jump into block 3 for a triple jump, repeats block 2, repeats block 1, and jumps out. The entire action is repeated from the other three sides of the square.

In Figure 2E, the player begins with a jump, hops around the circle and back into block 3, then exits with a jump from the first two blocks.

In Figure 2G, the *stop* blocks enable a player to rest and/or change feet.

Children compete in several ways:

(1) by finishing first
(2) by scoring one point for each successful trip
(3) by capturing the most blocks (explained below)

For use in a physical education program, the point system is recommended. If only one game is played (such as at a station), competition is individual; if there are several games, competition is by teams.

For summertime fun, capturing the most blocks is the usual method of competing. This style of play requires a thrower and unlimited time. Each player has a thrower (a small, flat object) that he tosses into block 1 before starting his turn; he does not step into block 1 as he travels down and back through the blocks. If he has a successful trip, he tosses the thrower into block 2 and repeats the action, avoiding stepping into block 2, and so on. When he misses, his thrower remains in place to indicate the block from which he starts his next turn. His opponent(s) may step in this block. When a player has completed a set number of successful trips, he writes his name in a block of his choice; thereafter, only he can step in that block.

Bases, cardboard, or sample carpet squares with tape on the back can be used to lay out a fast and temporary hopscotch pattern; bases may be used successfully on the playground. Sample upholstery squares sewn together work well on carpeted floors.

HAND TENNIS (5-6)

Highlights—striking a ball before and after a bounce, tennis-type scoring; *Equipment*—a lightweight ball—8"-10" in diameter, lines or ropes to mark off a court approximately 10' x 20', and a net or rope 2'-3' high. (See Points to Ponder for play without a net); *Area*—activity room or paved area; *Number of players*—two (singles) or four (doubles) per game.

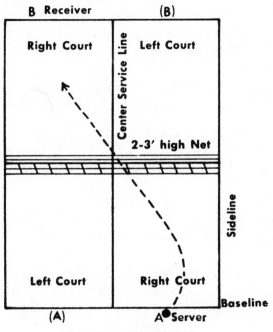

Figure 3 HAND TENNIS

Hand Tennis, a lead-up to tennis, is an exciting and popular game with tremendous carry over value. A court marked off in a driveway provides hours of summer fun.

The size of the court shown in Figure 3 is approximately 10' x 20'. The rules and the scoring are the same as in tennis. The ball is served and then played back and forth across a net and into the court until there is a miss. The ball is struck with the hand either before it bounces, or after it bounces once. The same player serves for an entire game. The first serve is from behind the right court; thereafter, it alternates from one side to the other.

Singles: In singles play (two opponents), each player stands behind his right court baseline. The server tosses the ball with one hand and strikes it with the other so that it travels over the net and

into the opponent's right-hand court. The ball may be struck underhanded or overhanded. A ball that hits a line is considered good.

The receiver *must* let the served ball bounce *once* before he returns it; thereafter, either player may volley the ball, or strike it after it bounces once.

The server has *two* attempts to serve successfully. If he misses on the first serve, it is called a *fault* and the server tries again. A serve is a miss if:

—the ball lands out-of-bounds
—the ball lands in the wrong court
—the ball is hit into or under the net
—the server steps on or across the baseline before striking the ball

A *let* ball is a served ball that touches the net and then falls into the correct court. It does not count as a serve and is served over. The number of *let* balls is unlimited. (During play, a ball that touches the net and then falls in-bounds is good.)

Doubles: In doubles play, there are two teams of two players each. The players on the serving team alternate between the right and the left courts after each point. The players on the receiving team remain in the same half of the court (one on right, one on left) throughout the game.

Scoring: Zero points: *Love.* One point: 15. Two points: 30. Three points: 40. Four points: *Game.* One point each: 15 *All.* Two points each: 30 *All.* Three points or more each: *Deuce.* Server makes one point after a *deuce* score: *Ad* (advantage) *In.* Receiver makes one point after a *deuce* score: *Ad Out.* Either team makes two consecutive points after a *deuce* score: *Game.*

After a score of either *Ad In* or *Ad Out,* the *next* score is always either *Deuce* (if the other team makes a point) or *Game* (if the same team scores a second point).

The server calls the score before each serve; he calls his score first. A score of 15-30 indicates one point for the server and two points for the receiver. A score of 40-15 indicates three points for the server and one point for the receiver. After calling the score, the server says, "Ready?" and the receiver responds, "Serve."

Points to Ponder

If the use of a net is impractical, use: a rope tied to bamboo poles or broomsticks, rotating those holding the poles into the action

after each game; a 3' neutral space in lieu of a net—the ball must clear the area and no player may enter it.

Encourage the use of only one hand in striking a ball.

A ball is not considered out-of-bounds until it touches the floor (or an obstacle); consequently, if a player strikes a ball that is obviously going out-of-bounds, the ball remains in play.

After the serve, a player may play inside the court. However, if he is hit by the ball, he loses the point.

Sometimes players find it hard to remember the score or which court to serve from next. Help them to learn that when the serve is from the *right-hand* court, the score is always *even*. Two points: *Love*-30 or 30-*Love* or 15-*All*. Four points: 30-*All* or 15-40 or 40-15. Six or more points: *Deuce*.

When the serve is from the *left-hand* court, the score is always *uneven*. One point: *Love*-15 or 15-*Love*. Three points: 30-15 or 15-30 or *Love*-40 or 40-*Love*. Five or more points: 30-40 or 40-30 or *Ad In* or *Ad Out*.

GRAND MARCHING (K-6)

Highlights—moving to a rhythmical beat, moving in unison with others; *Equipment*—lines or markers (plastic bottles) to mark off a rectangular area. Optional—a record player and a recording in march tempo; *Area*—activity room or paved area; *Number of players*—unlimited.

Children respond favorably to marching—with or without music. Although accompaniment adds to the fun, satisfaction is also achieved by stepping in rhythm to other foot beats. Primary-age children particularly enjoy following a leader while they tramp, tramp, tramp together. The older children are intrigued by the figures they can form.

Figures may be called by a student or followed in a set order. A student caller should have the ability to call a figure far enough in advance for it to be executed.

Marchers progress in several pathways: up the center of the area, across the ends, up or down the sides, and diagonally from corner to corner. They may travel singly (one line), with a partner (a double line), and in groups of four, eight, or sixteen. From a single line formation, it is interesting to let the leader choose a path for the group, whether across the stage, through a door and back, around several obstacles, or into a snail formation.

The following four suggestions are helpful in learning the *Grand March:*

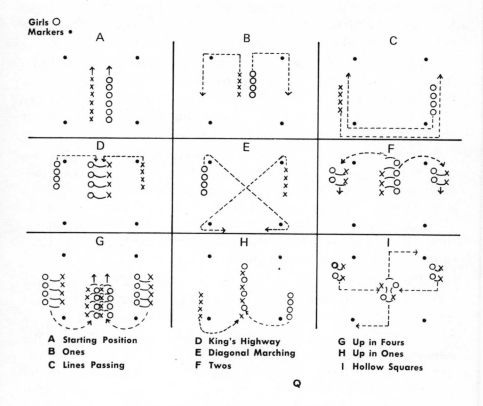

Girls O
Markers •

A Starting Position   D King's Highway   G Up in Fours
B Ones   E Diagonal Marching   H Up in Ones
C Lines Passing   F Twos   I Hollow Squares

Q

Figure 4 GRAND MARCHING

1. The first two couples should be good listeners because they guide the rest of the group.
2. Establish a rhythm by first marching *in place.*
3. When teaching a figure, have the first couples mark time after they have completed the figure until *all* have completed it.
4. For teaching purposes, use several marching commands:
   —"Forward—March!"
   —"Mark Time—March!"
   —"Class Halt!"

The following figures are basic marching patterns; they are shown in Figure 4.

Starting Position (Figure 4A): Couples (not necessarily boy-girl) stand side by side and in a double-file formation in the center of the area; the boy is on the left.

Ones (Figure 4B): Couples march forward; when they reach the end of the area, the boys turn left, turn the corner, and walk

down the side of the area in file formation. The girls do the same to the right side of the area. The two columns of marchers should be equidistant from the corners ("Keep up with your partner").

Lines Passing (Figure 4C): Marchers continue down the sideline, turn the corner at the end of the area, and march toward partners, still in single file. As they meet, the line of girls passes inside the line of boys as both lines continue to march to the corner and then down the (opposite) side.

King's Highway (Figure 4D): When single files meet, the first boy and first girl make a bridge by arching their hands overhead. Each couple, after going under the bridge, forms a bridge. Couples should go through side by side rather than one behind the other. When all have passed under the original bridge, the lead couple, followed by each couple in turn, goes "down the King's Highway" (under all bridges) and emerges to follow the next call.

Diagonal Marching (Figure 4E): When single files reach a corner, they march diagonally to the opposite corner; the girl (or the one on the right) passes in front of her partner when crossing.

Two's (Figure 4F): From a double-line formation in the center of the area, the first couple turns left, proceeds around the corner, and marches down the sideline. The second couple moves in the same manner to turn to the right. The succeeding couples alternate turning left or right. The result of this action is double lines marching down both sides of the area.

Up in Four's (Figure 4G): This figure is executed from the formation of double lines marching down the side. As couples turn the last corner and walk toward each other, each couple meets a couple in order, and joins hands with that couple to form a group of four. Each set of four marches side by side down the center of the area. (Build up to groups of eight or sixteen if space permits by having the groups of four meet, then eights, and so on.)

Up in One's (Figure 4H): From the formation of two single lines meeting, girls precede partners down the center of the area thus forming one long, single line of marchers.

Hollow Squares (Figure 4I): This is a method of changing partners. It is executed from the formation of double lines marching down the side. As couples reach the center of the sideline, they turn and march toward the *center of the room.* As couples from each side meet, each marcher turns his back to his partner and joins hands with

the new partner who is by his side. They then march down the center (line) toward the end of the area. One group of partners will be marching toward one end of the area, and the other group will be marching toward the opposite end. Each group turns right, proceeds around the corner, and down the sideline. One group marches slowly (or marks time) while the other group marches at a brisk pace to "catch up."

Points to Ponder

Children in the primary grades are generally able to master these figures: *One's, Two's, Lines Passing, Diagonal Marching,* and *King's Highway*.

Hollow Squares, Up in Fours, Eights, etc. are generally suited to the upper grades.

TETHERBALL (3-6)

Highlights—striking a moving ball, leisure-time activity; *Equipment*—a 9'-10' pole that is anchored, and a tetherball (a volley-sized ball attached to a 7½' cord) or two paddles and a small ball attached to a strong cord; *Area*—playground, paved area, or activity room; *Number of players*—suited best for 2-8 per game.

Tetherball is a game in which two opponents attempt to wind a tethered ball (a ball attached to a pole by a cord) completely around a pole in *opposite directions.* The ball is struck with the hand or with the paddle (depending on the size ball used) while the cord is at full extension *away* from the pole. One player (server) winds the ball clockwise, and the other (receiver) winds it counterclockwise.

Draw a line, or place a rope on the ground so that the area around the base of the pole is divided into halves. Each player stands or moves within his own half; he does not step on or across the dividing line.

The server, holding the ball so that the cord is fully extended and parallel to the ground, calls, "Ready?" and the receiver responds, "Serve!" The server swings or pushes the ball to his left, keeping the cord at full extension as he does so. The ball travels around the pole in a clockwise direction toward the receiver in such a manner that he can play it. If the served ball travels above the receiver's reach, or if it travels up and down, rather than around, it is served *again.* The receiver has the advantage of getting the *first* hit. Thereafter, each player continues batting the ball in an attempt to wind it around the

pole by hitting it above his opponent's reach and/or by hitting it each time he has the opportunity.

If, during play, the ball settles at full extension against the pole, it should not be picked up (this is a miss). The player on whose side the ball rests gives it a series of taps to set it *away from the pole* and in position for a successful, winding hit.

The game goes to the opponent if:

—a player steps on or over the line
—a player touches the pole
—a player stops, catches, or picks up the ball
—a player hits the cord with his hands or paddle
—the cord wraps around a player's arm or paddle

Each new game begins with the loser serving (clockwise).

Points to Ponder

Most children will need help in learning to strike the ball sideways in order to keep the cord fully extended and wind it around the pole. Their first attempts may be to strike the ball toward the pole—this causes the ball to swing back and forth rather than to wind around the pole.

Before competing against each other, let the children explore and experiment with different ways to strike the ball. Let them individually try to "beat the pole." The player wins if he can continue striking the ball and make the cord wrap tightly around the pole. The pole wins if the cord wraps only loosely around the pole and leaves the ball and much of the cord hanging.

Either hand may be used. If a regular tetherball is being used, both hands may be used. However, this is usually a defensive play.

As players become more proficient in the game, help them discover where they could best position themselves for offensive play and for defensive play. For the server, who is winding the ball clockwise, the far left side of his court is better for offensive play, the far right side is better for defensive play. For the receiver, the opposite is true.

Because the game involves only two players per game, set it up as a station at which a few players take turns.

Net standards may be used for tetherball poles. Simply attach a 7½' cord to the top of the pole. One may be improvised by setting a 13' pole in cement 3' in the ground. Of course, official poles and balls may be purchased at almost any sporting goods store.

Balls may also be improvised. For the large-sized ball to strike with the hands, cut two quarter-size holes approximately 2" apart (use a punctured or discarded volley-size ball), insert the end of a rope or cord through the holes and tie a knot. Attach the other end of the cord to the top of the pole. The ball should hang down approximately 6½'. To attach the ball to be used with paddles, make a small hole through the center of a tennis ball or rubber ball. Insert a small, strong cord and knot it. Equally good is a small ball placed inside a sock, which is attached to the cord.

Ping Pong or small wooden paddles may be used instead of purchasing official paddles.

LESSON PLAN GUIDE

June   Grades K-2

WEEK	MONDAY	TUESDAY	WEDNESDAY	THURSDAY	FRIDAY
1	(Long) rope jumping (Short) rope jumping	Line Up Hopscotch	Stations: 1. (Long) rope jumping 2. Hopscotch 3. Scoops 4. Walkie-Talkie	Classroom: What's Our Bag Today? Sock It to Me	Grand Marching Explosion
2	Peace Tag Line Up	Stations: 1. Hopscotch 2. (Long) rope jumping 3. (Short) rope jumping 4. Walkie-Talkie	Favorite Activities or Parachute	Obstacle Course Four Square Peace Tag	Grand Marching Drag Race
3	Jumping Brooks (Short) rope jumping (Long) rope jumping	Peace Tag Touché Turtle Drag Race	Stations: 1. (Long) rope jumping 2. Hopscotch 3. Swing Along 4. Walkie-Talkie	Classroom: Mousetrap Think and Do Stride Ball	Throw and Go Line Up
4	Stations: 1. (Long) rope jumping 2. Walkie-Talkie 3. Hopscotch 4. Monkey Tag	Grand Marching Cottontail Hop	Bowling Target Old Mother Witch	Favorite Activities or Parachute	Old Mother Witch (K) I See Jumping Brooks Spaceship (1-2)

June   LESSON PLAN GUIDE   Grades 3-6

WEEK	MONDAY	TUESDAY	WEDNESDAY	THURSDAY	FRIDAY
1	(Long) rope jumping (Short) rope jumping	Stations: 1. (Long) rope jumping 2. Throw and Go 3. Scoops 4. Walkie-Talkie	Kickball (3) Softball (4-6)	Tetherball	Drag Race Grand Marching
2	Bull in Pen Hopscotch	Stop Thief (3-4) Donkey Dodge (5-6) Tetherball	Grand Marching Explosion	Classroom: Exchange Tag Nervous Wreck Hot Potato	Stations: 1. (Long) rope jumping 2. Hopscotch 3. Tetherball 4. One Against Three (3-4) Donkey Dodge (5-6)
3	Four Square (3-4) King Square (5-6)	Kickball (3) Softball (4-6)	Target Bowling Defrost (3) Capture the Flag (4)	Partner Tag Hopscotch (3-4) Tetherball (3-4) Broom Hockey (5-6)	Stations: 1. Hopscotch 2. Tetherball 3. (Long) rope jumping 4. Give Me Ten (3-4) Donkey Dodge (5-6)
4	Couple Tag Tunnel Ball Drag Race	Obstacle Course Swing Along (3-4) Bird in Nest (3-4) Hand Tennis (5-6)	Stations: 1. Tetherball 2. Hopscotch 3. (Long) rope jumping 4. Bowling (4) Hand Tennis (5-6)	Classroom: Push Back Bicycle Race Heel Slap Crane Dive Endurance Hop	Throw It and Run (3-4) Hand Tennis (5-6)

THE CENTIPEDE

The centipede was happy quite
Till a frog asked in fun
Pray tell which leg goes after which
This threw his mind in such a pitch
He lay distracted in the ditch
And knew not how to run.

Author Unknown

LEARNING CENTERS FOR THE OPEN CLASSROOM

The open-classroom concept means different things to different people. The term itself may be a little misleading because it implies a physical structure. In reality, the single most important ingredient is an open-minded teacher—one who plans experiences that are child-centered, fun, and individualized so that each child finds both success and challenge.

Long before the open-classroom concept became popular, many dedicated teachers were successfully incorporating these ideas in their teaching using various methods. Although there is no one best method, recent trends are toward incorporating learning centers in the different curricular areas. If you are already using centers, whether in a self-contained classroom or a cluster-type arrangement, you will find the suggestions on the following pages useful for physical education centers. They require a minimum of space and noise. Treat them as you would other centers: (1) Use a few at a time. (2) Change any part necessary to better meet the needs and abilities of your children. (3) Change a center according to the children's interests. (4) Tasks may be placed on index cards and kept in a card pocket at each center, or, for variation and fun, they may be written on a spinning wheel. (Cut lightweight cardboard to make two wheels approximately 12" in diameter. Cut out a 3" square about 1" from the edge of one wheel. Place this wheel on top of the other wheel, and attach them in the center so that the top one can move. Tape the bottom one to the table. Through the cut-out square, write tasks all around the bottom wheel. A child finds his task by spinning the wheel.) (5) Use children's ideas for centers and for improving centers. (6) Store used centers for future use.

All of the following centers have been used successfully by hundreds of boys and girls; many were created by them. Grade levels are deliberately omitted because the concept is the same for all; use the variations suggested according to the abilities of your children.

NUTS AND BOLTS

Need—One board with several bolts of varying diameters and matching nuts as shown in Figure 5; *Task*—Place the correct nut on each bolt and turn it as far as possible; *Variation*—"I can do *Nuts and Bolts* in _____ seconds."

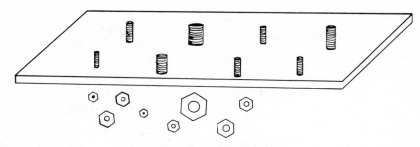

Figure 5 NUTS AND BOLTS

FOUR TO SCORE

Need—One clothespin for every four large bottle caps and two containers as shown in Figure 6; *Task*—"I can hold the clothespin in my right hand and move four caps from one plate to the other. I can do the same thing using my left hand"; *Variation*—"I can do *Four to Score* in _____ seconds."

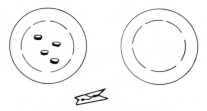

Figure 6 FOUR TO SCORE

JUMP ROPE

Need—One jump rope approximately 8' long; *Task*—"I can turn the rope and jump it _____ times before missing"; *Variations*—(1) "I can jump the rope _____ different ways." (2) "When I jump the rope, two ten's and three, I have jumped _____ times." (3) "I can jump the rope _____ minutes before missing."

PITCH YOUR SCORE

Need—One piece of cardboard and several shallow containers marked like the one shown in Figure 7 and five 2" rice bags (small beanbags); *Task*—Stand 3' away, toss each bag at the targets, and total your score; *Variations*—(1) Add your first three tosses, subtract the fourth, and multiply by the fifth toss to get your score. (2) Add your first three tosses, divide by your fourth toss, and multiply by your fifth toss to get your score.

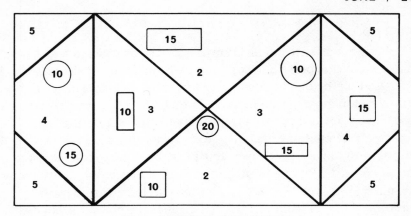

Figure 7 PITCH YOUR SCORE

TIC-TAC-TOE

Need—A tic-tac-toe pattern on cardboard, as shown in Figure 8, with pegs (round clothespins) and 6 plastic rings (cut from plastic sealers on various canned goods); *Task*—Find a partner, designate a distance, and play *Tic-Tac-Toe* tossing the rings to score.

Note: Use masking tape to make a pattern on a 3' x 3' piece of carpet. Use small carpet squares to toss. For younger children, paint various animals, put a peg in each, and let them try to ring as many animals as possible.

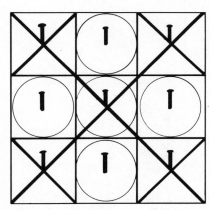

Figure 8 TIC-TAC-TOE

HUNGRY PUPPY

Need—A cardboard drawing of a puppy (or any animal) with an opening for the mouth and several beanbags or similar objects; *Task*—"I can feed the puppy _____ times out of five tries."

BAL-A-HOOP

Need—One suspended hoop of plastic or twisted paper, 3' in diameter, a balloon, and one or two paddles. Paddles may be purchased or made by shaping a wire coat hanger and covering it with a nylon hose or knee sock—stretch the hose over it, twist the hose, invert it, and repeat the process to the end of the hose. Tape loose ends around the handle; *Task*—Using the paddle to strike the balloon, how many times can you hit it back and forth through the hoop before it hits the floor? You may hit the balloon any number of times, but you score only when it goes through the hoop; *Variations*—(1) "I can score _____ times within 30 seconds." (2) "With my partner on the other side of the hoop, we can score _____ times together."

MIX 'N MATCH

Need—Boards, nails, rubber bands, related words and drawings similar to those shown in Figure 9; *Task*—Match the words and drawings by stretching a rubber band over the nail heads between a match. There is no limit to the possibilities for this center—colors, animals, arithmetic, language, measurements, emotions and feelings, science, and so on.

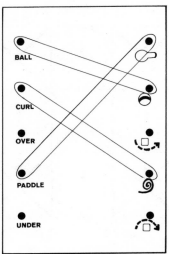

Figure 9 MIX 'N MATCH

Many of the activities found throughout this book easily lend themselves to learning centers. To prevent repetition, only example

tasks from a few activities are given below. Add other tasks appropriate to the activity and abilities of your children.

Examples of Tasks

(1) "I can complete one round trip of *Hopscotch* in _____ seconds." (2) "I can toss a beanbag and catch it on _____ [number] different parts of my body." (3) "I can go over the *Bottles and Canes* _____ [number] different ways." (4) "I can jump high, land softly, curl, roll, and balance." (5) "I can jump [standing broad jump] _____ inches." (6) "I can jump and click my heels together _____ times before landing softly on my feet." (7) "I can roll with good body control _____ different ways." (8) "I can run lightly in place _____ minutes before stopping." (9) "I can use a paddle and strike the ball to keep it in the air _____ times before missing." (10) "I can toss a ball and catch it in the scoop _____ times before missing."

Remember that one idea sparks another, and that the most meaningful centers will be those created by you and your children.

INDEX

GRADES		PAGE	What			How				Where			
			GAME/SPORT	DANCE	GYMNASTICS	INDIVIDUAL	PARTNER	SMALL GROUP OR STATION	LARGE GROUP	PLAYGROUND	CLASSROOM	ACTIVITY ROOM	PAVED AREA
	A Chinese Proverb	70											
	A Few Don'ts	94											
	About Dance	95											
5-6	Accents and Patterns	165		●				●			●	●	
K-6	Back Away	47	●				●			●			
K-6	Ball-handling Skills	28	●			●	●	●		●		●	●
K-6	Balloon Ball	180	●			●	●	●			●	●	
4-6	Bamboo Dancing	124		●				●			●	●	
4-6	Beat the Throw	207	●					●		●			
	Being Human	201											
K-6	Bicycle Race	76	●						●		●		
3-4	Bird in the Nest	164	●						●	●		●	
K-6	Bowling	77	●					●		●	●	●	●
K-4	Branding Cattle	146		●					●			●	
3-6	Bridge	61	●						●	●		●	●
4-6	Broom Hockey	219	●						●			●	●
2-6	Bull in Pen	203	●						●	●			
4-6	Capture the Flag	40	●						●	●			
	Centipede	242											
	Children Learn What They Live	114											
3-6	Chinese Get-Ups	175											
5-6	Club Guard	145	●					●		●		●	●
K-6	Coffee Grinder	175											
K-6	Cottontail Hop	193	●						●	●		●	
3-6	Couple Tag	204	●					●		●			
3-6	Creative Exercises	129		●	●	●	●	●			●	●	
3-6	Creative Games	157	●					●					
	Curiosity	136											
	Curriculum Fable	156											
3-6	Defrost	39	●						●	●		●	

249

GRADES		PAGE	What			How				Where			
			GAME/SPORT	DANCE	GYMNASTICS	INDIVIDUAL	PARTNER	SMALL GROUP OR STATION	LARGE GROUP	PLAYGROUND	CLASSROOM	ACTIVITY ROOM	PAVED AREA
4-6	Lane Soccer	58	●						●	●			
	Learning Centers for the Open Classroom	243											
	Lesson Plan Guides:												
	September	51											
	October	68											
	November	92											
	December	112											
	January	134											
	February	154											
	March	177											
	April	199											
	May	222											
	June	240											
3-6	Let's Make a Dance (with music)	107		●				●			●	●	
K-6	Let's Make a Dance (without music)	105		●				●			●	●	
3-6	Limbar	132		●				●		●	●	●	
K-2	Line Up	205	●					●		●			
K-6	Lummi Sticks	88		●		●	●	●			●	●	
K-2	Man from Mars	174	●						●	●			
K-6	Mended Hearts	149	●						●		●		
K-3	Midnight	137	●						●	●			
K-2	Monkey Tag	75	●					●		●		●	
K-2	Moon Man	46	●						●	●			
3-6	Motion	122	●						●		●		
K-6	Mousetrap	84	●						●		●	●	
1-6	Nervous Wreck	144	●					●			●		
K-6	Obstacle Course	171	●						●	●		●	

GRADES		PAGE	GAME/SPORT	DANCE	GYMNASTICS	INDIVIDUAL	PARTNER	SMALL GROUP OR STATION	LARGE GROUP	PLAYGROUND	CLASSROOM	ACTIVITY ROOM	PAVED AREA
			What			**How**				**Where**			
K-2	Old Mother Witch	63	●						●	●			
	On Attitude	180											
	On Being Consistent	115											
	On Communication	54											
	On Evaluation	226											
	On Feelings and Emotions	202											
	On Free Play	137											
	On Moving to Learn	28											
	On Responsibility	157											
	On Rights and Responsibilities	95											
	On Self-image	71											
3-6	One Against Three	60	●					●		●		●	
	Organization	19											
5-6	Par Three	99	●					●		●		●	
K-6	Parachute Activities	101	●						●	●		●	●
K-6	Parachute Games	103	●						●	●		●	●
K-6	Parachute Rhythms	104		●					●	●		●	●
1-6	Partner Tag	167	●						●	●		●	
K-3	Peace Tag	226	●					●		●		●	
	PHYSICAL EDUCATION												
K-6	Push Back	110											
1-6	Race Ball	160	●						●	●		●	
3-6	Rescue Relay	189	●						●	●		●	
3-6	Rhythmic Sports	109		●					●		●	●	
K-6	Right On/Left Off	67	●				●				●	●	
K-6	Rope Jumping	32	●			●	●	●		●	●	●	●
5-6	Rotation Dribble	100	●					●		●		●	

252

GRADES		PAGE	What			How				Where			
			GAME/SPORT	DANCE	GYMNASTICS	INDIVIDUAL	PARTNER	SMALL GROUP OR STATION	LARGE GROUP	PLAYGROUND	CLASSROOM	ACTIVITY ROOM	PAVED AREA
K-6	Scoop Ball	139	●			●	●	●		●	●	●	●
K-6	Seven Jumps	150		●					●		●	●	
K-2	Sevens and Threes	86		●					●		●	●	
K-2	Sing a Song of Sixpence	130		●					●		●	●	
3-6	Smush	80	●					●		●		●	●
K-6	Soccer Skills	54	●			●	●	●		●		●	
K-6	Soccer Steal	57	●					●		●		●	
K-6	Soccer Touch	57	●				●			●		●	●
K-6	Sock It to Me	39	●						●	●	●	●	●
4-6	Softball	210	●					●		●			
1-3	Spaceship	191	●						●	●		●	
3-6	Spud	37	●					●		●			
3-6	Stop Thief	121	●					●		●		●	●
K-6	Stride Ball	45	●					●		●	●	●	●
K-6	Strike It	182	●			●	●	●			●	●	
	Student Leaders	22											
K-6	Stunts	88											
3-6	Chinese Get-Up	175			●		●				●	●	
K-6	Coffee Grinder	175			●	●					●	●	
K-6	Crane Dive	88			●	●					●	●	
K-6	Endurance Hop	88			●	●					●	●	
K-6	Heel Click	110			●	●					●	●	
K-6	Heel Slap	110			●	●					●	●	
K-6	Push Back	110			●	●					●		
K-6	Swing Along	162	●			●	●	●	●	●		●	●
	Take Time	179											
K-6	Target	96	●					●		●	●	●	●
3-6	Tetherball	237	●			●	●	●		●		●	●
K-2	Think and Do	65	●						●		●	●	
K-6	Throw and Go	190	●						●	●			

253

GRADES		PAGE	GAME/SPORT	DANCE	GYMNASTICS	INDIVIDUAL	PARTNER	SMALL GROUP OR STATION	LARGE GROUP	PLAYGROUND	CLASSROOM	ACTIVITY ROOM	PAVED AREA
			What			**How**				**Where**			
3-6	Throw It and Run	207	●					●		●			
	Thus a Child Learns	53											
3-6	Touchdown	71	●						●	●			
K-2	Touché Turtle	43	●						●	●		●	
3-6	True or False	42	●						●	●	●	●	
3-6	Tunnel Ball	209	●					●		●			
1-6	Victory Lane	168	●						●	●			
4-6	Virginia Reel	131		●					●		●	●	
5-6	Volley Tennis	187	●					●				●	●
K-2	V-r-r-room	36	●						●	●		●	
K-6	Walkie-Talkie	50	●					●		●	●	●	●
3-6	Wall Ball	185	●			●	●	●				●	
K-6	What's Our Bag Today?	120	●						●		●		
1-2	Yogi Bear	173	●					●		●		●	
3-6	You Name It	143	●				●			●		●